Psychology Today

HERE TO HELP

calming
THE ANGER STORM

Psychology Today

HERE TO HELP

calming
THE ANGER
STORM

Kathy A. Svitil

ALPHA

A member of Penguin Group (USA) Inc.

To Ron, Jeremy, Matthew, and Jenna

ALPHA BOOKS

Published by the Penguin Group

Penguin Group (USA) Inc., 375 Hudson Street, New York, New York 10014, U.S.A.

Penguin Group (Canada), 10 Alcorn Avenue, Toronto, Ontario, Canada M4V 3B2 (a division of Pearson Penguin Canada Inc.)

Penguin Books Ltd, 80 Strand, London WC2R 0RL, England

Penguin Ireland, 25 St Stephen's Green, Dublin 2, Ireland (a division of Penguin Books Ltd)

Penguin Group (Australia), 250 Camberwell Road, Camberwell, Victoria 3124, Australia (a division of Pearson Australia Group Pty Ltd)

Penguin Books India Pvt Ltd, 11 Community Centre, Panchsheel Park, New Delhi—110 017, India

Penguin Group (NZ), cnr Airborne and Rosedale Roads, Albany, Auckland 1310, New Zealand (a division of Pearson New Zealand Ltd)

Penguin Books (South Africa) (Pty) Ltd, 24 Sturdee Avenue, Rosebank, Johannesburg 2196, South Africa

Penguin Books Ltd, Registered Offices: 80 Strand, London WC2R 0RL, England

International Standard Book Number: 1-59257-438-6
Library of Congress Catalog Card Number: 2005932824

08   07   06   05   8   7   6   5   4   3   2   1

Interpretation of the printing code: The rightmost number of the first series of numbers is the year of the book's printing; the rightmost number of the second series of numbers is the number of the book's printing. For example, a printing code of 05-1 shows that the first printing occurred in 2005.

Printed in the United States of America

Note: This publication contains the opinions and ideas of its author. It is intended to provide helpful and informative material on the subject matter covered. It is sold with the understanding that the author and publisher are not engaged in rendering professional services in the book. If the reader requires personal assistance or advice, a competent professional should be consulted.

The author and publisher specifically disclaim any responsibility for any liability, loss, or risk, personal or otherwise, which is incurred as a consequence, directly or indirectly, of the use and application of any of the contents of this book.

Trademarks: All terms mentioned in this book that are known to be or are suspected of being trademarks or service marks have been appropriately capitalized. Alpha Books and Penguin Group (USA) Inc. cannot attest to the accuracy of this information. Use of a term in this book should not be regarded as affecting the validity of any trademark or service mark.

Psychology Today is a registered trademark of Sussex Publishers, Inc., 115 East 23rd Street, 9th Floor, New York, NY 10010.

Most Alpha books are available at special quantity discounts for bulk purchases for sales promotions, premiums, fund-raising, or educational use. Special books, or book excerpts, can also be created to fit specific needs.

For details, write: Special Markets, Alpha Books, 375 Hudson Street, New York, NY 10014.

Publisher: Marie Butler-Knight

Editorial Director: Mike Sanders

Senior Managing Editor: Jennifer Bowles

Senior Acquisitions Editor: Paul Dinas

Development Editor: Phil Kitchel

Production Editor: Janette Lynn

Technical Editor: Editors of *Pyschology Today* Magazine

Copy Editor: Tricia Liebig

Cover Designer: Kurt Owens, Ann Marie Deets

Book Designer: Trina Wurst

Indexer: Heather McNeil

Layout: Specialized Composition, Inc., Rebecca Harmon

Proofreading: John Etchison

Contents

Foreword

Anger is unique among the emotions: it's a whole-body experience. When rage hits, your thoughts begin to race, your pulse climbs, your jaw tightens, and your entire body feels tense. Whether you're in a boardroom or in a bar room, your physical response often moves faster than the speed of thought. All of a sudden, you're 100 percent poised for action.

Anger also has real power. Properly harnessed and in the right context, anger can be a force for liberation, a motivator par excellence, a source of inspiration to right wrongs and restore justice. Anger in its rightful place is the spark that urges us to address difficult conundrums or to stand up to people who would dominate us.

But too many of us lose control and our anger gets the best of us. It ruins relationships. It fuels hatred. It saps us of health, happiness, and vitality. Unless we keep it in balance, anger can quickly become a tyrant.

Calming the Anger Storm helps you wrestle with—and master—this many-headed beast. It helps you understand different expressions of anger—why certain people scream and holler while others quietly seethe and keep their feelings tightly under wraps. It also explains why anger takes different forms in men and women and how to recognize signs of an anger problem in a child.

Author Kathy A. Svitil is a longtime science writer who has worked as an editor with many publications. After 11 years of marriage, her husband's temper changed, causing him to lose control in terrible rages. He eventually discovered that a medical condition was affecting his mood, and treatments have helped him regain some emotional stability. But in the meantime, Svitil learned firsthand how difficult living with an angry person can be. Her journey and the insights of the experts she has marshaled in these pages help you gain a full understanding of this powerful and often devastating emotion.

Calming the Anger Storm introduces the many tools available to help you and those around you tame rage, from traditional anger management classes to cognitive therapy to yoga. It helps you learn to defuse anger before it spirals out of control, and restore the emotion to its proper role in your life.

Kaja Perina
Editor in Chief
Psychology Today

Introduction

I never expected to write a book about anger. I also never expected that for a while my life would become completely overwhelmed by anger—my husband's, not my own, although at some point the distinction came to matter very little. And yet, as one of the women I interviewed for this book very astutely pointed out, you can't write the script of your life.

Nobody *plans* to be angry. After all, anger, unlike most emotions, is fraught with negative connotations. It can be ugly, embarrassing, a sign that we have lost control. But it is also completely natural—and necessary. Without anger, we lose the alarm bell that alerts us we're in danger, or being mistreated, or that something isn't right. Anger can be bad, but anger can also be good. That dichotomy is part of the essence of anger, and it is something I have tried to convey throughout *Calming the Anger Storm*.

Calming the Anger Storm doesn't tell you that you should *not* be angry. Everyone gets angry. What it *does* do, in addition to explaining the behavioral and biological roots of anger, is show you when your anger might be going too far or, often just as damaging, when you're bottling up valid and vital emotions you really should be expressing. You learn what the implications of your temper might be—to your health, to your intimate relationships, and to your life.

In addition, I introduce you to the latest, most effective (and sometimes controversial) methods for anger control: what they do and won't do, and how to stay the course and keep cool. And then, because anger affects not just the angry person but everyone in the path of his or her rage, you learn what you can do to repair the damage and help your loved ones, friends, and colleagues recover, heal, and, perhaps, forgive.

What You'll Find Inside *Calming the Anger Storm* is divided into four parts:

In **Part 1, "Understanding Anger,"** I go over the basics of anger—what it is (and isn't), how culture and upbringing can shape it, how it differs in men and women, and what causes anger in children. Finally, there is a primer on the biology of anger—how it is generated in both the mind and the body.

In **Part 2, "When Anger Hurts,"** I discuss what can happen when anger is out of control—how it can affect your health and also be rooted in other physical and mental conditions as well as how it damages intimate relationships, work lives, and your place in the world.

In **Part 3, "Taking Charge,"** you learn how to recognize that you have an anger problem and how to make the decision to change. You also learn about the options you have—traditional and unconventional—to get the upper hand on your emotions. I have also included a chapter on helping children with anger.

Part 4, "Managing Anger in Your Life," is about the aftermath. If you've overcome an anger problem, what do you do now? In these chapters, you learn tips to stay on course and also how to repair the damage your rage might have done to your life and relationships. Finally, I offer a chapter for family members, friends, colleagues, and caregivers of the angry person.

How to Use This Book In *Calming the Anger Storm*, I tried to touch on every aspect of anger: the causes, the impact, and, of course, where to go and what to do if you have an anger problem. The book should be instructional, but I also want you to find inspiration, hope, and help within its pages. The chapters are meant to stand alone; no need to read the first chapter to understand the fifth or the fifteenth. Flip through to find something meaningful or interesting to you.

The book is written primarily for the excessively angry person, who explodes too much and too often. But I have also tried to speak to the anger suppressors—who dangerously suppress their feelings—as well as to the family and friends of someone with an anger issue.

Sprinkled throughout each chapter you'll find a number of sidebars:

These sidebars consist of questions about related issues and answers from the experts.

Web Talk sidebars point you to sites with information that expands upon or supplements the text in that section.

PsychSpeak

PsychSpeak sidebars give definitions for terms that may be technical or that are not explained fully in the text.

GET PSYCHED

Get Psyched sidebars offer insight or inspirational messages from experts and from people who have dealt with anger in their own life.

you're not alone

You're Not Alone sidebars tell the personal stories of people, like you, who have had some experience with anger in their life—maybe their own, maybe a family member's—and have pulled themselves past it.

At the end of each chapter is a section called "What You Can Do," that summarizes what you've read and offers tips or advice that you might take away from it.

Acknowledgments I am not a therapist or an anger specialist. I'm a writer—a science writer, mostly—and that means my approach to this book has been to rely on the experts who know the subject best. *Calming the Anger Storm* would not be possible without their gracious help answering my seemingly relentless questions and keeping me on the right track. I am deeply indebted to:

Craig A. Anderson, Ph.D., chair of the department of psychology at Iowa State University; George Anderson, MSW, founder of Anderson & Anderson anger management; Rachel Greene Baldino, MSW, a licensed clinical social worker in Massachusetts; David Baron, Ph.D., chair of the department of psychiatry and behavioral health at Temple University Hospital and School of Medicine in Philadelphia; Karin Bruckner, a licensed professional counselor in private practice in the Dallas area; Jennifer Coleman, N.C.C., a divorce counselor in Raleigh, North Carolina; Darrell Burnett, Ph.D., a clinical psychologist and certified sports psychologist; Brad Bushman, Ph.D., a social psychologist at the University of Michigan; Deborah L. Cox, Ph.D., a psychologist at Southwest Missouri State University; Jerry Deffenbacher, Ph.D., a psychologist at Colorado State University; Evan Deneris, Ph.D., a neuroscientist at Case Western Reserve University; Eva Feindler, Ph.D., a psychologist at Long Island University in New York; Wendi Fischer, Ph.D., a clinical psychologist in private practice in West Islip, New York; Leon James, Ph.D., a psychologist at the University of Hawaii; Steven L. Katz, an executive coach in New York; John Lochman, Ph.D., a clinical psychologist at the University of Alabama; John McGrail, a clinical hypnotherapist in Los Angeles; Andra Medea, M.A., a conflict management expert based in Chicago; Raymond Novaco, Ph.D., a psychologist at the University of California at Irvine; Ari Novick, MS, clinical psychologist in private practice in Laguna Beach, California; Michael Rayel, M.D., psychiatrist in private practice in Newfoundland, Canada; John R. Rifkin, Ph.D., a clinical psychologist in Boulder, Colorado; Susan Reeve, a personal development consultant, author, and interfaith minister in San Francisco; Susan Romanelli, LCSW, Ph.D., director of the Hope Adult Program at the Menninger Clinic in Houston; Mitchel D. Rose, Ph.D., a licensed clinical psychologist in private practice in Boston; Charles Spielberger, Ph.D., director of the Center for Research in Behavioral Medicine and Health Psychology at the University of South Florida; Sara Salmon, Ph.D., psychologist and executive director of the Center for Safe Schools and Communities in Denver, Colorado; Sally Stabb, Ph.D., a psychologist at Texas Women's University; Sandra Thomas, Ph.D., psychologist and director of the Ph.D. nursing program at the University of Tennessee; Yvonne L. Thomas, Ph.D., a psychologist in private practice in Los Angeles; and Kiki Weingarten, M.Sc.Ed, MFA, a life and career coach and co-founder of Daily Life Counseling in New York City.

My deep gratitude goes out to the men and women who so openly shared their anger experiences with me. Thank you to Andra, Anthony, Brian, Cheryl, Deb, Elizabeth, Jamie, Jeff, Jeff, Jennifer, Jenny, John, Kurt, Magnus, Mark, Michele, Michelle, Mike, Paula, Sandy, and Susyn.

Thank you also to Paul Dinas at Alpha Books, for helping me understand a bit about the book business and for letting me slip on a few deadlines, and to Lybi Ma and Kathleen McGowan at *Psychology Today* for their encouragement.

Discover magazine was my professional home for a staggering third of my life. Thanks to Stephen Petranek and the *Discover* staff for giving me the opportunity to do this book, for commiserating with me, and for bucking up my flagging spirits when I felt overworked and overwhelmed.

I never imagined I'd write a book, so I am deeply grateful to Lori Oliwenstein for not only telling me I could, but making this one possible. Thank you also to my friends, including my amazing friend Gaylen Ducker Grody, for *always* being there and not minding when I dropped off the face of the earth, and to Mark Wheeler, for being the best not-really-my-brother older brother a girl could have.

Thanks also to my mom and dad, Ruth and Ed Svitil, for believing that everything I write is wonderful, and to my brother, Eddie, and my sister, Amy, for their love and support.

Huge thanks and tons of love to my perfect children, Jeremy, Matthew, and Jenna, for enduring many months of lost playtime, missed stories, and frozen food, and for putting up with my tired crankiness. And finally, a big, heartfelt thank you to my husband, Ron Fisher, for running interference with our kids so I could write, for always being proud of me (even when he didn't tell *me*), and for accepting, without hesitation, that I needed to include our own personal battle with his anger in this book. I love you all.

Part 1

Understanding Anger

Like it or not, we all get angry—and that's not necessarily a bad thing, if you have control of your anger and not the other way around. Learning about anger can give you the upper hand. In Part 1, you discover the basics of anger—what it is, how it originates in our body and mind, ways we experience it differently, and why it's such a powerful force for good and bad.

Anger Basics

Steamed, fuming, furious, enraged, seething, sulking, raving, hot under the collar, or just plain mad. Whatever word or phrase you use, and regardless of what sets you off or gets your blood boiling, the feeling is the same: anger.

Everyone gets angry and that's okay, because there is absolutely nothing wrong with feeling mad. Anger is as normal an emotion as sorrow or love or fear. At its best, anger has a noble purpose: It is a warning sign—a red flashing light—signaling to us that something is wrong, and the situation needs to be addressed.

Anger can motivate us to make a change in our personal life or our career, or to fix an injustice. It can be essential to survival. But, at its worst, anger can be destructive and debilitating. Anger can damage relationships, gnaw away at health, and irreparably ruin lives. Left unchecked, anger can escalate into aggression and violence.

In a sense, healthy anger is about balance. Just as it's not a good idea to *over*express your anger—using your rage to verbally (and sometimes physically) intimidate every person who irritates, frustrates, or disappoints you—neither should you keep that irritation, frustration, and disappointment bottled up. It will only come out in some other way—an ulcer, perhaps, or high blood pressure, or depression—because your needs and feelings, left unspoken, never get fulfilled. Regardless of how you act, those underlying feelings—and how you deal with them in your own head—give rise to anger.

The trick is to find a way to assert your feelings without damaging everyone within shouting distance. Before you can do that, you need to understand your own anger. What are its seeds? What triggers it? How do you respond?

What Is Anger?

Such a simple question should have a simple answer, but anger remains the least understood emotion, a confusing combination of both mental and physical responses.

PsychSpeak

Strong emotions can set off a wave of involuntary responses by the **autonomic nervous system:** blood pumps faster, the mouth gets dry, muscles tense, body temperature rises—leading to the hot-blooded state we experience as anger.

Ask a neurobiologist, and he might tell you that anger is a heightened state of physiological activity in the body's *autonomic nervous system.* The body pumps out an intoxicating brew of hormones that elevates blood pressure, gets the heart pumping faster, and raises body temperature. Those changes leave us physically aroused and energized, with our senses and reactions heightened so that we're primed for a quick reaction to whatever it is that got our blood up.

A psychologist, on the other hand, might say that anger is a complicated emotional response to a provocation, such as a displeasing person, situation, or thing. Sometimes, we get angry when our thinking is distorted—when we imagine, for example, that other people's actions are always intended to harm us: the "everyone is out to get me" mind-set. Psychologist and anger expert Raymond Novaco, Ph.D., of the University of California at Irvine, sees anger in a slightly different light. He describes anger as a "psychological fortification for a sense of worth" and "a guardian of self-esteem," which acts as a shield to protect us from things that we feel threatened by. "Ultimately it is about feeling safe," Novaco says.

These two definitions hardly seem to describe the same thing—a paradox that is part and parcel of the complexity of the emotion. How we experience and express anger is as unique as our genetic code, but our collection of anger responses do follow some patterns and can be described in three dimensions: behavioral, cognitive, and physiological.

Behavioral anger describes how we act: Do you cry when you get angry? Shout? Throw things? On the other hand, angry thoughts and images—usually exaggerated and an inaccurate depiction of reality—fall into the cognitive anger camp. Physiological anger is our body's response: rapid breathing, flushed face, clenched teeth, and tight muscles, for example.

> **GET PSYCHED**
>
> "Anger tells you to look for the problem. It also tells you to do something to make the situation better." –Ron Potter-Efron and Pat Potter-Efron in Letting Go of Anger (New Harbinger Publications, Inc., 1995)

Knowing When You Have an Anger Issue

Because everyone gets ticked off and anger is a normal emotion, there's no straightforward definition of what constitutes an anger problem. There are, however, some obvious clues. In broad strokes, if you get angry quite often over situations that don't bother other people, and you can't seem to calm down, your anger might be unhealthy. If it leads to aggression or violence, or if it interferes with your personal relationships or work, then it's a good bet that it *is* unhealthy. If your temper often drives a wedge between you and your closest friends and family members, weakening your relationships, that's another strong sign that it may be out of control.

Alternatively, if your anger is temporary and restrained; if you state your beef calmly and strive for a resolution of conflict; and if you can put your feelings to bed whether or not you've gotten your way, pat yourself on the back, because you're handling your anger well.

Anger Levels Some people are just more hotheaded than others. Scientists would say that they have high "trait anger," which simply means they have a propensity toward anger, or an angry disposition. They flare into a rage more quickly and more often, so their anger level is perpetually higher than a less irritable or easily frustrated person. Scientists haven't quite figured out why this is, but in some people it may be an innate personality trait, the adult form of the "difficult child" syndrome, which can be recognized in babies as young as a few days old. Psychologist John Gottman of the University of Washington has found that in couples, constant criticism and bickering can cause a surge of brain chemicals until one or both parties are primed to blow, and unable to listen rationally. Over time, they might start flying into this "flooded" state at the slightest provocation.

Another way to look at anger is in terms of a person's level of anger at the moment. How mad are you right now? What are you experiencing? Are you irritated? Annoyed? Crabby? Angry? Flat-out furious? Psychologists call this "state anger." Very angry people would tend to score higher on assessment tests for state anger, which means that at a given moment, they're more likely to be at a more intense level of anger than the average.

Is Anger Eating Away Your Quality of Life? To be honest, anger can be a thrill: the surge of adrenalin, the heightened senses, the feeling of power and control. There are people who get addicted to that high. Coming down and facing the aftermath, however, may not be pleasant, and that's not counting the potential detriment to your health and emotional well-being from being in a state of constant conflict. Your rage might have felt appropriate in the moment, but was it really worth it if it alienated a loved one, or made you a laughing-stock at work? Are your continued outbursts making anyone's life better, especially your own?

Very often, the best way to find out if anger is a problem for you is by talking to people around you. Your family knows the score. They might not be willing to say so if you don't ask (perhaps out of fear of your fury), but they definitely are in a position to tell you if your emotional outbursts are making a mess of *their* lives. You don't have to poll your entire family and every friend you have: if one person in your inner circle says your anger is making them uncomfortable or concerned, it's time to tone it down. Two votes in the "out of control" column, and your anger definitely has the better of you, and it's making people you care about miserable.

You might not have to ask anyone. Take your own mental inventory: Has anger had a noticeably negative impact on your quality of life? Has your boss reassigned you to a different project because you couldn't get along with your co-workers? Do your kids dread when you show up at their soccer games because you yell at the ref? Do you feel tense and crabby all the time? Then you know the score, too.

WEB TALK: Take an online quiz to assess how angry you are at:

www.angeresources.com/angerindex.html

On the other hand, if you never get mad—*ever*—regardless of the circumstance, you may have your emotions dangerously bottled up. That's just as much of a problem as going overboard. After all, if someone intentionally slams your hand in a door, you're entitled to be annoyed, at the very least. Reacting with a shrug while you're seething inside means you're suppressing your true feelings. You may be acting on anger in other ways and are not really aware of it. Do you avoid calling your mom because she's been critical of your boyfriend or nagging you to lose weight? Are you nit-picking at your husband because he hasn't finished repairs around the house? You may be avoiding or nagging because you're actually mad about something else they've done. Maybe you think you're avoiding an ugly confrontation by not mentioning that issue, but you're just avoiding your anger, period. Your subtle acts of hostility show that the problems aren't going anywhere.

When Those Around You Suffer One of the most insidious aspects of chronic anger is that it tends to hurt most the people we love best. Maybe you think that you are keeping your public anger—your annoyance at traffic or irritability on airline flights—separate from your family. Perhaps you believe you have buffered them from it, that they feel no effects. It's possible, but not likely. Like it or not, negative emotions and their consequences make waves that spread throughout your entire life.

I still cringe at the memory of one of my husband's many outbursts when he was ill. We needed a prescription filled from the hospital pharmacy before I could take him home. It wasn't ready, and he became completely enraged. He wasn't mad at *me*, but his anger was unreasonable, frightening, and, frankly, embarrassing.

Even if your bad moods aren't directed at your family, they will suffer. And if you *are* venting your anger at your spouse or kids or friends (as most of us do), it is going to take a toll. I simply avoided and ignored my husband when he was angry all the time. I started not to care, although the stress from his behavior had me emotionally drained.

What's worse is the effect on your kids. You love them and want to protect them—but what if they need protection from you? Your anger might make them feel bad about themselves. They might start acting out, have trouble sleeping, or have difficulties in school. Over time, they'll start to avoid you, a distance that will grow. Their own health and psychological well-being will suffer. Worse yet, you're setting in motion a pattern in their own behavior that might affect them the rest of their lives. Anger begets anger.

Anger, Hostility, and Aggression

To figure out what anger is, it's important to note what it is *not*. Anger is not aggression and it is not hostility, although they are often intimately linked. Anger is a feeling that arises and fades away. Hostility, on the other hand, is an enduring personality trait that predisposes a person to chronic anger.

When you get mad, you won't necessarily become aggressive or violent, but you're raising the risk that you will. The physiological changes in our bodies when we're angry lower the threshold for aggression.

GET PSYCHED

"I have learned in dealing with my son that it is better if I leave or walk away before I go back and talk to him, because when I scream at him it turns into a screaming match and nothing gets accomplished." –Deb, a nurse from Philadelphia who has grappled with an anger problem

you're not alone

"I inherited the worst of both my mother's and my father's tempers," says Michelle, a mother of two from Ohio. "My mother would get mad quickly—I used to compare her to a flash fire—and my father would get mad very slowly but then stay mad for a very long time. I got mad fast and then stayed mad for a long time.

"My mother must have recognized that tendency in me, because she tried to get me to contain my temper. She couldn't control her own temper so she didn't have any techniques to teach me. It was mostly through punishment. I wasn't allowed to get mad, or hit, or throw things. A lot of neighborhood kids got away with sh*t with me because they knew I wasn't allowed to get mad."

When Michelle was only 12, her mother got sick with complications of high blood pressure and started spending more time in the hospital; her father, an alcoholic who relied on his wife to help him stay sober, began to drink heavily. Michelle was put in charge of her younger brother and the household. When she was 14, her mother died and the job became permanent; when she was 16, her father died when their house burned down.

"During all this time, I handled my anger in the same way: if I was very angry, I might swear, or yell, or hit people. But after my father died, I went through a number of unfortunate things—I got raped, I was run over by a car. The guardian who had been appointed to me tried to have me put away so he could have control over the money I got after the car accident. As a result, I became horrendously depressed. Almost catatonic. I had kind of gone off. I think I was insane.

"When I turned 18, I was suddenly of legal age, and it was like someone had flipped a switch, because now I was allowed to live on my own, do things for myself. But I first needed to come out of this really passive, catatonic-like state, and when I started to do that, I realized that I'd lost any control I ever had over my temper.

"It took many more years for me to learn to control my temper. Now I really don't get mad very often any more. Some of it just got better with time, and having kids helped me—although in the beginning it made it worse. I also attribute a lot to my faith, which came much later down the road. And patience. The growth of patience."

It's like partially pushing the cork out of a champagne bottle; add a little more pressure and the cork is gonna fly. On the flip side, aggressive behaviors are not always rooted in rage. The soldier who blows up an enemy tank is causing intentional harm—and that's aggression—but he's acting on orders, not anger. Similarly, the armed man who jacks your car is terrorizing you, but he may be in complete control of his emotions as he does it.

Over the years, psychologists have come up with a number of theories to explain the origins of aggression, including that it is a basic human instinct, linked to our desire to acquire territory and resources. Even Sigmund Freud claimed that humans are born with an innate aggressive instinct; he argued that when our aggressive urge is foiled, the result is a hostile attack. In 1986, however, at an international behavioral science conference conducted in Seville, Spain, psychologists, neurophysiologists, and other researchers debunked that idea. They concluded that it is "scientifically incorrect to say that in the course of human evolution there has been a selection for aggressive behavior," and just as inaccurate to say that humans are inevitably predisposed to violence. In other words, despite humanity's history of violence and aggression, it is not our destiny.

Relationship of Anger to Other Emotions

Anger is entangled with many other responses and emotions. It can overwhelm other feelings—when you're furious at your spouse, you might be hard pressed to dig up any feelings of love for him—but there can also be considerable overlap. Feelings ranging from guilt, hurt, hate, envy, and confusion can be wrapped up in anger. Certain individuals express their anger by crying. If you never admit to your angry feelings, on the other hand, you may end up depressed.

PsychSpeak

The **amygdala**, a primitive part of the brain, connects fear and anger. That's why frightening situations can make us respond with rage.

Feelings of fear and anxiety can turn into anger, while anger, both our own and anger directed at us, can be frightening. When faced with danger, you might get scared or you might get angry. Your body's response is in many ways the same: a racing heart, shallow breathing, the hairs on your neck standing on end. In both situations, your body is getting prepared for action, whether it is to run away or stay and fight. That interplay of fear and anger makes sense on a biological level because the same region of the brain, an almond-sized clump called the *amygdala*, triggers both emotions.

Seeds of Anger: Fear, Blame, Frustration

Anger is individual to us, specific to our interpretation of the world, our experiences, and our feelings about ourselves. That's why the same event—say, a car weaving in and out of traffic on the freeway—might get you boiling mad but scare the daylights out of another guy. You're mad because you were just in a wreck and the last thing you need is for some jerk to get you in another one that will send *your* insurance skyrocketing; the fellow in the lane next to you is afraid because his brother died in a car accident.

How we feel about an event depends on the lens through which we view it and the world. That's why, says psychotherapist Ron Potter-Efron, children who grow up in an angry home, where angry behavior is normal and expected and used to solve problems, are prone to problems later in life.

Many psychologists don't disagree about the adverse impact of an angry upbringing, but believe that anger stems from blame. If you smash your thumb with a hammer, it's your son's fault for distracting you (or the hammer's, for being improperly made); if traffic is annoying and inconveniencing you, the other idiot drivers are responsible; if your emotional needs are not being met and you're feeling hurt or ignored, your wife is to blame.

After you have decided that the world is screwing up and conspiring against you and that you are being treated unjustly, the stage is set for anger. Shame fuels the rage. Cognitively, you give up control of your own feelings to the person who has betrayed you, failed you, or let you down: "She won't stop criticizing me!" "He's driving me nuts!" Someone else, rather than you, is now responsible for *your* furious feelings. The rage is also fueled by blaming *yourself* for your inadequacies and failures and feeling guilty or ashamed over it.

In that same vein, frustration—being denied or prevented from achieving some goal or desire—can also lead to anger. The more we want what we can't get, the angrier we can become, and that anger can lead to aggression. Therapists call it the frustration-aggression hypothesis. When the model was first developed in 1939, frustration was invoked as an explanation for *all* aggressive behavior. Now, frustration is thought to be the origin of only some anger, although it's sometimes used as an excuse by angry people who don't control their outbursts.

How Stress Amplifies Anger

The common thread connecting all of these is that they put extreme demands on your mind and body. That's stress, and it can take many forms. It might be a physical injury or ailment, money problems, trouble at work, an attack on your belief system, or worry about your son's health or your daughter's upcoming wedding. The reaction of your body to those stressors is a heightened state of arousal and awareness to cope with the challenges that confront you. Stress puts your mind and body on edge, and that can make you more likely to react to a trivial provocation that otherwise wouldn't bother you.

When you're stressed, any number of things can trigger anger. In the book *When Anger Hurts: Quieting the Storm Within,* psychologist Matthew McKay, Ph.D., clinical director of Haight-Ashbury Psychological Services in San Francisco, calls these thoughts the "psychological flint" that converts stress into anger. Everyone has different hot buttons, but the provocations range from a feeling of powerlessness and lack of control, to criticism, to the thoughtlessness of others, to physical danger. Cognitive triggers—those initiated in our own thoughts and not by an external event—generally fall into two categories: blaming, the idea that you are being intentionally harmed; and "shoulds," which stem from a belief that someone else ought to be acting differently than they are, and that their behavior is breaking the rules.

Psychologist Sandra Thomas, Ph.D., director of the Ph.D. nursing program at the University of Tennessee, has spent the past two decades studying women's anger, and, more recently, anger in men. Some of the common anger triggers she has found include:

- Unfair treatment
- Unmet expectations
- Powerlessness
- Offense to personal morals or values
- Stress and pressure
- Someone else's thoughtlessness or incompetence
- Disrespectful treatment
- Criticism

- Inability to control something or someone
- Interference with personal goals or plans
- Harassment
- Delays (traffic, long lines, and so on)
- Fatigue
- Irresponsibility from someone depended on
- Property damage or destruction
- Threats to self-esteem

What triggers your temper might be different. My husband, for example, says that feeling crowded, with many people talking to him at once, makes him overwhelmed, and then, often, angry. My own anger triggers are more garden-variety—injustices, when people don't believe what I say (and I *know* I'm right). You might not have any control over the things that set you off, but if you recognize what they are, you can learn how to react differently.

Anger Styles

Flip open five different books on anger management and you'll likely find five different lists of anger styles. Some experts break anger down into four different types, others six or ten. Although there may be merit in creating a recipe book of rage, most professionals prefer a simpler three—passive, aggressive, and passive aggressive. (Healthy anger, in which you accept and then assert your feelings in a respectful and productive manner, is separate from all of these.) As with many things involving anger, there are few hard boundaries, and your own style may slop over from one category to another.

Passive Passive people say and do nothing that would offend or annoy. Passive people are compliant and agreeable; they go with the flow, they try to make everyone happy—and they get walked on *a lot*. Unfortunately, they still have feelings and wants and desires, but they go unrecognized and unfulfilled, because they never tell anyone—or if they do, they're timid and unassertive.

Passive people do get angry, but they deny their anger, and in fact might feel guilty about it. Because passive people don't deal with their emotions outwardly, they're often in inner turmoil, which can manifest as stomach pain, headaches, and other problems.

Aggressive An aggressively angry person is the prototypical rager: they argue, shout, demand; they use humiliation, sarcasm, insults, and the threat of physical attack to coerce and dominate others. If they don't get what they want, they explode. It might work; family and friends might acquiesce to their will. They will likely also be feared, resented, and distanced from others. Others might also push back and resist the abusive attempts to control them, driving the aggressor into a more frenzied fury that can escalate into violence.

Aggressively angry people might feel guilty afterward over their blustering and brutality, and might try to mend their ways; but if they do so by denying their needs, the aggression will probably resurface.

Passive Aggressive The passive-aggressive person won't assert their feelings or openly disagree with you. They may seem happy, but that compliant exterior hides aggression that comes out in insidious ways. Prior arrangements will be ignored or "forgotten" (because they never wanted to participate in the first place), or they'll show up late (because they're angry that you were late for your last engagement). They'll say they don't understand you, be unresponsive, withhold affection—all the while denying any negative feelings. Some people do this strategically, with manipulative intent. But many people may not even realize they're acting out—in fact, they may not even recognize their own angry feelings.

I don't blow up like my husband does, but he accuses me all the time of being passive aggressive. As long as I'm not yelling at everyone, why is that a bad thing?

"I see marriage after marriage come into my office where there is the dynamic of a passive-aggressive person who is bringing in their partner, saying, 'Doctor, you have to fix this, my partner is exploding all the time. They have a problem with anger and I don't know what is wrong with them.' But that passive-aggressive person is 50 percent of the problem. They are not willing to deal with the dependency and the negotiation of relationships, so they make agreements and they don't keep them. And, yes, their partner blows up. What a surprise. People have no idea how damaging passive-aggressive behavior can be."
—*John R. Rifkin, Ph.D., author and licensed clinical psychologist in Boulder, Colorado*

The Yin and Yang of Anger: Suppressors and Expressers

As these anger styles make clear, it can be just as destructive to repress feelings as it is to bellow and berate. Psychologists have come up with a number of terms to describe the dichotomy: anger-in or anger-out, imploders or exploders, underwater or on-the-surface, suppressors or expressers ....

What it boils down to is that we can cope with our negative emotions by keeping them to ourselves, pent-up and unaired, or we can release those feelings to the world (hopefully in a productive way).

GET PSYCHED

"First, foremost, and always: breathe first, and then decide how you want to respond. Anger demands expression; if you have recognized it and owned it, then you will have a choice of when, where, and how you express it. Just saying *That makes me angry or I do not like it when …* may not be as satisfying as hitting someone, but it has far less serious consequences." —*Laura J. Petracek in* The Anger Workbook for Women *(New Harbinger Publications, 2004)*

PsychSpeak

Repressed feelings are disturbing or painful ideas that are denied or submerged into the subconscious.

We can also choose to calm down, on the outside by controlling our actions, and on the inside by trying to relax, learning to understand the origins of the feelings of rage, and trying to allow the angry feelings to subside (a much more difficult proposition). Which path we take often depends on the situation.

Physicians and psychologists have long known that being mad all the time can cause chronic health problems, in addition to sabotaging personal and professional relationships. More recently it has become clear that bottled-up emotions are equally detrimental, contributing not just to depression and anxiety, but also to medical problems such as headaches, migraines, high blood pressure, angina, ulcers, skin problems, and more. *Repressed* anger is equally troublesome. Recent studies in Spain show that women who repress their anger—generally to preserve harmony in their relationships—show higher rates of malignant cancers, although exactly how this happens is unclear.

Holding in your feelings can make you sick—and it isn't a very effective way of dealing with your anger, either. Anger suppressors usually blow up anyway. "What people report is that they hold back and hold back and then something happens and they just explode. They surprise themselves with the intensity of their reactions," says psychologist Deborah L. Cox, Ph.D., of Southwest Missouri State University.

Not only do the feelings remain, but they can intensify, say researchers at the University of Aberdeen in Scotland. In a 2002 study, psychologist Judith Hosie and her colleagues played an emotional film clip for groups of volunteers. One group was told to express their feelings of anger, another told to keep them in. The participants were then shown another emotional clip and were allowed to spontaneously air their feelings. The group that suppressed their earlier reactions had a much stronger response to the second film. They were angrier, more upset, and reported more desire to curse.

you're not alone

"I used to be involved in a violent relationship. I'd married a man 17 years my senior—he had a drug and alcohol problem, and didn't work. It was fine with our first baby, but by the time the second one came, he was smoking pot, drinking heavily, and incoherent a lot of the time. I decided to leave him after he slapped me and tried to choke me. That was in 1993.

"We endured a 10-year custody battle over the kids. During that time, my ex tried to run me over, broke into my house, stalked me. I was really very angry—probably justifiably so—and so I tried to turn him over to the naturalization authorities (he was Canadian), the IRS. We had restraining orders against each other.

"Eventually things calmed down—for two reasons. First, I stopped feeding it. When he would get mad, I stopped reacting. Second, he ran out of steam. I only had it because I thought I was doing what I needed to do to defend the kids. Now they are bigger. They can do it for themselves.

"We can talk now, but it's not always easy. Is that a happy ending? I don't know. Did Mrs. Doubtfire have a happy ending? Ours is kind of like that."
—Sandy from California

Sociologists have also found a link between repressing emotions and violence in men with a history of domestic violence. The violent men reported higher levels of stress than a group of nonviolent men, and yet did not admit to any increased psychological distress (depression or loneliness, for example) as a result of their stress. That suggests they were repressing the feelings that naturally develop under stress. Indeed, they were more likely to say that they did indeed bottle up and ignore their emotions.

"People who repress emotions are not necessarily free of distress, but are instead just free of the most obvious symptoms of that distress," says study co-author Kristi Williams, Ph.D., of Ohio State University. "This may lead to a buildup of frustration that results in an outburst of violence."

Does "Pent-Up Anger" Need a Release?

Clearly, keeping anger in is a bad idea. So should you pound a pillow or yell and scream to purge yourself of it? Thirty years ago, the answer would have been yes; but now psychologists generally agree that the violent venting of anger—called *catharsis*—isn't such a good idea.

The idea of catharsis goes back at least a thousand years to the Greek philosopher Aristotle, who wrote in his *Poetics* that viewing tragic plays was beneficial to both the individual and to society because it helped to rid people of their fear and pity. (The word catharsis derives from the Greek word *katharsis*, which translates as a "cleansing" or "purging.")

Sigmund Freud took the idea a step further in his hydraulic model of anger, in which he proposed that repressed anger could build up inside our psyche, creating pressure that leads to psychological problems such as hysteria or phobia.

WEB TALK: Read more about catharsis and other influential ideas in psychology, medicine, and a vast range of other areas in the Dictionary of the History of Ideas at:

http://etext.lib.virginia.edu/DicHist/dict.html

Getting what burns you off your chest through aggressive behavior or even by viewing aggression—in other words, through catharsis—can then, the theory goes, release that pressure and prevent the negative effects.

Q&A

Sometimes I get so angry I want to put my fist through a wall. How can I calm down?

"Our studies have shown that there are four things that seem to work. The first is to delay responding. Count to 10, or to 100. Take a walk. The idea is that when people are highly aroused, they have highly impulsive behavior, and they don't think about what they're doing. If you delay your response, the arousal can decrease and you can make better decisions. Second, distract yourself; think about something else. The more you ruminate on something, mull it over in your mind, the worse it becomes because it just keeps aggressive thoughts and angry feelings alive. Third, try to relax. Take deep breaths, listen to relaxing music. This also reduces your level of arousal. Fourth, try to do something incompatible with anger and aggression, such as petting a puppy, kissing your lover, or watching a comedy. It will also reduce your level of aggression and anger." *—Brad Bushman, Ph.D., social psychologist, University of Michigan*

The Case Against Venting Does *venting* work? Most researchers say no. Lashing out, punching a hole in the wall, or pummeling a punching bag may feel good in the moment and immediately afterward, but it does nothing to dispel anger. In fact, many studies show that it leads to more aggression.

"When people get angry they want to hit, they want to kick, they want to swear, they want to shout, and that is what comes most naturally," says social psychologist Brad Bushman, Ph.D., of the University of Michigan, who has conducted a number of studies about the usefulness of catharsis. "When they do it, they feel a sense of relief afterward … *ahhhh*. But our research shows that those good feelings don't translate into less aggression. They translate into *more aggression,* because those actions keep the angry feelings and the aggression alive. Venting anger is like using gasoline to put out a fire: you are feeding the flame, and it just makes things worse.

PsychSpeak

Venting is the attempt to release negative emotions, such as anger, through aggressive acts. Many studies show it only increases aggression and isn't a good solution for most angry people.

"For example, in one study, we asked people how they felt after hitting a punching bag when they were angry. Seventy-five to eighty percent said 'I feel good ... I feel better.' But the better they said they felt, the more aggressive they were later on. We think these 'good' feelings just reinforce aggressive behavior," Bushman says.

To bolster that view, he has conducted an analysis of every report that looked at the catharsis phenomenon. "There isn't any evidence that it works. It is very clear that venting produces more anger and more aggression, not less," he says.

However, the idea remains in the public consciousness—perhaps perpetuated, Bushman believes, by misguided endorsements in the media. In the movie *Analyze This,* for example, the character portrayed by Billy Crystal, reluctant psychiatrist to mob boss Robert DeNiro, advises his client to hit a pillow to get rid of his anger. "People want to do it—they want to kick a trashcan, and if they think it's going to make them feel better, they'll do it. But it doesn't work," Bushman says.

The Case for Venting Despite what Bushman and other researchers say, there are still psychologists and therapists who endorse catharsis. "I have a lot of trouble with research that says venting is bad, because they use simulated laboratory situations that are pretty artificial. It's very different from how people experience anger in real life," says Karin Bruckner, co-author of *The Anger Advantage,* and a licensed professional counselor in private practice in the Dallas area.

Bruckner uses cathartic exercises in her practice and finds them to be useful, although she admits that her patient's anger does initially increase. "You initially do see an outpouring of anger as the patients get in touch more with what they are feeling," she says. Kids will become more aroused with anger; they struggle with it more.

"But it is not that the anger is being invented or generated," she says. "It is because they have a release for this overwhelming backlog of anger that is inside them, like a glass filled to the brim and ready to spill over at any moment." Over time, Bruckner and others argue, the anger dissipates. "Because they've released their reservoir of anger, instead of it overflowing every time a little annoyance happens throughout the day, they can have room to absorb the emotions and can keep themselves on an even keel. It's a much more comfortable way to live."

For some people, then, venting may very well be a healthy way to release pent-up feelings—especially for people who tend to deny or repress their anger. But for people who already have a tendency to blow up or act out their anger or aggression in impulsive, destructive ways (bullies, for example), venting just might fuel the fire and make things worse.

What You Can Do

Anger is a confusing emotion—it hurts, it heals, it can be an overwhelming force on our thoughts and feelings and actions. We can become consumed by it, deny it, or embrace its value.

If you aren't handling your anger as well as you might like, or have a loved one that might have a problem, you've taken the first step down a healthier path. Here are some more:

☐ Remember that although it can go too far and do damage, anger does have a purpose. Your goal should be not to rid yourself of the emotion, but to learn how to control it and use it to your advantage.

☐ Take inner stock of your anger. Be honest. Are you out of control? Are you burying your feelings?

☐ Think carefully about why you get angry, and what sets you off. Start making a list of your triggers.

☐ Are you blaming everyone else for your outbursts? Is frustration driving you into a rage? Blame and frustration are frequent seeds of anger. Now is the time to find out if they're planted in you.

☐ Get the low-down from your family and friends. Find out how they feel about your behavior. And be open to what they say.

☐ If a family member or friend has an anger issue, sit them down, talk to them. Let them know your concerns.

☐ If they resist you—and they might—be patient, but be persistent.

An Unusual Emotion

Anger happens to all of us. We may express it differently and view it differently depending on our gender, perhaps, or our culture, but the emotion itself is absolutely universal, from humans to rats.

And although it's incredibly easy to brand anger as simply a 'bad' emotion—destructive, debilitating, and dangerous to our health—it is also wrong to do so. That's not the full story. Yes, anger *can* be those things, and often *is*, but anger is also a protective impulse, a messenger, a teacher, a motivation, an energy that powers change. That means there's no reason to feel bad about your anger. You just need to find a way to understand it, and put it to good use.

What *is* true about anger is that it may be the most complicated of the emotions, an interplay of the body, mind, culture, and context. Anger is a physiological response that is sculpted by our personality, filtered through our experiences and history, and shaded by social influences. We need to recognize that complexity if we are to understand our own relationship with anger—and use it to make our lives better.

What Is Anger Good for Anyway?

If you had lived 20,000 years ago, your anger might have focused on self-preservation—an innate, instinctual aggressive reaction to a threat from the hostile guy in the cave next door, or a reaction to flee from a bear in a bad mood.

WEB TALK: The full text of Charles Darwin's treatise on rage and other emotions is available online at:

http://human-nature.com/darwin/emotion/contents.html

Animals do the same thing, although their anger manifests in slightly different ways, with ruffled fur, raised hackles, hissing, or bared teeth. Many angry humans also sneer or snarl (think of the last time you saw someone really pissed off—they probably were baring their teeth as well). In *The Expression of the Emotions in Man and Animals,* Charles Darwin, the nineteenth-century biologist who developed the theories of natural selection and evolution, said that the expression revealed man's "animal descent."

PsychSpeak

An **adaptive** emotion, such as anger, is one that may now be occasionally unpleasant, but helped our ancestors respond to, and survive, difficult and threatening situations.

"Charles Darwin recognized that fear and rage were fundamental characteristics of both humans and animals," says Charles Spielberger, Ph.D., director of the Center for Research in Behavioral Medicine and Health Psychology at the University of South Florida and the developer of the world's most widely used psychological assessment test of anger. "The reason they are there is because they are *adaptive* emotions." If you are feeling angry, anxious, or endangered, he says, you will avoid that danger; or, if you are being attacked and hurt, you will use aggressive behaviors to protect yourself. "Those are essential to survival. Persons who have the most effective usage of those emotions are more likely to survive and procreate."

These days most of us don't have to worry about pillaging barbarians or angry saber-toothed tigers, but our reaction is the same to danger and threat, or unfairness, injustice, and anything else that causes us pain and frustration: we get angry, and then we act from there. Our negative angry emotions can be a surprisingly positive thing—*if* we can avoid acting in ways that are inappropriate or bad for us or the people around us.

Think about some of the major social movements of the twentieth century: women's suffrage, the civil rights movement, the overthrow of the Soviet Union. What was the catalyst? Anger. In every case, the mistreatment had become unbearable and people's rage reached a boiling point, and so they used that emotion to jumpstart the hard work that change requires. Environmental groups who try to protect old-growth forests and wetlands aren't just doing it because they really like trees and swamp grass, but because they're angry that nature is under threat. Neighbors who try to get a stop sign at the end of their block aren't just thinking of traffic control—they're furious at the speeding cars whizzing by their playing children.

Anger is always lurking underneath social movements, both large and small. Rage is crucial to the beginning of any movement, says social psychologist and anger expert Carol Tavris, Ph.D. in her book *Anger: The Misunderstood Emotion*. "It unifies disparate members of the group against a common enemy; the group becomes defined by its anger."

But that's not all that anger can do. In addition to propelling social change, Tavris says, one of anger's most important roles is its policing function: "Anger, with its power of forcefulness and its threat of retaliation, helps to regulate our everyday social relations: in family disputes, neighborly quarrels, business disagreements, wherever the official law is too cumbersome, inappropriate, or unavailable (which is most of the time)." In small groups where people have to get along because they're stuck with each other—whether in a book club or a Brazilian tribe—anger is "society's servant," she says. Although it's true that inappropriate anger is corrosive, these groups have unspoken rules that are enforced through what Tavris calls "ritual bickering." Toe the line or you're subjected to angry words and scorn.

The Power of Anger

Of course, anger isn't just society's servant. Use it well, and it can become your own servant. You don't have to go through years of intensive therapy getting in touch with your anger to make use of it, although for people whose anger stems from a difficult childhood or who have buried the emotion, therapy can be essential for figuring out what you feel and why you feel it. If your tendency is to deny your negative feelings, finally getting angry can push you to see what's upsetting you and then make changes and decisions, says Karin Bruckner, a licensed professional counselor in the Dallas area who has studied anger extensively.

Q&A

I hear all the time that anger is a "red flag" telling me that something is wrong. What if I don't know what that something is?

"There are a number of things you can do to get in touch with your anger—to raise your anger 'consciousness.' One way is to engage in physical activity, because stimulating your body physically helps you get in touch with the adrenalin rush that accompanies anger, so you can kind of go in through the back door. Another way is journaling, writing about your feelings, which is a more passive way. And there is also always therapy, with a therapist who views anger as a positive thing rather than something that needs to be controlled." *—Karin Bruckner, co-author of* The Anger Advantage *and therapist in private practice in the Dallas area*

Bruckner and her collaborators have interviewed hundreds of people (mostly women) about how they deal with their feelings of anger, aggravation, and frustration, with some surprising results. "In doing the research, we started hearing stories about these 'aha' moments that women were having. They got furious about something, and that was the night or the moment when they finally made decisions about what they needed to do to change or fix their lives: 'I have to leave this man,' or 'I have to change jobs,' or 'I have to stop drinking.' When they went with their anger," Bruckner says, and allowed themselves to finally get mad at a cheating spouse or a manipulative boss instead of repressing or denying the problem, "it led them to a very powerful place, a place of insight."

John R. Rifkin, Ph.D., an author and psychologist in private practice in Boulder, Colorado, places anger among a triad of negative emotions, along with fear and sadness, which are each generated by pain or injury. Sadness is our psyche's way of honoring or grieving the injury, he says, while fear is generated by the injury to keep us from getting hurt again. And anger, Rifkin feels, provides the energy and motivation to fix what is hurting us.

"After you understand your anger, you can use it for what it is meant for, which is really addressing the injury—whatever it is that caused you pain," he says. With that energy, you can take action. It can come in a couple of forms. Direct it at yourself— by taking a bath to calm down and relax, or going for a run to burn off your brewing rage—and it's self-nurturing; direct the

> **GET PSYCHED**
>
> "The catchphrase is 'You've got to feel anger to heal anger.' Healing it means allowing it to be there, allowing yourself to feel what you feel, and trying to figure out what you are supposed to do with those feelings."
> —John R. Rifkin, Ph.D., author and licensed clinical psychologist in Boulder, Colorado

energy to the world—by talking to your boss about the raise you didn't get, or starting a petition drive to get a proposed sewage treatment plant out of your town—and "you're getting the world to take care of you and bring you what you want. That's empowerment," he says.

Overcoming the Legacy

you're not alone

Kurt grew up the youngest of six children in an angry home. "My father had a very explosive temper. There was never physical abuse, but definitely daily terrorizing of all the kids in the house. The time between stimuli and response was zero for him. Anything or absolutely nothing could set him off into a rage. It was a very scary place for kids to be."

Now a successful architect in the Boston area, Kurt didn't recognize that he had any of his own anger problems until his then girlfriend pointed out some of his behavior and the problems that his temper was causing. "It practically destroyed our relationship," he says. At her urging, he went into therapy, where he soon realized that his father's rage had been imprinted on his own personality. "It was almost like a hardwired response in my brain to act like that—to act out aggressively for sometimes no reason at all. I realize now that my childhood is where my own anger problems stem from. When I look back, I can see myself in situations where I acted exactly like my father had. I recall being in business meetings with clients and getting very angry, for maybe a good reason or no reason at all. It just sort of *happened*. When you're starting a new business, that kind of thing can be very damaging to a long-term client relationship."

One surprising benefit did emerge from Kurt's anger-filled childhood: "I developed a hypervigilance to things, from immediately having to size up a situation, what my father's moods were the instant he came in the door. That tendency has almost poisoned my personal relationships, but it has helped me very much in my business. That kind of instinct keeps you on your toes."

After several years of therapy, Kurt now considers himself free of his anger. "I'm actually very proud of myself because I feel that it's almost not an issue anymore. It so seldom comes up. What I try to do is capture in my mind a place where I don't have those angry feelings. It's almost like a mental vignette of how it feels not to be angry. That's how I want to feel, and by capturing it and remembering it, it's easier for me to stay there. When I start to go away from it and into an angry pattern, I can see what I'm doing and I keep myself from going into the angry loop. It's like if you're young and you go out drinking with your friends and you get a terrible hangover the next day. That hangover is your deterrent from getting drunk the next time. To know how badly it feels to be angry and how bad it makes everyone feel— that is my deterrent from doing it."

An Emotion Like No Other

One of the hallmarks of anger is that it is an intensely physical experience. When we feel angry, we really *feel* it. This is the case with all emotions, from love to fear to sorrow, but with anger the effect seems to be particularly profound. Even Charles Darwin was aware of anger's effects on both mind and body. "A man may intensely hate another," he wrote in *The Expression of the Emotions in Man and Animals*, "but until his bodily frame is affected, he cannot be said to be enraged."

It's not so surprising, then, that some people resist getting angry. They suppress it, deny it, refuse to admit even to themselves that they experience anger, because in that anger is a certain loss of control—not just of their feelings but of their own bodies. People like to be in control of themselves, and if anger gets the upper hand, it can take that control away.

Good vs. Bad Anger

Anger has power. It can make people pay attention to you, notice you, get you what you want. On a broader scale, anger can help reinforce the laws and rules of a culture and of social interchange. That's anger putting on its best face.

Clearly, not all anger is good. The anger that creates mistrust with your co-workers is bad. The anger that leads to your neighbors calling you a nut is bad. And the anger that drives away your friends, intimidates your spouse, and scares your kids is undoubtedly bad. Can you have one without the other? Ideally. But accepting anger in your life means you also have to accept the dichotomy, the good and the bad.

If you have a hard time doing that, you're really depriving yourself of a heck of a lot of useful energy. You can't make the best of your anger, after all, if you're denying that it exists.

GET PSYCHED

"Anger, like love, is a moral emotion. I have watched people use anger, in the name of emotional liberation, to erode affection and trust, whittle away their spirits in bitterness and revenge, diminish their dignity in years of spiteful hatred. And I watch with admiration those who use anger to probe for truth, who challenge and change the complacent injustices of life, who take an unpopular position center stage while others say 'shhhh' from the wings." –Carol Tavris, social psychologist, in Anger: The Misunderstood Emotion (Touchstone, 1989)

Cultural Taboos

One of the more fascinating aspects of anger is that it takes so many forms in different parts of the world. That's not to say anger isn't ubiquitous; cross-cultural researchers have found that the facial expression of anger is universally recognized, as are five other emotions: disgust, fear, happiness, sadness, and surprise. Everyone, everywhere, feels anger. But how we feel and display that irritation or annoyance or rage—and how it is received—is knit tightly together with our social upbringing.

Researchers have found that the expression of angry feelings differs dramatically from group to group and culture to culture. As Carol Tavris says in *Anger*, "Cultural masks overlay the face of emotion .... People everywhere get angry, but they get angry in the service of their culture's rules."

In hunter-gatherer societies, basic survival usually makes the rules. The !Kung of Africa's Kalahari Desert, for example, depend enormously upon each other. They are nomadic, traveling from area to area in their seasonal pursuit of food, and so there is no permanent town to offer stability—and no place to go when they're on the outs with their village mates. As a result, the !Kung frown upon overt displays of anger, because dissention and conflict threatens their existence.

WEB TALK: Learn how you can channel your anger into social change at: **www.advocacy.org**

In other cultures, the rules governing anger are no less powerful, even though they may be a few steps away from basic survival. In Latin and Middle Eastern cultures, it's perfectly natural to have a quick, flashing temper. The Japanese, on the other hand, are models of emotional restraint, a practice that dates back to the days of the Samurai. "Traditional Japanese culture would have that you don't get angry," says psychologist and anger researcher Deborah L. Cox, Ph.D. of Southwest Missouri State University. To the Japanese, an outburst of anger is not just impolite. It means that you have lost control, and that means losing face.

"Asian women I've interviewed say 'I don't get angry about these things that you are saying you get angry about. I just don't get angry,'" Cox says. "And so in families and in family systems in that culture, there is a lot of shame around showing anger in general. I think anger is an individualistic emotion, so it makes sense to me that a more collective culture would frown on anger, because it does highlight the individual's needs and wants in the moment." Not surprisingly, other cultures that place high emphasis on community, such as the Scandinavians, also tend to get less angry.

In the United States, anger is not by any means prohibited, but it can be viewed as a no-no. "Anger is still quite a taboo, surprisingly," says Karin Bruckner. "Our theory is that the foundation of the taboo has a huge confusion between anger, which is the emotion, and aggression, which is a destructive acting out. Although we can say anger is healthy, useful to us, and informs our living and our life, aggression is rarely if ever helpful, constructive, or positive.

As a result, we look askance at people who can't seem to control their temper. They might be dangerous. We also carry a heavy dose of confusion over how we are *supposed* to act. "We are told in one breath not to rock the boat, and in the next that the squeaky wheel gets the grease," writes Carol Tavris.

Americans may also be less forgiving of negative emotions in general than are other cultures, where the negative emotions in life are accepted far more readily. "In America, we need to be 'Happy! Happy! Happy!' And if we're not 'Happy! Happy! Happy!' we need to do something quick to fix it," says Karin Bruckner. The problem with a quick-fix attitude, of course, is that we might not be able to change what is upsetting us, and that can make us angrier. If you have a boss who is condescending and constantly criticizes your work even though you know you're doing a good job, can you change him? Not likely. You can leave, but that might not be economically feasible. So you're stuck—and ticked off about it.

Our Angry Society

We might think of ourselves as optimistic and upbeat all the time, but Americans can be a pretty angry lot. Our ire, some say, is increasing. We're enraged about the war in Iraq, or angry that other people are criticizing it; unhinged about the erosion of

you're not alone

To foreigners, the American propensity for anger can be uncomfortably confusing. Such was the case for Magnus, a Swedish-born computer security specialist raised with typical Scandinavian stoicism, who moved to southern California several years ago when he married an American woman. Magnus doesn't consider himself an angry person—in fact, he says he only gets angry a few times a year—although that's not uncommon for people who are raised in Scandinavian countries. "In Sweden, the culture tells you that you should never complain, you should never get angry," he says. "It's not that you don't stand up for yourself, but being angry is usually considered stupid and rude, because you are not putting other people first. In Sweden, the community is considered more important than the individual. That is not the case in America: People here put their own happiness first, the basic attitude is 'me, me, me' and they get angry over small, stupid things, such as traffic, that they can't do anything about anyway."

"moral" society, or irate that some groups would try to dictate how we live; annoyed about rising health-care costs and high gas prices; fed up with politicians and the media and traffic and crime and pollution …. The list is endless.

Popular culture—violent video games, "rage rock," mayhem in movies and on television—seems to embrace and feed that anger, rather than demonstrating and encouraging a conflict resolution through communication and compromise. The more we see raging people who get away with being angry and get what they want to boot, the more it seems okay for us, too.

It doesn't help, some experts say, to slap cute labels on rather unattractive (and totally unacceptable) behavior. In addition to road rage and air rage, we've now got desk rage, shopping rage, parking rage, and even surf rage. Call it what it is: that little incident where you ran another car off the highway was more than road rage—it was assault!

There are other factors at play. Your grandmother will tell you that kids these days are not taught to be as polite as she was in her day, and she's probably right. Without the skills for civil discourse—and practice in doing it—we allow ourselves to be rude to one another, and that just makes everybody mad.

Charles Spielberger suspects that as our lives get more and more complicated, we have more things to be frustrated about. "Frustration does lead to anger," he says. Spielberger also blames Americans' rising rage on simple laziness. Because we're not as physically active, we don't have that outlet for our frustrations. We don't blow off steam plowing a field or walking that mile into town. We blow up.

Adding to the problem, Americans also often *want more* than the members of other societies. It's the American dream to have it all, isn't it? That can brew up a fair amount of anger. "When everything is possible, limitations are irksome," writes Tavris in *Anger*. "When the desires of the self come first, the needs of others are annoying. When we think we deserve it all, reaping only a portion can enrage."

Is Overstimulation to Blame?

Could it also be that we just have and do too much? Although there isn't any scientific proof that our increasingly busy lives have caused a general rise in surly behavior, it isn't a stretch to suspect the connection. After all, it's hard not to be overwhelmed when the TV is blaring, the phone is ringing, the kids are bickering, dinner needs to be made, and there's work to be done. In a toddler, that kind of overstimulation can bring on a whopper of a temper tantrum.

What about in adults? Maybe so. It really depends on your own temperament. Some people don't mind a bit of sensory overload and can thrive in chaos. Other people need things to be calm so they can focus, and when they don't get it, they get flustered.

What You Can Do

Is anger good for anything? It can be destructive, but it doesn't have to be. Anger can provide power and purpose and energy. Learn to use it to your advantage.

- ☐ Slow down. Appreciate your life—what you have, what you've done, the people you love. Being thankful for what you have lowers your anger threshold so that daily frustrations may not seem so frustrating.

- ☐ Accept that you can't be happy all the time, and that you can't always get what you want.

- ☐ If you're angry and passionate about an injustice or a social cause, embrace the feelings, then channel the energy. Take action.

- ☐ If a work situation has you fuming, don't just stew—stir things up. Tell your boss, calmly and assertively, why you are unhappy. Tell her what would improve your situation. Or start looking for a new job, update your resumé, and make contacts.

- ☐ Learn to appreciate the cultural differences in how people express their emotions—inclugding anger. Remember that a person of Hispanic heritage might express his feelings much more readily and vividly than a Japanese American, but their emotions are equally valid and may be equally intense.

- ☐ That said, if you're stuck in your own cultural mold and find that it is causing problems in your life or relationships, don't assume you have to stick with the programming. You can retrain yourself to express your anger in ways that work better for you.

What Sex Has to Do with It

Ever watched somebody of the opposite sex get mad? It's fascinating, even if it's bewildering, because they sure don't get mad like *you* do. Men yell and fight; women pout and cry.

Okay, so that's a generalization ("a *sweeping* generalization," as my high school English teacher would say), and it's certainly not true for every man or for every woman. But there's definitely something different about what gets men and women mad, and about how they deal with their anger. Here's what biologists, psychologists, and other researchers have learned about anger's gender divide.

Grouchy Men, Bitchy Women?

Consider some of the labels used to describe angry men: assertive, powerful, strong, and motivated. Or they might be considered vicious bullies, hotheads, and violent wife beaters.

Now, what about women? Well, if they actually *get* angry and let their feelings out, they're bitchy, a nag, overbearing, rude, perhaps shrewish, and scolding. They might have PMS. "Good" girls are supposed to be soft spoken and agreeable, to not make a lot of waves. "Both sexes, when asked, will say that women ought not to be the recipients or instigators of anger and aggression, poor fragile creatures that they are," writes social psychologist Carol Tavris, Ph.D., in *Anger: The Misunderstood Emotion.*

Sarcasm aside, it's clear that our society attaches stereotypes to anger in men and women. You can dismiss the stereotypes as social misperceptions that have nothing to do with how we experience anger. But we absorb the stereotypes as we grow up, and they can affect how we feel about anger—and, in fact, how we feel the emotion.

you're not alone

A Private Note to My Friend Ambre, Writ Publicly

Dear Ambre, every now and then, despite the fact that we are so fundamentally alike, you and I will disagree with one another—and we'll say so. Sometimes, we say so over and over again, caught up in a desire to change the other's mind. And every time it happens, at some point during our back-and-forth I'll smile to myself and think, "I bet she doesn't know how happy this makes me. I really need to tell her." But then I get sucked back into the debate, and I forget.

I'm remembering now. And I'm thanking you.

You may be wondering why arguing with you makes me happy. Let me go back a bit. My parents officially announced their intention to divorce when I was 11. But in all the years of their marriage, I can remember only two fights. Ever. Two. One of them is particularly vivid; we were at the new house of one of my mother's best friends and her husband, and I began to feel sick. Turned out I had a high fever. So my folks borrowed some blankets and put me in the car and drove me home. It was snowing hard, and very cold. And on the way, they got into an argument about which direction to go, and they raised their voices a bit. I began to sob, scared and sick in the back seat, and they fell into silence. When we got home, I was so distraught and feverish that they came into the room and hugged each other to prove that everything was okay. (It wasn't. As it turned out, my father was sleeping with my mother's friend, and if I'm remembering correctly, that was the night my mom found out. As an aside, every time I think about that hug, I wonder just how much self-esteem and self-respect that cost my mother, and am awed by how much she was willing to sacrifice for me.) Then they went back into the living room of our tiny apartment, and watched TV. If they argued any further, I didn't hear it, and I would have, given my proximity to where they were.

This really isn't a huge aside; I think of it as somehow explaining an awful lot about who I am today. All I know is that I've never, ever felt comfortable confronting people or standing up for myself. I've gone through my life as a people-pleaser, somehow figuring that I'd be better off having people like me than saying what I feel or think. That has included friends and even lovers. I've always had the fear, in the back of my mind, that if I would dare disagree with a friend, said friend would banish me from their life forever. Better to be agreeable than sorry, I always said.

I knew that my husband and I would end up being just fine together when I got to the point where I could get angry enough at him to scream at him, and not assume that meant our relationship was over. (To be honest, that point didn't come until *after* we were already married; it takes me a while.) Now, while we very rarely have that kind of explosive exchange, I don't fear the repercussions of it; there may be a number of reasons why I don't always say what I have to say to him, but it's not because I don't trust him to stick with me even if he sees my "ugly" side.

That's the way I feel about you, too. I can launch myself into an "I think you're full of it and here's why" rant without a second thought to whether or not you'll still be my friend after we've both said our piece. That tells me just how important you are to me; that I'm willing to be me, all of me, in front of you. It tells me that I trust you with my most vulnerable parts. And that's huge for me. Huge.

This essay originally appeared on a blog called Tiny Coconut (http://tinycoconut.blogspot.com). It is reprinted here with the permission of the author.

What Provokes Us: The Gender Rift   Without that socialization, would we really be that different? In some ways, yes.
Psychologist Sandra Thomas, Ph.D., director of the Ph.D. nursing
program at the University of Tennessee, has led several extensive
studies of anger in women as part of an eight-year-long Women's
Anger Study, and more recently has been probing anger in men.

Her research has turned up several key distinctions. For one
thing, women and men don't tend to get mad about the same
things. Women tend to get angry when they feel powerless,
when they experience or witness injustice, and when others are
irresponsible. Their anger often emerges in their most intimate
relationships—with a spouse, children, other family members,
friends, or close co-workers. Women get mad when they are let
down or when too much is expected of them. They are frustrated when they pour their energy and intensity and devotion
into a relationship, and get less in return.

"Lack of relationship reciprocity is a frequent trigger of a
woman's anger," Thomas says. "The woman feels pressed,
stretched, and almost pulled apart by multiple demands, and she
wants someone or something to change but often feels powerless
to make this happen."

Those things might also peeve a guy, but other stuff gets his
goat more. Thomas has found that men get mad about what
they can't control and can't fix—whether it is an inanimate
object such as a computer or a car, a situation at work, or their
son's wild fastball. They get angry when people they can't control
("control" is the buzzword here) act illogically or improperly—the
stupid driver who didn't wait his turn at the stop sign—or vio-
late their sense of how things should or should not be done. (It
often doesn't matter that "their way" is not necessarily the right
way, or that there are alternatives.)

Men's anger is generally provoked by strangers, not loved ones; by faulty mechanical objects (often the tools of their work); and by "global societal issues in which a principle was at stake or an injustice was perceived," writes Thomas. Does that mean they don't get angry at their family members and other intimates? Not likely. They might just not report it as often.

> ## GET PSYCHED
>
> "Situations where my opinion or outlook differs from someone else's and you have to come up with a solution can be a huge problem for me. I get lost and frustrated, then that frustration builds up and I get angry."
> —*Jeff, a contractor*

There are other distinctions: women often cry when they are angry, and often report being "hurt." It's a feeling women have a hard time distinguishing from anger, perhaps because women have been trained by society to believe their anger is unacceptable. (We'll get to that later.) "When we talk to women, they'll say, 'I'm not angry, I'm just upset,'" says anger researcher Karin Bruckner, Ph.D., a psychologist in private practice in the Dallas area. "They can't use the 'a' word because of all the negative connotations." Men, on the other hand, don't cry when they're mad (at least, they don't say they do), and they very rarely say they feel hurt, Sandra Thomas's studies show.

Men and women even use different imagery to describe their internal feelings of anger. Men talk about their rage as a flood or fire or some other powerful force that sweeps them along, while women use words such as "simmering," "slow boiling," and "stewing" that illustrate how their anger often lingers without release.

What Do We Do with Our Anger?

If you're a woman, the answer might be nothing. Psychological tests reveal that although women are generally regarded as the more emotionally expressive sex, that's not necessarily so with anger. In fact, women are less inclined than men to admit angry feelings to themselves and others. Those feelings crop up just as frequently in women as in men, but they're less likely to act on them.

PsychSpeak

The **State-Trait Anger Expression Inventory** is a psychological test that can reveal your anger patterns—if you express or suppress anger, how you control it, and more.

On one commonly used scale, women generally score high on measures of "anger-in"—anger that is felt but directed inward. Just because women tend to hold in their feelings doesn't mean it's easy or instinctual. "Women wrestle with angry feelings and how to communicate them to a huge degree," says Bruckner. It also doesn't mean that any individual woman will follow the pattern and hold in her rage; lots of women express, assert, and act on their angry feelings—sometimes too much.

The suppression doesn't usually last. It can emerge in passive-aggressive behavior, or might build up and then erupt in a volcanic angry outburst. This usually doesn't help much to resolve the underlying issues causing anger, and often makes women feel guilty and ashamed. Men go the other way and have higher "anger-out" scores; they're more likely to express and assert their feelings.

In the course of research to create a new anger scale, Raymond DiGiuseppe, Ph.D., chair of the psychology department at St. John's University in New York, has also found gender differences.

Women stay angry longer, are more resentful, and are more likely to write off the people who've made them mad, axing them out of their lives. They also let out their feelings in a variety of indirect ways: blaming, sarcasm, sulking, indecisiveness, and manipulation, among others.

Men are more impulsive in dealing with their anger and more physically aggressive. They more often seek revenge through their anger, and are more inclined to use anger to coerce others into doing what they want.

Men also score higher on passive-aggressive behavior. That may seem surprising; our society tends to think that men who have anger problems are overly aggressive— the blowhard, or the bully. Because women tend to let out their feelings in indirect ways, it seems they should also score higher on passive aggression.

> ## GET PSYCHED
>
> "The power of anger can be used to achieve conditions of justice and equality. To claim their power, however, is frightening to women because they equate power with destructiveness and selfishness .... It is *effective* power that we advocate: power that enables women to make positive, proactive changes in their lives."
> —*Psychologist Sandra Thomas, Ph.D., R.N., University of Tennessee, in the Journal of Advanced Nursing (1998)*

Not so. Passive-aggressive behaviors more often crop up in men. Ever known a man who didn't follow through on agreements, or who procrastinated? Who withheld his opinion or feelings and then got upset when you didn't know what he wanted? Other behaviors are common in passive-aggressive men, just as in women: sarcasm, sulking, belittling. The passive-aggressive man is the one who pushes all of his girlfriend's or spouse's buttons, gets her riled up, then says that *she* has a problem with anger. It's the boss who hems and haws about decisions, leaving his employees dangling. These men aren't trying to drive their partners crazy (although that's often the result).

They generally have a fear of conflict or confrontation, and try to avoid it by ignoring their feelings—but those feelings come out in other ways, or the emotions get turned inward, leading to anxiety, stress, and health problems.

But contrary to stereotypes, many men are not proud of their anger. The men interviewed by Sandra Thomas all emphasized the destructive potential of their anger—which they consider a "problematic and uncomfortable emotion." It seems we're all unsettled by anger, regardless of how we show it to the world.

Is Biology to Blame?

Men and women have such obvious physical differences that it seems equally obvious that gender variation in anger must also have some physiological cause. Obvious, but not necessarily true.

Scientists still aren't quite certain how biology fits into the picture. There are some intriguing hints, however, that suggest at least a tenuous connection between our emotional differences and basic biological processes.

For example, take an August 2002 study in the *Proceedings of the National Academy of Science* by researchers at the State University of New York at Stony Brook, which found that emotionally charged photographs (say, of bodies and guns) were more readily remembered by female volunteers than by their male counterparts. Scans of the subjects' brains when they viewed the photos revealed an increase in the blood flow to nine areas of the women's brains, compared to only two areas in the men's.

That means women really are better at remembering the details of emotionally charged events—which explains how some women seem to remember every word (especially the nasty ones) spoken during an argument. They're also better than men at recognizing an angry face on a woman, discovered Lisa Goos of York University in Toronto. That may seem sexist, but it makes sense evolutionarily: men, being physically stronger than women in general, have less reason to worry about whether or not a woman is angry. Knowing when another physically strong guy is angry, however, has survival benefits for a man.

Finger size, of all things, also offers clues to the relationship between our biology and our angry behavior. Psychologist Peter Hurd, Ph.D., of the University of Alberta, and his grad student Allison Bailey have discovered that the length of a man's index finger relative to his ring finger is a good predictor of how physically aggressive he is.

The link, reported in the March 2005 issue of *Biological Psychology*, isn't as ridiculous as it sounds. Scientists have known for more than a century that the ratio between index finger and ring finger differs between men and women, and more recently have found that finger length is related to the amount of *testosterone* that a baby is exposed to while in the womb. High testosterone means a short index finger (again, relative to the ring finger)—and a lot more physical aggression (but not verbal aggression), say Hurd and Bailey.

> **PsychSpeak**
>
> High levels of the male hormone **testosterone** have been linked to increased aggressive behavior.

Testosterone doesn't just affect the sex organs. The brain is slightly altered, too; several regions grow larger when exposed to testosterone, including parts of the hypothalamus, which is crucial for sleep, appetite, respiration, heartbeat, and sexual desire; and the amygdala, the brain structure that helps process fear and anger. With bigger amygdalas, men could theoretically be more anger prone, although the size of one part of the brain doesn't necessarily relate to behavior.

A Creation of Culture?

Although biologists still debate whether the physical variation in our bodies leads to the differences in how men and women feel and express anger, there is little doubt that society's clearly defined gender roles shape our relationships with anger.

Even today, boys are often taught not to express emotions such as fear or hurt or anxiety. "Growing up male, we are taught to avoid anything that is seen as the least bit feminine. We are taught that men 'do' while women 'feel.' As a result men are taught to keep all emotions under wrap," says Jed Diamond, a licensed psychotherapist and author of *The Irritable Male Syndrome.* "We cannot show we are hurt, afraid, worried, or panicked. The only feeling that is sometimes allowed many men is anger."

WEB TALK: Read about irritable male syndrome, male depression, and other male issues at Jed Diamond's site:

➤ www.menalive.com

Girls, on the other hand, might learn that anger is unfeminine, unattractive, and unladylike. Because many girls are still taught that being pleasant, appealing, and ladylike are important female characteristics, is it so surprising that they resist showing anger?

Stereotyping can take a toll on kids at a very young age. Through interviews of children in the Dallas public school system, psychologist Deborah L. Cox, Ph.D., of Southwest Missouri State University, observed that as early as the fourth grade, girls who were previously relatively open with their angry emotions started to pull away from their friends and not talk about their feelings when they got mad. They still get angry—studies show that men and women (and boys and girls) experience anger at the same frequency—but the girls are no longer inclined to act on it. "They assume they are going to be made fun of when angry," Cox says, and so they tend to suppress their feelings, which can lead to behaviors such as not eating and social withdrawal, "things that look like depression," she says. "There is a lot of criticism for girls who don't know how to moderate or control their anger," concurs Karin Bruckner.

A feminist might tell you that anger is perceived as an instrument of power, which makes it taboo for women, because men are in control. Another reason women deny their angry feelings could be the notion that women, as the more "nurturing" gender, are supposed to devote their emotional energy to taking care of both the people around them and their relationships. Some women can address negative feelings (their own or someone else's) in a healthy way and maintain their emotional equilibrium. But other women aren't so good at it, in part because anger is rather universally frowned upon, and so they shut down that emotion. "Society has simply done a superb job of assigning them the tasks of preserving relationship harmony, even if the needs of the self—and feelings such as anger—must be set aside in the process," says Sandra Thomas.

The socialization runs deep, says Cox, who thinks the social construct of gender is so powerful that it shapes how we experience and display anger outwardly, and in a way that psychologists call *affectively*. "Learning so well that you shouldn't be angry can translate into not really feeling it," she says. "If you query a woman, 'What are you feeling? What is going on in your body right now?' you might get responses such as, 'My chest is tight, my palms are sweaty, my heart is racing,' but she might not call that anger because she's not supposed to."

PsychSpeak

Affective pertains to emotions, feelings, or mental states. Our **affect** is how we display our emotional state.

By the time little boys become toddlers, they kick, push, wrestle, and hit more often than girls do, and they are prodded to be tough and fearless. Being encouraged to show aggression may seem preferable to stifling your feelings, but the anger box men are forced into fits them no better. Although many conform to standards of "aggressive masculinity," they aren't particularly thrilled about it, says Sandra Thomas. In a 2003 study about the meaning of anger in middle-class men, Thomas found that men were unhappy about the social pressure that pushed them into their angry, manly roles, and often as uncomfortable and conflicted about anger as women.

"In speaking of boyhood experiences, they pointed out that becoming a successful fighter did not make them feel good about themselves. Many men described decades of inner conflict regarding anger and its expression," she says. They "were emphatic in stating that anger was never a good feeling for them, even if they discharged its force in decisive action."

Studies that look not at gender but at *gender roles*—whether masculine, feminine, or androgynous (regardless of their actual gender)—bear out the importance of socially defined roles. People who are highly feminine are more likely to suppress their anger and to get angry at their co-workers and intimates, whereas extremely masculine personalities are more aggressive, more prone to anger, and less able to control it. Interestingly, androgynous people, who don't identify strongly as either masculine or feminine, have the healthiest anger traits: they are less prone to anger, suppress it less, and control it better, which just goes to show that extremes in anything are rarely good for you.

you're not alone

For Louisa, a 40-year-old government worker from Virginia, getting angry was never an option during her childhood and adolescence. "When I was growing up, I would never yell and scream the way other people—my mom and dad—did when they were angry. My parents didn't get angry that often, but when they did, it was frightening to me, and so in my mind anger in any form was bad, a negative thing. So I wouldn't blow up or make a scene. As far as I was concerned, I never actually got angry. What I *would* do is get 'upset,' however, and I would cry when I got frustrated or something violated my sense of fairness."

It was only in adulthood that Louisa came to accept her own angry feelings. "I had a terrible boss who treated me incredibly unfairly. She lied, screwed me around, and generally treated me like dirt. I blamed myself for the longest time, figuring it must have been something I'd done. But then I started seeing that she was treating other people badly too, and I caught her in blatant lies. It dawned on me that I was incredibly angry."

After the "evil boss" transferred to another state, and her career got back on track, Louisa got a healthier handle on the angry feelings she suppressed and denied for so long. "I still sometimes cry, and I still won't blow up, but I've gotten better at discussing with other people what is bothering me. Maybe part of it too is just getting older and having more experiences, and caring less about what other people think."

Anger and Sex

When you're discussing men, women, and anger, it's impossible to pull sexuality out of the picture. Look at some of the words used to describe anger: heat, passion, boiling, bursting, and so on. Don't they bring, oh ... *sex* to mind?

Is there an intimate connection between anger and arousal? Perhaps, although the nature of the link hinges on whether you're looking at men or women. For example, although some studies show that men might view sex as a way of resolving conflict—smoothing over the fight—women don't usually see sex as a solution. It's often the last thing they want when they're pissed off at their partner.

Q&A

Is there any truth to the adage that sex is better after couples fight?

"It may be for some people—if the anger is pretty well resolved. There is a pattern where people have fights and then make up, and then they feel closer to each other, and sex can be part of that. Anger also leads to pure physiological arousal. When you get angry you get pumped up. If your partner stops being a jerk and starts acting sweet, and the situation gets resolved, that physiological arousal can switch to something else."
—*Sally Stabb, Ph.D., psychologist at Texas Women's University*

Indeed, our physiological desire for sex appears to be influenced by anger, and here, too, men and women part ways. In a series of detailed online surveys to examine the link between anger and sexuality, psychologist and anger researcher Sally Stabb, Ph.D., of Texas Women's University, found that sexual arousal and the desire for sex drops in women when they get angry. The effect is more profound in women with a history of abuse, who are also less likely to discuss their anger about sexual issues. In men, on the other hand, anger is much less likely to diminish sexual arousal; in fact, some studies suggest that it can increase their ardor, although other reports have found no such effect.

In a separate survey of more than 200 women, Stabb found that how a woman deals with her anger parallels her feelings about sex and her own sexuality. Women who tend to repress their anger, for example, have negative views of their bodies and of sex, while women who have the highest levels of anger report low sexual satisfaction.

WEB TALK: Read about research on women's anger at the Anger Project:

www.angerproject.com

What is the cause and what is the effect? It's not clear. Women might be angrier because they're not sexually satisfied, or they might not be sexually satisfied because of their problems with anger and its underlying cause—which might have to do with their partners!

What is certain is that sex can be a big source of frustration and hurt feelings—and anger—in relationships. When couples go into therapy, Stabb says, the most common complaint of men is that they're not getting enough sex. "When their request for sex gets denied, they feel rejected, but in their social role they are not allowed to feel rejected, so they get angry instead," she says. Their anger might manifest as hostility or critical comments to their partner, "and she will get further turned off because she doesn't want to have sex with someone who is hostile and critical," perpetuating the problem, she says.

What Are the Consequences?

If you believe that men and women are simply acting the parts that they've been assigned, for whatever reason (biology, psychology, social prodding), then you'll also probably feel that the scenes play out between them as they should.

Men should be the more assertive and vocal and physical gender when it comes to their anger; it's what makes them men. Women should be more cautious with their words and actions, finding other ways to express their feelings and get what they need.

Most of us, though, don't want to be forced into a rigid role based on stereotypes, and we aren't very good at meeting society's expectations anyway. That's one reason why both men and women tend to have such strong and complicated feelings about how their anger relates to their gender roles. Another reason is that the strictest interpretation of these roles—a shouting, bullying man and a passive woman—doesn't help anyone get their needs met in a healthy and constructive way. Men—most of them, anyway—don't like losing their temper or getting into heated confrontations. The volunteers in Sandra Thomas's study of male anger were uncomfortable and conflicted about their anger just as often as women. Those she spoke to were often concerned about being controlled by anger, which they often felt was an emotion that *they* couldn't entirely control. And although they were ashamed of their behavior when they lost control and acted aggressively or violently, men also felt shame when they did not act "according to internalized norms of masculinity," Thomas says.

GET PSYCHED

"If we have a variety of supportive relationships, we do better with managing stress, but we ultimately need to be talking to just about everyone we get angry with. It may be hard in some circumstances, but it will keep those relationships connected."
–Deborah Cox, Ph.D., psychologist and anger researcher

Women who try to bury their anger, on the other hand, end up isolating themselves emotionally—which hurts not just them but the spouses, parents, children, and friends around them.

"As women, we fear our anger so much that we avoid talking about it, and we're so afraid that we're going to hurt someone by telling them that they've made us mad that in a sense we take ourselves out of the relationship," says Cox. The paradox is obvious: women may be socialized to be "relationship creatures," Cox says, but because of their unhealthy attitudes about anger and concerns about damaging those relationships, they inadvertently sabotage them, while alienating themselves. "We sacrifice our connectedness out of the fear that we will be left all alone, rejected, and annihilated, inside our relationship. There may be a short-term risk in expressing our feelings, but in the long term it seems like more honesty pays off."

Swallowing anger also rarely gets rid of it for good. It comes out somehow, sometime. You might not take your husband to task for forgetting, again, to put his dirty socks in the laundry, but you're still annoyed. With every dirty sock, that annoyance builds to irritation, then anger, then rage, and then you blow— maybe not about a sock at all, but probably something equally minor. Your husband, on the other hand, may think you're being unnecessarily naggy about the socks—or he might not give it a thought at all, because other than your occasional reminders to pick up the things, you don't tell him it's driving you mad. When you do explode, he'll never think it's *really* about socks. He'll just think you're acting nuts.

All these gender-stereotyped behaviors might be easy enough to settle into—it's what we're taught, what our parents did, and how our friends and neighbors might act. But being common doesn't make it at all healthy.

What You Can Do

Men and women can be very different creatures when it comes to emotions, and anger especially. Those differences can breed confusion and conflict.

It doesn't have to be that way. We might have been socialized as little girls and boys to behave a certain way, and told how—or how not—to feel. And our own biology might be butting in. But we can still make changes, learn new patterns, and take a fresh path.

☐ Think about the things that get you mad. Is your anger rooted in relationship strife or in your need to have control? You certainly don't have to fall into those traditional female/male boxes, but it can be enlightening to keep them in mind when you evaluate your own behavior.

☐ Take a look at your own family. How does your mom get angry? Is your dad a yeller, or does he keep everything in? The tactics we use to cope with our own anger very often come from our parents. Their behavior can be a mirror to our own.

☐ Think about the messages you are giving your own kids about their anger. Have you ever told your son that boys shouldn't cry, or told your daughter that it's not ladylike to get mad?

☐ If you haven't before, now is the time to tell your kids— sons and daughters alike—that they have a right to feel and express their emotions, respectfully and without yelling.

☐ If you and your mate find sex to be most passionate after a fight—lots of us do—don't use that as an excuse *to* fight. There are healthier ways to stir up passion: have a romantic dinner or take a bath together. Give each other a massage. Tenderness is better than a tantrum.

☐ Don't get caught up in the passion of a fight (or the aftermath) and forget to resolve your problem. Sex might be better in that moment, but eventually the intimacy will be lost.

Kids Get Angry, Too

To parents, relatives, guardians, teachers, and other caregivers, an angry child or adolescent can be both frustrating and heartbreaking. But in children and adolescents, just as in adults, anger has a purpose, and it can be both useful and powerful.

Kids are supposed to get angry. They *should* get angry. In them, as in adults, anger can be a blaring alarm that something is wrong and it needs attention: they need help or need to act. Anger also helps children define their boundaries, their likes and dislikes, and where the world ends and they begin. But anger can also get *way* out of control.

Sometimes a child's problems are obvious: your child may constantly get into fights, argue with you, and defy your authority, or he may act out in class or vandalize school property. Such fury can be difficult to understand and cope with, and it often seems hard to help, although even the most onerous tempers can be tamed, experts say. In other kids, angry emotions are buried under passivity, sarcasm, withdrawal, neediness, or self-destructive behaviors. You might not recognize that your child's actions are planted in angry feelings—but they may well be.

If you think you've got it tough as the parent or teacher of an angry kid, put yourself in his shoes. Talk about an uncomfortable fit! For many reasons—biological, psychological, even social—children and adolescents are poorly equipped to deal with their angry thoughts, feelings, and impulses. They don't understand their anger, and they don't have the skills to control it. And that often leaves them conflicted, guilty, and ashamed.

Anger in children, when it is unaided and unhealed, can lead to anger in adulthood—which is very often much more severe— perpetuating a cycle that can last a lifetime, even for generations. But children can learn control, too, experts say; there is always a path to control and calmness, however hard it may be to find.

Are Kids Getting Angrier?

Maybe so. Kids are more stressed out, less patient, less polite, and quicker to rage. They're often overworked and overscheduled. Media and television violence, along with violent video games, have led to an increasing level of anger and aggression in children and adolescents (which we'll discuss a bit later).

> **GET PSYCHED**
>
> "Parents and teachers must allow children to feel all their feelings .... Strong feelings cannot be denied, and angry outbursts should not always be viewed as a sign of serious problems; they should be recognized and treated with respect."
> –*Luleen S. Anderson in* The Aggressive Child

"It's definitely getting worse," says psychologist and former school superintendent Sara Salmon, Ph.D., executive director of the Center for Safe Schools and Communities in Denver, Colorado. Although it's hard to quantify just how many kids are coping with angry feelings these days, experts such as Salmon point to increasing violence as proof of rising rage. Anger can lead to aggression and violence, and violence—especially in children—rarely happens without anger in the picture.

Youth violence has decreased in some respects since the "epidemic" that plagued the United States from 1983 to 1993, but it hasn't disappeared by any means. For example, a recent report by the Centers for Disease Control (CDC) revealed that in 2003, 1 in 10 high school students reported being threatened or injured with a weapon on school property during the prior 12 months.

Students, the CDC says, are increasingly unwilling to go to school because they fear for their safety. They're not just worried about weapons; studies show that roughly one-sixth of U.S. children report being bullied. The actual numbers may be higher. Those picked-on kids can go on to develop serious *post-traumatic stress* and depressive disorders, while the bullies may become more and more antisocial; both groups often have academic problems.

Some child violence turns deadly. These rare cases tend to get all the attention, but for every murderously violent child, tens of thousands—likely many more—are struggling to control their anger. Perhaps their relationships with parents and family members have become strained. Or if a difficult home life with troubled parents is the *cause* of their anger, they might be acting out at school, having trouble making and keeping friends, or resorting to bullying and other brutish behavior.

PsychSpeak

Post-traumatic stress disorder, or PTSD, is an anxiety disorder associated with a severely traumatic event or series of incidents. Bullied kids can begin to exhibit signs of PTSD.

How Kids Express Their Rage

What makes it tough for adults is that they don't always know if and when a child is angry. The rare child will be able to directly communicate how they are feeling. With children, as with adults, however, that's pretty darned rare—and, if they're assertive, honest, and communicative, they're probably able to manage their anger before it becomes a problem.

Children tend to mask the anger behind other actions, displace it onto other things, or vent it indirectly. They might be aggressive, or not. They might be physical, or not. They might lash out at others, or themselves, or sulk or pout or cry. It can be quite a challenge to figure out where anger lurks—especially when even your child may not know it's there.

To help the confused parent, child anger experts have identified a number of clues that indicate a child is feeling angry. (Children do tend to be much more expressive than adults, which is a help.) In addition to the physical signs—clenched teeth, rolling eyes, tense body, funny noises (little kids may make growling noises when they're mad), kids who are feeling angry might begin to speak faster or get restless and jumpy, or they might start whining. Behavioral problems in an otherwise obedient child can be a sign of unspoken anger, as can sorrow without an obvious cause. Licensed clinical psychologist Bernard Golden, Ph.D., has identified a host of behaviors that children may use as anger management strategies. The list includes ...

- **Verbal aggression.** Yelling, teasing, name-calling, or the use of inappropriate language can be indirect ways of expressing anger. The intent is not to express whatever is making him angry, but to inflict hurt on the recipient of the verbal barrage—a hallmark of bullying behavior.

- **Physical aggression.** This can be an assault on someone who has made a child mad, or on an object—smashing a toy, for example. Most adults won't resort to pushing, shoving, or breaking things unless they're furious, but it's common in children (especially toddlers) and is often their first instinct when they're mad.

- **Displacing anger.** Displaced anger is focused on someone or something other than the cause of the feelings. Self-destructive and risky behavior, such as driving recklessly and substance abuse, can be anger that is displaced inward, as can self-destructive behaviors such as cutting. Body piercing and tattoos, although disturbing to many parents, probably aren't a sign of buried anger. (Although if the piercing starts to seem compulsive, you might want to talk to your child about why they feel the need to do it.)

- **Withdrawal.** Children who feel that their anger will be ignored or that they will be rejected for expressing it might simply withdraw emotionally from a situation. (In some situations, however, withdrawal can be an effective and healthy way to control anger.)

Lateness, stealing, anxiety, physical ailments such as headaches and stomachaches, extreme neediness, sarcasm, self-denigration, academic underachievement, and sexual promiscuity—all of these can also be manifestations of anger.

If you see any of these signs in your kids and you suspect that anger might be behind them, sit your children down, talk to them, express your caring and your concern, and try to get to the heart of their feelings. Be sure your kids know that anger is a perfectly normal emotion that they should feel free to express, as long as they're not acting out in hurtful ways. One way to encourage your kids to talk about their feelings is to set aside regular family time to address their issues and concerns. (And actually be willing to discuss things; if your child is angry about a decision you've made—that they can't go to the mall, for example—explain your reasons, rather than just saying "I'm the mom so you do what I say.") You might also work with your kids to come up with alternative behaviors. What can they do instead of yelling? How might they deal with their feelings?

It might be fruitless at first—a teenager who is used to locking down emotionally and who has crawled out of touch from you isn't likely to immediately pour out his pain and frustration— but you'll at least be starting a dialogue.

Types of Aggressive Children

As you've read in previous chapters, not all angry people are aggressive, and not all aggression stems from anger. Remember, anger is the emotion; aggression is an action with the intent to cause harm. The two, however, are often quite closely linked, and this is true for children as well.

Aggression in children "begins with inept discipline," says social psychologist Carol Tavris, Ph.D. Parents punish often, but the punishment may have little to do with a child's behavior; they fail to establish clear rules and consistent consequences, and they don't praise good behavior or require that their kids actually comply with their punishments.

What comes next isn't surprising: kids listen less and disobey more; parents respond by exploding, perhaps with verbal and physical assault. And more and more, kids learn to be aggressive.

Clinical psychologist John Lochman, Ph.D., of the University of Alabama, has been studying aggression in children for nearly 30 years. He's found that aggressive children can be divided into two groups: reactive aggressive and proactive aggressive.

Reactive Aggressive: Kids Who Lash Out These children "are the most obviously aroused with anger at the time of their aggressive acts," Lochman says. "They are responding to a provocation, getting quickly angry about it, and then they respond impulsively." Reactive-aggressive kids only lash out when they feel they've been threatened or pushed into it.

"This is the most common pattern seen in children," Lochman says, and they can be helped to control their temper and its consequences with relaxation techniques, distraction, and other tactics that teach the kids how to avoid those knee-jerk, aggressive reactions.

> **GET PSYCHED**
>
> "'Authoritative' parents know when and how to discipline their children. They neither demand total obedience nor abdicate all rules; they set standards and enforce them firmly, while also explaining the reasons behind their discipline and demands. They use authority when necessary, yet also recognize their children's rights."
> —*Carol Tavris, Ph.D., in* Anger: The Misunderstood Emotion

Proactive Aggressive: Kids Who Scheme Proactive aggression, on the other hand, is a means to an end. The kids aren't provoked or threatened. Their behavior is calculated, a way to get something they want. "They are angry, but it is more of a simmering anger," Lochman says. They might perceive an enemy and resolve to act aggressively against them, "but it is not that instantaneous surge of rage that occurs in reactive aggression," Lochman says.

Kids displaying a subclass of this behavior that Lochman calls *instrumental* aggression act to acquire something tangible they want—a concrete object. Toddlers who kick a playmate or scream at them to get a toy fall into the instrumental-aggressive category.

Angry Bullying Bullying is also a type of proactive aggression, says Lochman. Bullying begins to crop up in early elementary school, "when kids really are preying on other kids," he says. The aim, however, is to inflict some kind of harm, whether it is psychological or physical. Bullies aren't trying to acquire something. The only purpose of the intimidation, teasing, or abuse is to cause another person distress.

WEB TALK: Get information on bullying of all kinds at:

www.bullyonline.org

Bullies also come in different flavors. Some are "pure" bullies. Their goal is really only to make someone else suffer. Pure bullies can be tough nuts to crack; they don't much care about the impact of their behavior on other children, nor do they have any internal motivation to change, so in trying to stop their behavior, "you really have to rely on external consequences, such as the removal of privileges or work chores," Lochman says.

More commonly, however, kids are bully victims, who seek to torment others—kids who are smaller or weaker or lower on the social totem pole—because they themselves have been tormented. In these children, Lochman says, anger management techniques and other methods can be effective because they really are responding to their rage at being victimized.

"These kids are easier for a clinician to work with, because you can ally with the part of them that has been victimized and help them think about how to cope with it," he says. "They don't like to feel that way, so they are willing to work on it."

Are Young Brains Predisposed to Snap?

With so much anger and aggression and violence turning up in young kids and adolescents, it's hard not to wonder if there might be some underlying biological cause—and not just our screwed-up society, faulty school management, and bad parenting.

It's foolish to overlook the huge impact of those things, but there might well be something going on in the brains of children and adolescents that can make it hard for them to handle anger. Neuroscientists used to think that because the brain is almost adult-size by the age of 6, most of our personality, behavior, and academic promise would be fully formed by then.

Not so. In fact, the brain continues to change—quite a lot—well through adolescence and into early adulthood. In 2001, neuroscientist Jay Geidd of the National Institute of Mental Health and neurologist Paul Thompson of the University of California at Los Angeles discovered that during this time, the *prefrontal cortex* of the brain is undergoing extensive changes. This part of the brain is often referred to as the brain's chief executive officer because it manages the activities of so many other areas and functions. Among them— you guessed it—our expression of anger.

With so much construction going on in this critical brain region, teenagers really might *not* have the same level of control over their actions, be they risky behaviors or a hair-trigger rage. They might have a harder time anticipating the consequences of their actions the way an adult would, and they may not be able to plan ahead. All of this underscores the

PsychSpeak

The **prefrontal cortex,** part of the brain's frontal lobe, behind the forehead and between the temples, exercises executive control over anger and other emotions. Without that control, we'd act impulsively and recklessly.

important role that parents have in guiding their kids toward making the best decisions, scientists say.

Other studies show that adolescents are less able to read the emotions of others than adults are, particularly expressions of fear and anger. In adults, this function happens in the prefrontal cortex, but in kids, it happens in more primitive and emotional parts of the brain. That means kids often misinterpret the actions and motivations of others. They might ascribe evil intent to a harmless remark (and get into a fight), or think their parents are scolding them when they're not. Such miscalculations breed frustration, conflict, and anger.

Moreover, some children (and adults) might have a genetic predisposition to anger and irritability. Child-development experts have discovered that just a few days after birth some infants already show signs of a bad temperament—they cry more, are anxious, and are generally difficult. Babies so young have not yet been affected much by their environment, which suggests that this crankiness may be innate.

It's important to remember that children, being children, are not emotionally mature. They don't have the psychological and social skills to deal with their feelings the way adults should be able to. They haven't yet fully developed the capacity for introspection, so they can't adeptly reflect on their own behavior and its consequences or completely understand the causes for their feelings. They're not terribly good at soothing their own damaged psyches, which means they tend to lash out, and they have low tolerance for frustration and poor impulse control. It's only natural.

That doesn't mean you should excuse unacceptable or out-of-control behavior. To the contrary, this should remind parents and educators that they have an enormous responsibility to help the children in their charge to become healthy, emotionally balanced adults.

WEB TALK: Kids and their parents can learn about anger and how better to express it at psychologist Lynne Namka's Angries Out site:

www.angriesout.com

Do Depressed Moms Rear Angry Kids?

There are a lot of other reasons that kids might have problems with anger and violence. Some might reach all the way back to infancy, finds psychologist Dale Hay of Cardiff University in the United Kingdom and her colleagues. The researchers screened 122 mothers in south London for signs of depression during pregnancy; 3 months after the birth of their children; and when their kids were 1 year old, 4 years old, and 11 years old. The kids were interviewed at age 11.

The study, published in 2003 in the journal *Developmental Psychology*, revealed that moms with postpartum depression were more likely to rear kids who had problems with violence. (Although most kids weren't violent at all.) Children of mothers who had more than one depressive episode after giving birth had the biggest problems: more than one-third described trouble paying attention and keeping their emotions in check, and they were prone to fights in school that often led to injury and suspension. Other family difficulties, such as financial problems or a biological father in jail, were ruled out as primary causes of the kids' behavior.

The researchers don't know if the mother's depression is a direct cause of the violence (due to some hereditary, biological connection between anger and violence) or if children who grow up to be more violent are also more difficult as babies, which could make their moms frustrated and depressed. Depressed moms might not be as successful at talking to and soothing their upset newborns, Hay says, which is how babies learn to calm themselves. Without those skills, the babies might grow up unable to manage their distress and agitated feelings—and are primed for anger and aggression. Postnatal depression is an "easily identifiable risk factor" for social development problems in children, say the researchers. They suggest that children of these mothers should be targeted for programs that prevent antisocial behavior. Mothers who worry that their own mood might be adversely influencing their kids' might consider talking to a therapist or counselor about their concerns. Most likely, the kids will be unaffected—but it can't hurt to get the opinion of a professional and some help if necessary.

Do Angry Parents Raise Angry Children?

There is no question that growing up in a rage-filled home can confuse and complicate a child's emotional development. How a child learns to experience and express their anger and respond to anger in others, however, will be shaded—sometimes darkly—by their upbringing. Children who are often exposed to boiling rage can become angry, hostile, aggressive, and just as abusive to others. Not every child will emulate their father or mother (or both) and fly off the handle at the slightest provocation, but some might. The effects of an angry childhood can linger for a lifetime.

According to a 1998 review in the *Archives of Pediatric and Adolescent Medicine* by Li-yu Song, Ph.D., of Case Western Reserve University and colleagues, being exposed to chronic anger is the most significant "trauma symptom" that leads to later violent behavior. "Growing up in a harsh and frustrating environment in which violence is frequently modeled may be the common theme for causing free-floating chronic anger or alienation from larger society," says Song and colleagues.

you're not alone

Child in Conflict

"Three different custody judges told my parents that theirs was the worst divorce they had ever seen," recalls 25-year-old Jamie, a psychology graduate student from Texas. Jamie's parents divorced when she was five, and for years she and her two sisters were dragged back and forth between homes as her parents fought angrily over who would have full custody. "We were in custody court every 13 or 14 months to decide again who would get us. We were pulled back and forth between our parents all the time."

Jamie reacted to her parents' fury at each other by denying her own emotions. "I think what their fighting conveyed to me was that their anger was more important than mine. We were put on the back burner as far as what we thought and what would make us happy. It was more important for them to win than to take into consideration our feelings, and so I didn't express anger a lot when I was growing up. I think I was angry at my parents, but I didn't express it much. I mostly internalized my anxiety and anger. I kept to myself. I did a lot of writing."

The custody battles finally ended when Jamie was 11, with the death of her father in a farming accident. "My mom got remarried; things settled down. I got into a routine, a pattern, being able to live in the same household for more than a year. It was the time of my life when I finally got to relax, even though I was grieving immensely for my father."

In high school, Jamie started to express her feelings a bit more, "and then in college I started to be able to express my anger. I think the turning point came when my older sister's fiancé was killed in a car accident and it pulled up a lot of the anger from my dad's death. I went to group therapy and started to talk about what I was angry about. It is still hard for me to express my anger, especially with authority figures, but I'm getting better at it. I've been working on it for a while—expressing my anger positively, so that I am able to get something as a result of what I am angry about."

Other children take an alternate path and become afraid of losing their temper or seeing others do so. They might suppress or repress their negative emotions—perhaps for fear of setting off a touchy parent or because they've learned that their own feelings don't matter in the family.

Alternatively, they might start to take it all out on someone or something else: a younger sibling, the family dog, a wall.

In *Healthy Anger: How to Help Children and Teens Manage Their Anger*, Bernard Golden compares mismanaged and ignored anger to compressed gases that seek a way to explode through "the slightest opening." This, says Golden, "is the anger that may lead to bullying, social withdrawal, underachievement, substance abuse, anxiety, depression, excessive guilt, and shame, or, in the extreme, devastating violence."

Psychologists looking back at the upbringing of aggressive children often find a disturbed family dynamic. Instead of peaceful discussion and conflict resolution, there is lots of yelling, name-calling, threats, and, sometimes, physical abuse. Children are outstanding mimics—and seemingly more adept when it comes to unflattering actions—and they will behave as they see others behave. Show them an angry face, pummel them with angry words, and they very frequently learn to do it, too.

Of course, angry parents aren't the only ones to foster anger in their children. Having a hard-driving *Type A*–personality parent can also lead to hostile and angry children. In a 2003 study published in the journal *Child Development*, Finnish researchers repeatedly interviewed 1,004 children over a 15-year period, starting at age 6. Their parents were divided into three groups—an average group, a "negative" Type A group, and a "positive" Type A group.

Parents in the negative group reported low life satisfaction and high job involvement, but they were often impatient with their kids. Their behavior promoted hostility (the researchers defined it as cynical, mistrustful, and paranoid behavior) in their kids. Parents in the positive group, on the other hand, were hard driving and competitive but much more involved with their children. Their kids were not as hostile.

> **PsychSpeak**
>
> The **Type A** personality is characterized by extreme ambition, competitiveness, impatience, and a sense of time pressure.

Provocations to Anger

A child doesn't have to be in an angry home or go to a violent, gang-ridden school to be exposed to anger-provoking situations. Life is tough, even—or perhaps especially—for children. They have little control over their surroundings and environment, after all, and that can inspire enormous frustration and flares of temper even in a well-adjusted child with the social and emotional tools to cope. For children who don't have those skills, a difficult home life and the regular traumas of school can be devastatingly difficult.

At Home At home is where children are supposed to feel protected and safe and loved. It doesn't always work out that way. My own children, sadly, know this from personal experience.

When my husband's rage was at its worst I had to deal with his temper, my oldest son's anger at his behavior, and, of course, my own anger over our situation (although I tended to suppress those feelings).

GET PSYCHED

"I grew up in a loud household. Most people have discussions. The discussions we had were at a high volume and occasionally accompanied by flying objects. I was the same way, and I thought it was normal, but when I went to college I realized pretty quickly that I had a huge problem." —*Jeff, a construction site foreman*

My son understood a bit about the biological reasons for his father's actions and he loves his dad tremendously, but he was also incredibly mad at him. At the time, my son didn't feel that he could talk to his father, whose behavior was too often irrational, so he took out his foul moods on me and his younger brother and sister. (He knew we were no threat.) He didn't understand his own behavior, of course—he was only 8 years old; there's no reason he should have. As he got a bit older (and as my husband began getting the right treatment), my son began to become more aware of his feelings—particularly his anger. With the help of a therapist, he started to recognize the signs of his anger and began to talk about those feelings rather than simply lashing out. He still tends to hold in his emotions, but it's easier to coax them out—which is great progress.

Any stressful family situation, whether caused by illness, family conflict, financial difficulties, or some other problem, can frequently cause anger—expressed or buried—in children. Children of divorced parents are frequently angry, bad tempered, and even nasty to their already-guilty parents. They might be furious at their parents for disrupting the family and their life and try to use their anger to get their parents to change, to get back together, or to fix their world. Anger is easier for them to deal with than the pain they'd otherwise feel over the loss of their family.

For parents, it can be understandably frustrating. After all, you're not getting a divorce to upset your child; you're trying to create some emotional stability in all of your lives. To get through it, talk to your kids and encourage them to get out what they're feeling inside. Let them know that anger is a normal, healthy, and appropriate emotion—especially in the situation that they're in. If you can get them to open up, don't expect to always love what you hear. They might tell you that you're ruining their life, that they hate you, that they're miserable. If you can't handle that, find a family therapist or other adviser for your kids.

The child of a parent with an addiction (drugs, alcohol, gambling, shopping, or whatever else compels them) might feel left out and ignored. As the parent focuses on the addiction, he or she fails to meet the emotional needs of the child. Those kids may become resentful and fixated on what they're not getting. They might also experience frustration, grief, betrayal, loss, rejection, abandonment, and a host of other difficult feelings. They might fear asking for anything from their parents, out of concern that their parents might reject them even more if they dare to need something.

"In later years, the child goes through life trying to get others to make up for what his parents did not provide," says psychologist Lynne Namka, Ed.D., who has worked extensively with angry children and runs Angries Out, a website for angry kids and parents. Because these kids generally haven't learned the social skills that would allow them to interact smoothly with people, they might not be able to establish beneficial friendships and be accepted by their peers. To deal with the failure, "he learns to substitute irrational anger, cruelty to others, addictive substances, workaholic behavior, or material objects to fill his neediness," Namka says.

Neglectful parents aren't the only source of anger. Overindulgent parents can also breed angry children. Giving a child everything he wants will only make him think he should *always* get what he wants—and when that doesn't happen, his rage will brew.

In School School is no picnic. Kids can get teased and criticized, bicker with their friends, or have trouble relating to their teacher. And usually they have to cope with the slights and fights without getting overtly angry.

"Kids today don't have the option of being angry in school. They are expected to go the whole day without communicating any anger," says Karin Bruckner, co-author of *The Anger Advantage* and a licensed professional counselor in private practice in the Dallas area.

At some schools, divisiveness and hatred are allowed to take root, says Sara Salmon. Salmon describes public high schools where gangs have been allowed to take over a certain part of the parking lot, and others where hate groups are allowed to proliferate. "They are giving in to the kids' demands," she says, "and when you allow that, violence grows. It's a societal problem."

WEB TALK: For facts and statistics on school violence, visit the National Association of Students Against Violence Everywhere (SAVE) site:
www.nationalsave.org/main/facts.php

Q&A

My son comes home from school in such a bad mood and loses his temper at his little sister over nothing. What can I do?

"It is really important to talk a lot with both our sons and daughters about how there are healthy ways to be mad and not so healthy ways to be mad. Tell them you know what is going on, how they have no control over things sometimes and how frustrating that is, and tell them to come home and tell you about it. 'Let's talk instead of your pinching your brother or teasing your sister.'" —*Karin Bruckner, author and licensed professional counselor in the Dallas area*

Other Influences

Say you have an emotionally healthy home and your kids go to good schools. There should be nothing to incite their anger and aggression, right? Not so fast. Do your kids go to movies? Do you have a television? A computer? A PS2 or XBox or GameCube? Then your kids are being subjected daily to a blinding barrage of violent images and actions. And, psychologists say, it may be contributing to aggressive behavior.

For example, a study in the February 2005 issue of the British medical journal *The Lancet* reviewed five meta-analyses (studies that combine the effects of other studies) of media violence and uncovered a significant link between watching violence—either passively (on television or in movies) or actively (through computer and video games)—and more aggressive play and behavior in children.

Keep in mind that kids didn't become *angrier* as a result of exposure to violent media—remember, anger is an emotion; aggressiveness is a behavior—but their increasingly aggressive tendencies mean that the next time they do get mad, they're more likely to respond by clobbering someone or something, not by discussing their feelings.

"Parents and caregivers might be recommended to exercise the same care with adult media entertainment as they do medication or chemicals around the home," writes researcher Kevin Browne, Ph.D., of the University of Birmingham in England. "Carelessness with material that contains extreme violent and sexual imagery might even be regarded as a form of emotional maltreatment of the child," he says.

Television and Movies As far back as the 1960s, social psychologists recognized that children's aggression is influenced by their surroundings. Young people learn by watching and imitating—social psychologists call it social learning—and if they're viewing violent acts, they become more inclined to behave in the same way.

Research has shown that viewing violence on TV and in movies also decreases our concern with the suffering of others and our sensitivity to violent acts. In young children, the impact is more profound. Scholars have puzzled out a model of how it works. As we view violent imagery, our own aggressive thoughts immediately increase and then our aggressive feelings and emotions increase. Our heart starts pumping faster, priming our body for quick action.

This cascade of aggressive thoughts, feelings, and behavior becomes second nature, and aggression starts to feel like the most natural solution when we are faced with conflict; nonaggressive solutions fall by the wayside. The effects stick around for the long haul. Psychologists have consistently found that children who watch quite a bit of TV violence are more likely to be arrested for criminal acts as adults.

Video Games Experts such as social psychologist Craig A. Anderson, Ph.D., chair of the department of psychology at Iowa State University, say violent video games are even more likely to lead to such behavior among children, in part because children are engaged and involved in the action and they repeat the behavior over and over again, reinforcing the effects.

WEB TALK: Recent articles on violent media and aggression are available from Craig Anderson's website:

www.psychology.iastate.edu/faculty/caa/index.html

Q & A

How do I know what video games are okay for my child?

"Anything with an 'M' rating you can be assured is inappropriate for anyone under age 18. It will have a lot of violent content in it. You can almost guarantee that any 'T' or teen-rated game will have a lot of violence, although it won't be as graphic or as gory as the M-rated games. Even a number of E-rated—appropriate for everyone—video games are basically first-person or third-person shooters: violent video games that happen to have cartoonish characters and happy music, so they look like they are built for children. We now have research showing that when children and college students alike play these violent, E-rated games, their aggressive behavior increases.

"There is a lot of discrepancy between how labels describe games and what the content is, so parents really have to look at the game. They have to watch someone playing it who knows how to play. Ask yourself what is the main point of the game. Does the character you control reach a goal by hitting or kicking or shooting or stomping or in some way harming another game character? How often does this happen? Every two seconds? In a 5-minute period, are there 10 or 20 or 30 instances where one character is trying to harm another?

"A television show or a novel where there is one homicide and the rest of the show or novel is spent trying to solve it is a lot different from a video game where the body count numbers in the hundreds." —*Craig A. Anderson, social psychologist and media violence expert at Iowa State University*

And just how big is the impact? *Really* big, says Anderson, who has been studying media violence for 20 years. "To put it in context: the media violence effect is bigger than the effect of exposure to asbestos on certain types of cancer. It is bigger than the effect of lead exposure on IQ in children. The United States has decided that the asbestos and lead risks are serious enough to have spent a lot of money to make major changes in the construction industry and the automotive industry to deal with them. And yet they aren't as big as the effect of media violence exposure on later aggressive behavior, which we've done almost nothing to deal with."

The Future

If you think—or know—you have an angry child in your life, don't despair. The problem is not hopeless. "The toughest thug can be taught to manage anger," says Sara Salmon of the Center for Safer Schools and Communities. Your surly 7-year-old or furious 14-year old isn't destined to a life of rage, aggression, and violence.

Many kids who have trouble expressing their anger need to understand that their feelings are acceptable, that they can talk about them; kids who are prone to rages need to know that they are loved no matter what and that there are alternatives to lashing out. Yes, an aggressive child is more likely to become violent in later life, but that's only if nothing is done. You've caught it now, you've recognized the problem, and now you need to take some steps to help him or her out. (We'll discuss the specifics of those steps in Chapter 13.)

What You Can Do

Seeing our children angry can be frustrating, infuriating, and worrisome. What is going on? Why won't they knock it off? How did I fail?

It helps to remember that anger is just as normal an emotion as any other your child might feel. Yes, it can get out of hand, and yes, you might need help. But it is not an intractable problem. The following ideas might help you get through:

☐ Make it a point to talk to your child more about how he feels, especially if you see him struggling. Let him know—again and again—that he can always come to you.

☐ Let your kids know that their anger is okay and that it is something everyone experiences.

☐ Get your child's back—literally. If they've been plagued by a bully, have them confront the child, with you standing right behind them. Let your child do the talking. They'll be strengthened by your show of support, and they'll learn to stick up for themselves.

☐ If bullying is really becoming a problem for your child, talk to his teacher and principal. Be sure they're aware of the problem, and discuss what all of you might do to resolve the situation.

☐ If you sense that your own child is bullying others or having anger problems, get help. Talk to your family physician or spiritual adviser, or find a therapist who specializes in working with children.

☐ Evaluate your own behavior. How do you express anger? Are you setting a good example?

☐ Praise your kids when they've dealt with their anger in healthy ways. Acknowledging their good behavior and progress will make them want to keep it up.

☐ Take stock of your child's video and computer games. Watch him or her play. If you find games that are violent or that promote aggression, pull them out of the inventory.

☐ Keep a closer eye on your kids' TV habits, to see what they really watch. If it's inappropriate, lay down the law.

☐ Don't be afraid to curb your children's TV time—for any programming.

The Biology of Anger

Anger is an intensely physical experience—our heart beats faster, our breathing changes, and we get flushed and sweaty and ready for action. Only after our body is on full red alert does our mind become aware of what is going on, and only then can we make decisions about what to do.

Neuroscientists and physiologists have made great progress over the past several decades mapping out the changes in the body and tracing their origins back through the body to primitive areas of the brain. Here's what we know.

The Call of the Primitive Brain

Anger is experienced by animals and humans alike because it—like love and fear—is the product of the limbic system, a brain circuit that first evolved in the very earliest mammals. The limbic system isn't the only source of anger and aggression; cold, calculated revenge and acts of aggression that don't involve anger—a soldier killing an enemy on the battlefield, for example—originate in the *cerebral cortex*, the part of the brain that is responsible for planning, problem-solving, logic, and reason.

PsychSpeak

The **cerebral cortex,** or gray matter of the brain, is responsible for our higher, "thinking" functions. It can keep in check irrational acts of anger—but may actually be in control when aggression is calculated.

This brain circuit controls motivation and drive, regulates sleep and appetite, promotes social bonding, and plays host to our deep emotional memories. Sensory information from the neurons (or nerve cells) connected to the nose feeds directly into the limbic system, which explains why odors can have such strong emotional impact.

How Anger Ignites As irrational and out-of-control as our anger can seem, it follows a formula. When we are confronted with something that gets our blood boiling (say, the sight of our child getting clobbered by a bullying classmate), that sensory information travels into the amygdala, an important part of the most primitive limbic system. The amygdala acts as both relay system and processing center for emotionally charged input, and it operates on an instinctual, gut-check level.

Recent brain research has illuminated the importance of the amygdala not only to the perception and interpretation of danger but emotional processing in general. For example, when the amygdalas of lab animals are destroyed, the animals become indifferent to danger and lose the ability to interpret social situations. (Researchers believe this is because they can't read facial expressions in other animals.) Stimulate the amygdala, and animals become violently aggressive. Destroy the amygdala, and emotions can become blunted. In humans, damage to the amygdala can render patients unable to read the emotions of other people in social situations and select an appropriate behavior, and unable to identify the emotional significance of events—whether something is frightening or completely nonthreatening. Some researchers think autism may be caused by amygdala damage.

you're not alone

"I've done some horrifically stupid things when I was angry," admits Jeff, a construction site foreman from southern California. "I've been in fights. Not good—and also illegal. I've never hurt anyone, but I've done things that would be considered violent a few times in my life.

"Anger has always been a problem for me. In fact, it is still a huge problem, although the last couple of years it has gotten much better. I have to make sure I don't expose myself to situations that I've identified as being kick-off points—the trigger things that get me going. I can't always avoid them because there are too many. Early on it was a frustration with things not being fair—but the problem is, what's fair? What I thought was fair may or may not have been. Fair is not an absolute. I'm also kind of a control freak. I always want to be in control. That's hard to admit.

"I have to catch myself before it escalates—stay disinterested in things that just aren't important, other than someone's safety at work and my kids' safety at home—because if I get to the point where I invest in the moment, I'm screwed. It's nonstop after that, a runaway train. There's a funny little zone where if you roll over into it, there's no coming back. I can actually make someone wish they weren't born in about five seconds without touching them. There is no end to what I can do to someone verbally. That happens two to three times a year now, whereas eight or nine years ago, it was probably every weekend.

"The problem is that it is not just a mental thing. There is this whole physical response as well. It feels like if you threw your hand out in front of you hard enough, blood would start to shoot out the ends of your fingers. I've had it take me two days to recover. That physical part of it caught me way off-guard for a lot of years. In my younger years, I thought 'I must be right, look at the way I feel!'"

Where the Alarm Call Goes The first stop for the anger impulses that leave the amygdala is the hypothalamus, a part of the limbic system responsible for a number of basic functions, such as appetite, sex drive, and the regulation of body temperature. It translates the alarm message from the amygdala into a physical response, ultimately causing the adrenal gland to produce cortisol, the body's "stress" *hormone*.

Cortisol both raises the blood pressure and initiates the breakdown of fats, carbohydrates, and proteins stored in tissue to raise the amount of glucose in our bloodstream—boosting energy. The adrenal gland also releases the hormones norepinephrine and epinephrine, or adrenaline.

A Body Primed for Action When we see something that alarms us, adrenaline and norepinephrine jolt the body into a heightened level of awareness. The prodding works via what's known as the sympathetic nervous system, which ratchets our body into an energized state. Its counterpart, the parasympathetic nervous system, calms the body down later after danger has passed.

These chemicals generate a number of dramatic changes: our pupils dilate, sharpening eyesight; blood starts pumping harder and faster through our heart and leg and arm muscles but is shunted away from the stomach, slowing digestion; body temperature rises; saliva production gets cut, leading to dry mouth; the liver produces more glucose for fuel; and the muscles in our airway are relaxed, allowing us to breathe faster and more deeply. (However, the muscles in the chest can tighten—especially when we're anxious—leading to a feeling of tightness in the chest and shortness of breath.)

What all of that amounts to is the body's fight or flight response—the ancient instinct to respond to danger by either staying and doing battle or running away. We become ready for anything, eager for action, and acutely aware of our surroundings. There are slight differences in our response to fear and to anger, caused by variation in the exact balance of the two hormones; when we are afraid, for example, more blood is shunted away from the face and extremities than it is in anger, so we look ashen and feel clammy. When enraged, however, we get red-faced and feel hot.

How Memory Shapes Anger What next? What that physical arousal becomes depends on our psychological state of mind and the response we've been conditioned to have by past experiences. Even before we have a chance to think in some rational way about what we have seen (that is, our child being bullied), our brain is comparing that information with memories socked away in the hippocampus, a seahorse-shaped structure that is also part of the limbic system.

The hippocampus is like the mental filing cabinet for our memories and experiences, and it is especially important to long-term ones that can last a lifetime. Even in animals such as rats and mice (upon which most of the research on this part of the brain has been done), the hippocampus provides a quick-and-dirty evaluation of a situation based on the highly charged emotional memories it stores. What happened before when I was in this circumstance? Was I hurt? Did I hurt someone else? Was I mad, or afraid?

This primal processing allows animals to quickly evaluate situations and escape from danger or decide to attack, even though they don't have the more advanced capacity for analysis that we and other higher animals do.

What's Thought Got to Do with It?

We, of course, *do* have the capacity to evaluate our situation. Slightly after the limbic system is alerted to danger, the same sensory information reaches the prefrontal cortex, which controls advanced thinking and analysis. Our thinking brain lags behind our reacting brain.

That lag is not such a bad thing. The body's quick reaction to potential threats can be our salvation if we really are in danger and really do need to act fast. Those quick responses are what saves small and unsophisticated animals such as lizards from larger and brainier beasts such as cats.

WEB TALK: Read a talk with neuroscientist Joseph LeDoux on the relationship between thinking and emotions at:

↗ www.edge.org/3rd_culture/ledoux/ ledoux_p1.html

Fractions of a second later, the prefrontal cortex takes proper stock of what is going on and makes decisions about what to do. If the threat is real or we have legitimate cause to be mad, our body might stay on alert. Now, however, our response can be modulated by at least a bit of insight.

If there's no real reason to be agitated or angry, we can consciously take control and override the automatic response. This is what happens when we are startled by something harmless, such as a thunderclap. Even though our heart is pounding, our brain quickly tells us to calm down. The parasympathetic nervous system kicks in, soothing our heart and lowering our blood pressure. That's why it is vitally important that we learn to recognize the early physical signs of our anger. After we become aware that our body is entering its supercharged state, we can put the brakes on it if we have to and cool down before we boil over.

The Stress Response

The physical changes that happen when we are confronted with an anger-inspiring situation represent the body's stress response—our instinctual reaction to any kind of stress, whether physical or psychological.

Facing a tight deadline at work while coping with a sick child will undoubtedly stress you out, and your body will begin to react as if you were under attack. Your heart rate and blood pressure rise, your breathing gets faster, your pupils dilate, your digestion slows, and you get a burst of energy and strength.

Unfortunately, when dealing with a pile of files, you really don't *need* increased strength, agility, and speed. In fact, in most of the stressful situations we confront in our daily life, our body's hypervigilance can work against us, making it difficult to do what we need to. Over the long term, the stress response can be more foe than friend: being in a continual state of stress can interfere with your immune system, making you more likely to get sick; foster digestive problems such as cramping, diarrhea, irritable bowel syndrome, and other discomforts; and lead to chronic high blood pressure, headaches, muscle pain, insomnia, and a host of other maladies.

Stress can also make us more prone to lashing out—and not just because we're tense and under pressure. Researchers studying rats have found that high levels of corticosterone (the rat equivalent of our cortisol) launch the animals into aggressive, attack behavior. If the same is true in humans, it could explain why being stressed for any reason can make us short-tempered.

The "Anger Gene"

Most of us lose our temper occasionally, but for some people, anger seems to have especially deep roots. That may be true. Several years ago, researchers suggested that variations in a particular *gene* might make some people more prone to both anger and high blood pressure. The research was criticized by many experts. Then, in 2003, a team of experts at Case Western Reserve University in Cleveland, Ohio, published stronger evidence for an anger gene.

you're not alone

For a time during her late teens, Michelle, a contract negotiator living in Ohio, used to explode in flashes of anger. Her rage had a precedent, she says: "My mother's temper was violent, unpredictable. She admitted once that when she got like that she generally didn't see whatever she was angry at. She just wanted to kill it. I've experienced a little of what my mother was talking about. I've had that reaction. My blood pressure would rise to the point where literally my eyes would fill with blood and I couldn't see.

"It would feel like foam was coming up my esophagus—like one of those baking soda and vinegar volcanoes—and I would have to try to stuff the foam back down the pipe. When I did, my blood pressure would come down, my sight would clear, and I would look up and see what had set me off, which was normally not a big thing.

"I remember one specific example. I was a waitress. I went into the kitchen and reached for a side dish—beans or something—and one of the other waitresses reached for it at the same time. I said, 'That's mine.' She said, 'No, that's mine,' and suddenly, boom, there I was, pushing the foam down. When I looked up and I could see her, I said, 'Okay, fine, take the beans,' and she had her hands up near her face, like, 'Don't shoot me.' She told me to take them.

"Later I apologized and told her that I didn't know why I got so mad. She told me she'd never seen anyone look like that before. I don't know what goes on with my face while I'm struggling, but it must be pretty effective because the other person always backs down."

In mice, a gene called PET-1 seems to keep anxiety and aggression under wraps, neuroscientist Evan Deneris, Ph.D., has found. Mice that lack this gene attack unfamiliar mice almost immediately. In addition to high aggression, the mice show signs of anxiety. For example, although mice are by nature curious creatures, mice without PET-1 won't ever explore.

PsychSpeak

A **gene** is the basic unit of heredity, passed on from parent to child. The predisposition to excessive anger—and other emotional problems—may have a genetic component.

In previous research, Deneris and colleagues found that PET-1 is involved in serotonin-producing nerve cells, and they have since found a gene much like it in human brain cells. That's significant, because serotonin is probably involved in human anxiety and aggression. When serotonin levels are low, the result can be depression, anxiety, and other disorders. Drugs such as Prozac, Paxil, and Zoloft act by boosting levels of the chemical in the brain. Insufficient serotonin has also been blamed for irritability, impulsive anger, and aggression, and some studies have shown that raising serotonin can reduce those behaviors. By identifying the gene, researchers may someday be able to identify people who are at increased risk for anger and anxiety disorders—and perhaps develop new types of treatment.

Q&A

Would having a problem with this gene mean I'll suffer from excessive anger or some other mental problem?

Not necessarily, says neuroscientist Evan Deneris, Ph.D. of Case Western Reserve University in Cleveland, Ohio, although a person with a defective gene could be at increased risk for mental disorders such as depression, anxiety, or aggression. There are probably many other genes involved in the development and function of neurons that produce serotonin and that play a role in determining your risk (as does your environment and experience).

The "Atkins Attitude"

Can what we eat change our emotional responses? Yes, say some researchers. It's not just a matter of not eating enough, although low blood sugar can cause irritability and crankiness—as can the annoying restrictions that diets bring. Rather, the foods we choose can alter our moods, and a low-carbohydrate diet has been fingered as one of the biggest culprits.

The "Atkins attitude" (after the Atkins diet, the most popular low-carb, high-protein regimen) is characterized by high levels of anger, tension, and depression. Cell biologist and nutritionist Judith Wurtman, Ph.D., of the Women's Health Program at the Massachusetts Institute of Technology and the Adara Weight Loss Center, both in Boston, says this effect is well documented. Her research on rats fed a low-carb, Atkinslike diet also points to serotonin. The chemical plays an important role in bolstering feelings of happiness and well-being, and low-carb diets may cause a drop in serotonin.

Other researchers aren't so sure that low-carb diets arouse anger. In a study published in the *New England Journal of Medicine*, scientists from the Veterans Administration Hospital in Philadelphia found no difference in the moods of people consuming a low-carb versus a low-fat diet. Another study published in the *British Journal of Psychiatry* reported moderate mood problems in women on low-carb diets, but only if they already were battling depression, a disorder linked to low serotonin.

Addiction to Anger

The scientific jury is still out on whether it is possible to become addicted to anger in some physical sense, but at least a few psychologists suggest anger can indeed become an obsession for some people. The idea is that these "rage-aholics" are intoxicated by the biochemical changes that anger produces in the brain. When life gets dull, they may throw themselves into situations that produce more rage, or conjure up conflict where there might otherwise be harmony, to recapture the hormonal high. This may be a dynamic in relationships that seem almost unnaturally chaotic—what psychologist Lynne Namka, Ph.D., calls "operatic marriages," where "couples fight constantly and operate at a level of extreme emotional arousal."

Others suspect that "anger addicts" are just in a rut. "The study of anger addiction is a work in progress, but I'm not sure if it is an addiction so much as a terrible habit," says Rachel Baldino, MSW, author of *The New Age Guide to Loving Simply: Eliminating Drama from Your Intimate Relationships* and a licensed clinical social worker in Massachusetts. "It is the coping mechanism that they have developed—a bad coping mechanism, but a familiar one."

Anger can be an overwhelmingly powerful feeling. During a rage or immediately after, our bodies are energized; we feel strong and invincible. It's hardly surprising that some people are drawn to that feeling—just as a more traditional adrenaline junkie (a race car driver, extreme skier, or cliff diver, for example) is constantly seeking another rush.

> **GET PSYCHED**
>
> "My wife says that after I've bitten everyone's head off, I'm ready to go to Disneyland. I don't know how it is with women, but I'd feel great [after I vented my anger], and that made me think that I was doing the correct thing, when I was probably damaging my heart, my brain cells. It's not good." *—Jeff, recovering from an explosive anger problem*

WEB TALK: Read about adrenaline addiction at Adrenaline Addicts Anonymous:

www.adrenalineaddicts.org

Alternative Explanations for Rage

Not every culture views anger in the same light. Other systems of medicine and religion have their own interpretations of the emotion.

Anger in Ayurvedic Medicine According to the 5,000-year-old Hindu medical science Ayurveda, anger is not so much a product of hormonal action on the brain as it is a problem of imbalance. Ayurvedics believe that the universe, and everything in it, is made up of five elements: earth, air, fire, water, and ether.

Those elements combine into pairs to form three dynamic forces, the doshas. If you are healthy, all three doshas exist in balance. If you are habitually angry, the problem is too much pitta (which can also cause liver problems, hypertension, ulcers, and acne, among other things). Yoga, walks, oil massage—even cooling foods (bland instead of spicy, for example)—are said to be pitta pacifiers.

Anger in Buddhism Buddhists believe that anger has no place in a healthy psyche. Although the emotion, like other negative feelings, exists in all of us, to a Buddhist, there is no such thing as virtuous anger or justifiable aggression. Instead, anger is a delusion—destructive, unrealistic—the result of feeling frustrated at what we cannot control. The only constructive way to deal with it is to channel it, transform it, or redirect it.

Many Buddhists believe that creating and cultivating a state of mindfulness—a constant awareness of what we are thinking and feeling—can guard against anger.

What You Can Do

Just because anger is a biological process doesn't mean it's out of your control. The earlier you can catch your body heating up to a boil, the sooner you can lower the temperature.

- ☐ Learn to recognize your body's anger cues. Do your muscles get tense? Does your face get flushed? Does your stomach get tied up in knots? Stay vigilant recognizing the signs.

- ☐ When you become consciously aware that you're getting angry, your thinking mind can step in, evaluate the situation, and take control.

- ☐ Do what you can to reduce your stress—exercise, meditate, practice deep breathing, and so on. Anger and stress are intimately linked, so lowering one can help reduce the other.

- ☐ If you suspect your low-carb eating might be making you irritable, reevaluate your diet. In people who are already disposed or predisposed to mood disorders, a low-carb diet might trigger more problems. Your doctor or a nutritionist might have other options.

- ☐ If you suspect you might be an anger addict, talk to a professional. But remember: the jury is still out on anger addiction, and "I can't help it—I'm an addict" is no excuse for your behavior. All addicts, whatever their poison, have to accept responsibility for their actions.

Part 2

When Anger Hurts

Do you sometimes explode in anger? Keep your emotions inside? Both ways to handle anger are unhealthy—and both can take a toll. Anger can be damaging in many ways—physically, mentally, and emotionally. It can harm relationships and careers. In Part 2, you learn how anger may be hurting you and the people you know and love.

Mind and Body

Anger is the result of a delicate choreography between brain and body, but that doesn't mean it is necessarily good for us. Chronic anger, whether we allow it to explode or keep it simmering inside, can be debilitating, throwing a monkey wrench into our health and happiness. It can sometimes also be a clue that something else is wrong with our physical or mental health.

Is Your Anger a Side Effect of a Physical Problem?

Although unhealthy anger can throw the body out of whack, most of the time anger problems aren't the result of an underlying physiological problem. It's important, though, to keep in mind that this does happen. A variety of medical conditions—neurological, hormonal, and otherwise—can manifest in an irrational temper or flares of rage. If you or someone close to you suddenly begins to have troublesome anger without any obvious cause, you may want to be on alert for one of the following problems.

Brain Damage Every year, an estimated 1.5 million Americans suffer a traumatic brain injury—the kind that comes from a car accident, a fall, or a helmet-crunching collision on the football field. And if it does happen to you, it's understandable that you might be cranky. Head injuries *hurt*, after all, and in serious cases, the physical damage can devastate not just your health but your career and your relationships as well. That's enough to make anyone justifiably mad.

But could the heightened irritability, impatience, anger, and low stress tolerance that trauma victims often experience be caused by brain injuries? Scientists think so. Even moderate trauma (say, a mild concussion) is sufficient to modify, however slightly, a person's moods and behavior for a few weeks or months. In cases of severe brain trauma, those changes can be permanent.

Damage to the prefrontal cortex, the most forward part of the brain's frontal lobes right behind the forehead and the gatekeeper for our more rational side, is most likely to lead to emotional changes. (That's also the part you're most likely to smack on the windshield in a car accident.) The prefrontal cortex allows the expression of what it deems reasonable and acceptable and puts the brakes on inappropriate emotions and actions. Remove or handcuff that moderator, and behavior can turn capricious and improper. Or, in extreme situations, much worse: a bad mood morphs into a fit of temper, temper turns into fury, and fury spirals out of control into violence.

Anger is also not unexpected after a *stroke*, which afflicts an estimated 600,000 people in the United States each year.

PsychSpeak

Hemorrhage and blood clots can also cause **stroke**. The injury, and the depression that may accompany it, can increase angry behavior when regions of the brain that regulate mood are damaged.

Their injuries can put stroke victims at high risk for depression, and that alone can lower their tolerance to everyday annoyances, making them quick to anger. After my husband's subdural hematoma—a type of stroke in which blood pools between the outer two of the brain's three layers—and the two surgeries to relieve it, he suffered from both depression and unpredictable rages.

But researchers suspect the stroke itself may cause brain damage that can lead to a bad temper. In a 2002 study, Jong S. Kim, M.D., of Asan Medical Center in Seoul, South Korea, examined 145 patients for up to 12 months after a stroke. Although none had anger problems before their injury, 47 reported uncontrollable anger or aggression afterward.

The damage was often in three distinct areas of the brain that produce the chemical communicator serotonin, which helps modulate our moods and emotions. Low levels of serotonin can cause depression—and have been linked to aggressive, impulsive, and angry behavior—which may explain the emotional upheaval seen in stroke patients. If that's the case, drugs such as Prozac, Zoloft, and Paxil, which increase the amount of available serotonin in the brain, might stop stroke victims from boiling over.

Angry outbursts, forgetfulness, and thinking problems in a person who recently had a stroke or who has existing heart disease might also be caused by vascular dementia, the second most common form of dementia after Alzheimer's disease, which occurs when brain cells suffocate from oxygen deprivation (usually because of clogged arteries). There is no specific treatment for vascular dementia, also known as multi-infarct dementia, although therapies and interventions that reduce the risk of further strokes—such as anticoagulant drugs, reducing high blood pressure, and smoking cessation—can keep it from getting worse.

Alzheimer's Disease and Other Dementias Inappropriate flares of rage might suggest Alzheimer's, a disease that affects some 4 million Americans. In Alzheimer's and related diseases, the neurons of the brain and nervous system waste away and die. Among the inevitable side effects are disorientation, forgotten memories, and distorted thinking. Changes to personality are just as likely and can be early warning signs of trouble in the brain. People with Alzheimer's also may have wildly changing moods, from happy to enraged in the blink of an eye; a normally calm person can become euphoric or agitated, while a high-strung soul turns dispassionate and apathetic. There is no cure for Alzheimer's disease, but drugs now under study may slow its progression and seem to improve, at least temporarily, some cognitive problems. Behavioral problems and mood swings can sometimes be eased by reducing stressors and creating a calm, soothing environment for the patient.

A number of medications are also commonly prescribed—antidepressants such as Prozac, Paxil, and Zoloft for low mood and irritability; anti-anxiety drugs such as Ativan for anxiety, restlessness, and disruptive behavior; antipsychotics such as Clozaril, Zyprexa, and Risperdal for aggression, agitation, uncooperativeness, and delusions; and anticonvulsants and mood stabilizers such as Depakote for hostility and aggression.

In a less-common disorder called frontotemporal dementia, personality changes might be the *only* noticeable symptoms in the early years. This disease chews away at the neurons in areas of the brain important for regulating our social behavior and judgment—and for anger control. In Parkinson's disease, motor neurons are

> ## GET PSYCHED
>
> "Anybody can become angry, that is easy; but to be angry with the right person, and to the right degree, and at the right time, and for the right purpose, and in the right way, that is not within everybody's power, that is not easy."
> *–Aristotle*

attacked, progressively destroying the ability to move and leading to rigidity and tremors. Here, too, however, anger, depression, and early mood changes can sometimes strike before any
other physical symptoms.

Other, much rarer, neurodegenerative diseases can also cause
anger and bizarre behavior in their preliminary stages, such as
Huntington's disease, a rare inherited illness, and Creutzfeldt-
Jakob disease. If you're experiencing episodes of anger, you're
almost certainly not afflicted with a rare disease. But if your
anger or that of a loved one is accompanied by memory loss,
difficulty performing familiar tasks, disorientation, poor judgment, inappropriate behavior,
weakness, numbness, tremors,
balance problems, vision loss,
or any combination of these
symptoms, it wouldn't hurt to
see a neurologist.

WEB TALK: To learn about neurodegenerative diseases from the National Institute for Neurological
Disorders and Stroke, go to:

➤ **www.ninds.nih.gov**

Brain Tumors It's something you'd expect to see on a soap
opera: a formerly mild-mannered person suddenly becomes
plagued with headaches—and turns maniacally mean.

Diagnosis: brain tumor.

Melodramatic, maybe, but here fiction does mirror fact—*in a
very small number of people.* According to the National Brain
Tumor Foundation, 190,000 people in the United States are diagnosed with brain tumors each year. About half, particularly
tumors in the frontal and temporal lobes, alter mood and
personality.

The outcome is impossible to predict. Moods range from
depression and apathy to anger and anxiety to euphoria.

WEB TALK: For more information on brain tumors, their effects, and how to cope, visit the National Brain Tumor Foundation at:

www.braintumor.org

Previous personality traits might become exaggerated—a neat-freak could become obsessively orderly, for example. Alternatively, a tumor patient might have a major personality change: a shy person might completely lose their inhibitions, or a gregarious individual might withdraw from their closest friends. The most extreme personality disruptions are generally seen when tumors are fast growing, giving the brain little time to bounce back from increases in pressure and swelling.

Alarming, yes. But keep in mind that these tumors are rare—and are nearly always accompanied by blinding headaches and other symptoms such as seizures, blurred vision, nausea, speech problems, and general trouble thinking or remembering. A recurring headache plus a bad mood does not automatically—or even very often—equal a brain tumor.

Hyper Hormones The body maintains a delicate balance of hormones, both in the brain and in other systems; when hormones are off-kilter, one result can be heightened anger. For example, hyperthyroidism, an overproduction of hormones from the thyroid gland, can trigger irritability, restlessness, anxiety, and mood changes, in addition to physical symptoms ranging from rapid heartbeat and trembling to weight loss.

High levels of steroid hormones such as testosterone can also elevate anger, which is why body builders and athletes who take steroid supplements to bulk up and increase speed and performance sometimes struggle with "'roid rage."

Premenstrual Syndrome (PMS) The last thing a woman feeling angry and out of sorts wants to hear is that she's "PMS-ing." And yet if you *are* feeling angry and out of sorts in the week or so before your period, and if that foul mood is accompanied by bloating, skin breakouts, cramps, and other signs of premenstrual syndrome—well, there's a good chance you really are suffering from PMS.

The trouble here is believed to be an imbalance between levels of the hormones *progesterone* and *estrogen*. In women with raging PMS, progesterone levels tend to be lower than normal, and estrogen levels tend to be higher—although whether progesterone is decreased or estrogen is elevated is still a matter of debate.

PsychSpeak

Fluctuations in the body's levels of **progesterone** (a natural anti-anxiety chemical), and **estrogen** (an antidepressant) can cause mood swings.

Menopause Low levels of estrogen, on the other hand, are to blame for the physiological and emotional roller coaster many women experience during menopause, when the ovaries slow their production of the hormone. Not every woman will be thrown into an altered emotional state during menopause, but some will undergo rapidly fluctuating moods—crying jags followed by unrelenting rage followed by attacks of debilitating nervousness. Any previous psychological conditions, such as anxiety or compulsiveness or depression, may get magnified by the hormonal havoc.

In my family, we joke that my mother turned into a furious lunatic when she started going through menopause. (We joke about it *now;* at the time, her endlessly wavering moods and fits of anger were not much to laugh about.) Hormone-replacement therapy (HRT) tamed her rage, although many menopausal women now decline to take supplements because they've been shown to increase the risk of stroke, blood clots, heart disease, breast cancer, and dementia. If you choose not to use a HRT, talk with your doctor about other ways to control your mood swings and other emotional symptoms of menopause. Some women find antidepressants such as Prozac to be helpful—although if you'd rather not take meds, rest assured that menopause doesn't last forever and the symptoms will abate.

Low Blood Sugar Glucose, a simple sugar, is food for the cells of our body and brain. Because the brain depends on glucose to function properly, having extremely low blood sugar—a metabolic disorder called hypoglycemia—muddles our ability to think and make rational decisions—and it'll put a person in a foul mood. That's because the body responds to low blood sugar by pumping out cortisol, a hormone involved in the body's stress response—and in anger.

As a result, very low blood sugar can cause extreme irritability and anger, far beyond the crankiness you might experience if you had to skip lunch or if you are craving a cookie. Actual hypoglycemia is quite rare; it can occur in diabetics who take too much insulin (because insulin pulls glucose out of the bloodstream), but also in people whose bodies produce too much insulin. If your angry mood is accompanied by shakiness, sweatiness, weakness, clammy skin, headache, and hunger, of course, it might be a good idea to have a sip of orange juice or a spoonful of honey—and then make an appointment with your doctor.

"I didn't know that my husband was an angry person when we met. If you'd asked me then, I'd have said he was the least likely person in the world to ever scream at me or blow up at his kids. He was kind and happy, full of life, joy, and love. It was, however, immediately clear that he was more expressive with his feelings than I was. In my own family, arguments are rare; I remember my parents fighting about three times during my childhood. My family wasn't blissfully happy—we just bottled up our emotions and pretended they didn't exist. My husband grew up in a family where 'argument' was synonymous with 'discussion.' Our opposite anger styles created some conflict, but his being high strung seemed to complement my being low key, and we somehow got in tune.

"The harmony didn't last. As the years wore on, he got mad more quickly, with less provocation. I didn't understand it. I'm not sure I tried very much. I figured he'd changed, as people do, and I grew increasingly angry with him. We argued. Often. I'm not proud of that. Worse, the conflict was devastating for our three kids, who had already learned to back away from their daddy because he was 'grouchy all the time.'

"In early 2003, he found he had a goose-egg-sized, fluid-filled cyst in the right temporal lobe of his brain. Among other things, the temporal lobes are important for processing emotions such as anger. Although the cyst was benign, his neurosurgeon said that the pressure it exerted on the brain might be contributing to his mood swings and irritability.

"Over that summer, he had surgery to remove the cyst and then two more brain surgeries because of a large hemorrhage that blanketed two-thirds of his left frontal lobe in a layer of blood. We were lucky; pressure from the blood clot could have caused irreparable damage to his brain. But he wasn't unscathed. Now, in addition to the cyst (which, for a nasty bit of irony, grew back soon after the third surgery), he had brain trauma. He was afflicted with mini-seizures (thankfully controlled by medication) and memory problems (thankfully minor). And he suffered rages—sudden, face-contorting, and irrational. He remembered very little afterward, but it was terrifying for me and the kids. We never knew when it would strike or what might happen.

"Several months later, he was diagnosed with bipolar disorder, a disease producing swings between mania and depression with normal periods in between. His manias weren't creative, euphoric highs, as is sometimes the

continues

105

continued

case. He was irritable and snappy, with a hair-trigger temper. All of these conditions—the cyst, the brain trauma, and the bipolar disorder—are probably involved to some degree in his off-kilter temper, as is his angry upbringing. It's probably impossible to completely separate the effects.

"Now, we know our enemies, and he's beating them back. Medication has helped his bipolar disorder. His brain is healing from the trauma. And yet he still deals with anger problems, and the rest of us are still coping. You would think it would be easier to know that your furious husband is not just being a jackass. That he actually can't always control his behavior. It really doesn't help. I feel like I should be understanding, but I'm not quite there yet. *—Kathy Svitil, author of this book*

The Impact of Anger on Health

Your own anger probably doesn't involve brain tumors or hormonal upheaval. But if you or a loved one suffers from bouts of anger that come on suddenly and are out of character, there might be something else going on—especially if there has been a recent head injury or the odd emotions are accompanied by other mental problems or unusual physical symptoms. If that's the case, it's a good idea to talk to your doctor to get it checked out. He or she will likely find nothing and then you can focus your efforts on healing whatever else you need to; if something does crop up, at least you'll know where you stand.

In fact, anger is more likely to cause a physical ailment than to be the result of one. Occasional anger won't drag your body down. If you're always angry or always suppressing your feelings, however, that chronic state of stress and agitation can cause a host of problems, from your heart to your immune system to your gut and more.

High Blood Pressure and Cardiovascular Disease There is no longer any doubt that too much anger leads to heart disease. Combine the tendency to express anger (what psychologists call anger-out) with the tendency to try to control anger (fighting against your own nature), and "this contributes to *myocardial infarction*, or heart attacks," says psychologist Charles Spielberger, Ph.D., director of the Center for Research in Behavioral Medicine and Health Psychology at the University of South Florida and the developer of the State-Trait Anger Expression Inventory, a psychological assessment test of anger.

You needn't have battled a lifetime of anger to reel from the effects. In a 2002 study that tracked more than 1,300 former medical students for an average of 36 years, researchers at Johns Hopkins University found that young men who respond to stress by quickly getting mad are five times more likely to have a heart attack at a relatively young age (under age 55) than are their more relaxed counterparts.

PsychSpeak

Episodes of anger also slightly raise the risk of **myocardial infarction,** the death of heart muscle due to oxygen deprivation, possibly because anger raises heart rate and blood pressure and constricts blood vessels.

Anger—or, more precisely, hostility, a personality trait characterized by negative beliefs about other people, mistrust, and cynicism, and behavior with the intent to cause harm to other people that predisposes a person to chronic anger—is also the link between heart disease and the Type A personality (hard-driving, aggressive, ambitious, competitive, pressed-for-time people).

So what's going on here? Scientists are still testing all of the reasons why anger damages the heart and can lead to a heart attack, but it all comes back to those hard-wired physiological responses that are basic to anger. Blood vessels constrict, raising blood pressure, so if you're constantly angry, you also have chronic high blood pressure. Cholesterol moves into the bloodstream, where it can get deposited on the insides of vessels, producing artery-clogging plaque deposits. The blood also gets thicker and stickier, which makes it more likely to produce clots that themselves clog arteries.

Scientists have also found other intriguing connections between anger and heart disease. For instance, studies by scientists from Ohio State University published in April 2000 revealed that angry people also have elevated levels of a chemical called homocysteine. High levels of the chemical, which the body produces when metabolizing meat, can damage the cells that line the insides of arteries, leading to more plaque development. Other evidence ties angry moods with a compound called C-reactive protein (CRP). In 2004, Duke University scientists found that especially angry and hostile subjects had CRP levels that were two to three times higher than their cooler counterparts. This protein may lead to inflammation inside arteries— and that inflammation can cause plaque to accumulate, clogging up the bloodflow.

WEB TALK: Learn how to reduce your cardiovascular risk through lifestyle changes (including stress reduction) from the American Heart Association: www.americanheart.org/presenter.jhtml? identifier=3004354

Gastrointestinal Problems When our body is on edge and ready to confront danger or deal with conflict—as when we are angry—an intense chemical concoction (chiefly the hormones epinephrine and norepinephrine) causes blood to be shunted away from the digestive system. The plan is to marshal energy, oxygen, and nutrients for the areas of the body that might need them more, such as our leg and arm muscles, to give us strength in a fight. As a result, our digestion is slowed. It's no big deal in the short term; our system quickly kicks back to normal when we calm down. Over the long haul, though, constant anger can deliver a beating to the digestive system.

Anger has been linked to a higher incidence of irritable bowel syndrome, along with bloating, nausea, cramping, diarrhea, constipation, and stomach ulcers. (Although most ulcers are now known to be directly associated with a bacterial infection.) Researchers have found that angry people produce more stomach acid and have brighter red stomach linings compared to subjects who are fearful or depressed. That extra acid can predispose angry people to ulcerative colitis, an inflammation and ulceration of the lining of the colon causing pain and alternating episodes of constipation and diarrhea, and gastritis, an inflammation of the stomach lining that leads to nausea, loss of appetite, and discomfort after eating.

Immune Suppression Epinephrine and cortisol, the body's stress hormone (also produced when we get angry), may prime our body for quick and powerful action, but their effect is exactly the opposite on the immune system: our resistance to disease breaks down.

Our immune system gets dampened in some areas so that more invader-fighting white blood cells and immune molecules are available to places that might be injured in a scuffle. That reaction to stress (and, again, in anger) might protect our skin, but it leaves the rest of our body vulnerable to infections and illness. Anger can be, quite literally, sickening.

Other Health Problems It's bad enough that constant anger impairs our heart and cardiovascular system, our gut, and our immune system. It's also not all we have to worry about. When we're angry, our brain's production of a pain-relieving hormone called *endorphin* gets clamped down. Chronic anger, therefore, can increase our susceptibility to headaches, arthritis and musculo-skeletal pain, and other discomforts. And being in pain certainly

PsychSpeak

The hormone **endorphin** functions like a natural opiate in the brain, raising our pain threshold, leading to pain relief. Endorphin is responsible for the famed "runner's high."

won't make us inclined to come out of our bad mood! We also feel fatigued—it makes sense that a body that's always revved up would get a bit burned out, doesn't it?

The activated, angry body pumps out thyroid hormones, which rev up our metabolism but can lead to insomnia and other sleep problems and an even crankier mood—as well as leave us exhausted when we come down from the metabolic high.

Even our teeth can suffer when we're mad all the time: some people clench and grind their teeth—what doctors call bruxism— to release anxiety, anger, and aggression. That can damage our teeth and jaws and cause headaches and facial pain. I know this one—I clench my jaw in my sleep, especially when I'm stressed. When I was still in high school, that unconscious habit (and a painful dislocation) led to arthritis in my jaw and so much damage that I had to have surgery to repair the joint. In other, less extreme, but quite common cases, grinding the teeth, clenching the jaw, and nervous behaviors such as chronic gum chewing and nail biting can lead to temporomandibular joint, or TMJ, disorder, a painful condition characterized by stiffness, headache, ear pain, bite problems, clicking in the joints, and locked jaws.

Are You Cutting Your Life Short? If all of that wasn't reason enough to keep your anger in check, just think about the toll these health problems might take. Say you're chronically angry; you're developing heart disease, you've got constant stomach upset and headaches, and you seem to catch every cold that goes around. Add up those problems and untold others, and you end up subtracting time off your life.

How much time is impossible to say. No valid studies pin a number on how much anger might shorten your life—it's too individual a measurement for one thing, and the effects of anger are too difficult to separate out from every other variable. Intuitively, however, it makes perfect sense: your body is taxed, tired, tense, and possibly damaged by your anger, and that can cost you.

Holding in Anger Also Has a Physical Toll

As damaging as it can be to be explosively angry all the time, holding in your anger (suppression) or denying it completely (repression) can also have some nasty physical consequences.

Suppressors, who still *feel* anger and experience its effect on their body, are at higher risk of high blood pressure and hypertension, and, some studies propose, chronic headaches. Held-in anger has also been implicated—although not all investigators agree—in a host of other stress-related disorders, including ulcers, heart attack, asthma, arthritis, and more. Repressed anger, says psychologist Charles Spielberger, has even been linked to a higher rate of cancer.

Don't think that any of this gives you permission to yell and scream at everyone who crosses your path. It only underscores how critically important it is to release your angry feelings constructively.

GET PSYCHED

"[I]t doesn't matter whether anger is expressed or suppressed. It's just plain bad for you. Chronic anger that is expressed prolongs and supercharges all of the associated hormonal changes. Chronic suppressed anger mobilizes the sympathetic nervous system responses without providing any release of the tension. The effect is the same as flooring the accelerator of our car at the same time as slamming on the brakes."–*Psychologist Matthew McKay, Ph.D., et al., in* When Anger Hurts: Quieting the Anger Storm

Anger Erodes Happiness and Your Quality of Life

Although anger is very often an attempt to obtain some control over your life, it could end up doing just the opposite. When you put so much stock in the behavior of others to determine your mood, you're putting the responsibility for your happiness in their hands—and taking it out of your own. That can lead to a suffocating sense of helplessness. Again, remember, we're talking here about chronic, constant anger, not the occasional flare or the anger that we use to inspire us or prod us into constructive action.

Anger and Mental Health

We've already discussed some of the medical conditions that can generate anger in patients. Mental health problems very often do the same thing—and can, in fact, be one of the recognizable signs of mental illness. Some conditions with anger as a symptom or side effect include ...

- **Intermittent explosive disorder (IED).** Impulsive and unpredictable episodes of extraordinary anger and aggression. IED may be confused with a number of other more common mental conditions, including borderline personality disorder, attention deficit/hyperactivity disorder, acute mania, and psychosis. The condition may be due to a serotonin imbalance in the brain.

- **Depression.** Depression is typically characterized by persistent sadness, hopelessness, disinterest, and low energy, but irritability and anger are actually quite common in depressed people. One 1993 study in the *American Journal of Psychiatry* found that 44 percent of depressed outpatients experienced anger attacks—sudden and intense fits of anger. Treatment with fluoxetine—Prozac—reduced the attacks in more than 70 percent of the patients.

- **Bipolar disorder.** Patients with this mood disorder swing between periods of depression and spells of mania, with normal moods in between. The mania can manifest as grandiosity or euphoria, but it also might erupt in bouts of extreme irritability and anger.

- **Borderline personality disorder (BPD).** People with BPD display unstable moods and instability in interpersonal relationships, behavior, and self-image, which can prove quite destructive. The intense flares of anger in BPD can flash on and off suddenly, lasting from a few hours to as much as a day. (The anger or irritability in a bipolar patient may persist for weeks.)

- **Post-traumatic stress disorder (PTSD).** An anxiety disorder that can develop after a particularly frightening event in which physical harm occurred or was threatened. We often hear about soldiers suffering PTSD after a particularly terrifying battle, but it can also afflict rape or assault victims, people in serious accidents, survivors of child abuse or domestic abuse, and more. Irritability, aggression, and anger are frequently apparent in PTSD patients and can be even more prevalent among combat veterans with the disorder.

- **Attention deficit/hyperactivity disorder (ADHD).** This learning disorder, which begins in early childhood but can persist into adulthood, is characterized by inattention, poor impulse control, and hyperactivity. About half of children with ADHD suffer behavior problems—including explosive anger.

Q & A

Is excessive anger a mental illness?

Not according to the *Diagnostic and Statistical Manual of Mental Disorders (Fourth Edition)*, or the *DSM-IV*, psychiatry's gold standard for defining mental disorders and disease. Anger is a symptom or manifestation of many other disorders, ranging from bipolar disorder to borderline personality to post-traumatic stress disorder. But a diagnostic category in its own right? No. Not yet, anyway. A faction of psychologists led by Raymond DiGiuseppe, Ph.D., of St. John's University in New York propose creating a new category for anger in the *DSM-IV* that would include a number of different subtypes, including pervasive-anger disorder, impulsive-aggressive disorder, suppressed-anger disorder, and overcontrolled-anger disorder.

The Emotional Consequences of *Not* Expressing Anger

Even if you don't get sick from socking away your feelings, they can do quite a number on your emotional health. Say you don't let your husband know that it really upsets you when he goes out after work and doesn't call to let you know he'll be late. Will you avoid what might be a difficult confrontation? Maybe. But the cost could be great. Suppressed anger can balloon into more anger, which might explode over something unrelated to what originally angered you.

Some psychologists say that anger turned inward becomes depression; other therapists might argue that depression can also cause anger, or that the two could be unrelated. If you don't get depressed in a clinical sense, you might still feel sad and hurt because your husband doesn't understand how you feel, or guilty because you're mad and he doesn't even know why, or frustrated because your needs are not being met. You might feel like your life is out of your control, you might feel insecure, or you could feel isolated or inadequate.

In short, denying your feelings might seem like a solution in the short term, but in the long run, you're only alienating yourself, not just from other people, but from yourself as well.

you're not alone

"I think I've always had anger problems, outbursts of anger. My parents fought a lot, and my dad was both verbally and physically abusive. There was a lot of anger in our home, and I guess I thought everyone lived like that.

"In the fifth or sixth grade, I started to fight. I'd been constantly picked on by a group of kids, mostly one boy. A teacher told my parents that although she didn't believe in fighting, she thought that in my case it was necessary, and so my dad gave me permission to sock him one the next time he bothered me. Had I not, I might have had more problems from always holding my anger in—but I think that was the beginning of a lifelong series of explosive events.

"I finally started to realize that it was getting to be a serious problem before my first brain surgery, which was in June 2003. I was feeling stressed out all the time—*everything* was bothering me; minor things would get me enraged. Everyone in my family—my kids, my wife—had distanced themselves from me. They didn't want to get yelled at. Nobody wants to get yelled at! But I didn't actually do anything about it until more than a year later, when I was diagnosed with bipolar disorder. It was all too much, and the surgeries and the brain hemorrhage messed with my brain, so I didn't know anymore what I was doing or what was wrong, or that I even had a problem.

"Now, I have my good days and bad days. Usually, I'm able to stay cool. Other times it feels completely out of my control—the anger is like a balloon that you put too much air in and you know it's going to break. You feel the pressure building up, from your brain down into your gut. I suspect that's because of the brain trauma. At those times, I do deep breathing to relax, I count to 10. I'll leave the house if my temper starts to get out of hand. Hopefully, I'll learn to control it better, but I think this is going to be a lifelong struggle." *—Ronald Fisher, husband of the author of this book*

Drug and Alcohol Addiction

Angry people can also have more problems on their plate, including a propensity toward alcohol and drug abuse and addiction. It's almost a chicken-and-egg kind of situation. Addiction can drive anger; anger can drive addiction. Both can be true or neither one.

The idea that alcohol might breed a bad temper sounds odd; lots of people become not a bellowing brute but mellow and easygoing under the influence of alcohol. Having a few drinks can, however, increase the chance that you'll be irritable or lash out. (There are so many drugs of abuse that it's impossible to generalize about their effects.)

But alcohol intoxication also impairs our ability to make good decisions, upping the odds that we'll act irrationally, and lowering our inhibitions, raising the risk that we'll behave boorishly and perhaps in anger. For alcoholics, the link is clearer. In people who are dependent on alcohol, brain levels of serotonin, a hormone responsible for regulating mood, can drop. One effect is depression. Another, increased aggression.

Addiction Driven by Anger The relationship between anger and alcohol or drug addiction is complicated. Some people drink or do drugs *because* they are angry (or agitated, or upset, or depressed, or frustrated). Often those feelings stem from a childhood of abuse or neglect or from an ongoing destructive relationship.

"Sometimes, a lot of times, it has to do with something that happened earlier in the addict's life," says Susan Romanelli, LCSW, Ph.D., the director of the Hope Adult Program at the Menninger Clinic in Houston. "I often work with young people who basically got the message from their family that no matter what you do, you are going to be a failure, so they decide at an early age, 'Well, I guess I'm going to prove you right because it doesn't make a difference anyway.'"

Whatever the cause of those bad feelings, the addiction—to drugs, alcohol, shopping, gambling, whatever the poison—can arise from an attempt to forget or to quash them.

Anger Driven by Addiction In other cases, addictions cause angry and damaging behavior. A few drinks or a few hits off a joint might bring to the surface a lot of buried emotions. Under normal circumstances, it can be a good thing to unearth those inhibited feelings, but you can't bank on that kind of soul-cleansing catharsis. It's also likely that your alcohol-fueled out-burst will cause more problems.

Q&A *My son is an addict, and I'm furious at him. How do I deal with that?*
"Find out what the anger is about. Most people feel that addiction is a choice, and so they are angry at the addict for making that choice. We had a counselor here who made a very good point: no one wakes up in the morning and says 'Hmm, I know what my life goal is. I'm going to be an addict!' A lot of times the anger comes from fear as well. They're afraid that the next phone call they get won't be their child calling from jail, or the ER, but that it's going to be from the morgue. You have to understand why you feel the way you do." —*Susan Romanelli, LCSW, Ph.D., director of the Hope Adult Program at the Menninger Clinic in Houston*

And then, of course, there are people who are angry because of their addiction. An addict could be angry at herself for losing control, or for not having the strength to quit. She might be angry at others who try to point out that there's a problem. She might just be angry at the world because her life as an addict is unfair, difficult, and quite frankly sucks. The addict's family members could be equally incensed (although they might not be willing to admit it) at their loved one's behavior. "There is a lot of anger from other family members toward the person with the addiction because they are changing the entire family structure," says Romanelli.

Sobriety Relapses Angry feelings are a huge challenge to recovering alcoholics and addicts. Alcoholics Anonymous and other groups particularly advise recovering addicts to be alert for feelings of anger, because that can often push a person into relapse. Anger and irritability (along with other extreme mood changes) can also signal the onset of a relapse. To a recovering addict, mismanaged anger is a big red flag. It points to a general problem in coping with life's regular stresses—and that could mean other trouble is on the horizon.

Hot Under the Collar and Prone to Smoke

Can you think of anyone who has both a problem with anger and a hard-to-break nicotine addiction? It may be no coincidence. A February 2004 report in the journal *Cognitive Brain Research* revealed evidence that people with a propensity to anger and aggression may also be predisposed to getting hooked on nicotine.

Steven Potkin of the University of California at Irvine and his colleagues first used personality tests to pin down the personality traits of 31 smokers and 55 nonsmokers as either hostile or not hostile and then slapped nicotine patches on them. The subjects' brain activity was imaged as they performed tasks designed to elicit aggression.

In the hostile group—smokers and nonsmokers alike—nicotine induced drastic changes in brain regions that control emotion, social response, and other behaviors. In the happy-go-lucky, not-hostile group, the nicotine patches had no effect. Their brain, for whatever reason, just wasn't as interested in the drug. This could explain, the researchers say, why some people are more likely to get hooked on cigarettes and why they get so relentlessly irritable when they try (often unsuccessfully) to quit.

What You Can Do

Because anger is so intensely physiological—felt physically as much as emotionally—chronic anger can affect our bodies and health. It may also be true that anger has its origin in a physical or mental health problem—all the more reason to keep tabs on your moods and to learn better ways to express them.

☐ Remember that your anger *can* hurt you. If you're chronically angry and chronically under stress, you might also be chronically sick. For that reason if no other, it is in your best interest to change.

☐ Remember also that always holding in your anger has a physical and emotional price.

☐ Note any sudden changes in your emotions—sadness, anger, or any other moods that are out of character for you—especially if they are accompanied by health problems such as headaches.

☐ Report any changes that concern you to your doctor or a mental health professional, and be sure to mention when the problems started, along with any other physical changes.

☐ If you are worried about the behavior of a loved one, do a little information gathering: talk to other family members and friends, observe their behavior, look for signs of a problem. Then talk to the person you're worried about and tell them your concerns. If they won't get help, it can't hurt to seek the advice of a medical or mental health professional.

☐ Anger and addiction often go hand in hand. Someone who becomes hostile or loses his temper while drinking or doing drugs may have a substance abuse problem.

Intimate Anger

Do we always hurt the ones we love? Maybe not "always," but when we're angry, we do it often. Too often.

Certainly, no good can come of too much anger in a family. It can corrode the ties that bind you to other people and sometimes contribute to abuse. Kids, afraid of seeing their parents screaming mad, might resolve to never be angry and start a lifelong pattern of suppressing and displacing their feelings. Or they might come to believe that screaming is the only way to make their feelings known.

A burst of rage might be confined to one moment, but the ripples can spread far into the future, into many other parts of our lives. This chapter is about those patterns and ripples and how they affect our most intimate relationships.

Lashing Out at Loved Ones

You have a hard day at work and then come home and snap at your kids or your spouse—not because you're mad at them, but because it's easier to vent than to confront your boss about having too much work or your office mate about how his constant humming is driving you up the wall. You might get short with your best friend or get in an argument with a neighbor when, really, they've done nothing wrong.

"I really think it is true that people with angry personalities will lash out at the people closest to them," says Rachel Greene Baldino, MSW, LCSW, a therapist in Worcester, Massachusetts, and the author of *The New Age Guide to Loving Simply: Eliminating Drama from Your Intimate Relationships*. A child, for example, might be upset about something at school, not say anything there, and then come home and yell at his mom (as my son has). He knows she loves him unconditionally, so he knows he can do that without suffering permanent repercussions. Our family and close friends will put up with our anger longer than will our colleagues and acquaintances. Unfortunately, that means they more often bear the brunt of it. "We will push harder against the people we are intimately bonded with," Baldino says.

you're not alone

"I've always had a really strong temper, but it was never really a problem until I had kids," says Jennifer, a 35-year-old mother of two from rural Pennsylvania. "Certainly my anger has gotten worse since then, because of the stress and exhaustion and how my life has changed. And when you lose your temper in front of your kids, you feel like you are ruining them forever. So it is a combination of my anger being worse now and the stakes being higher. It means more now.

"I am not a patient person, so the repetition of parenting can rub me the wrong way. Having to tell your child eight thousand

The Erosion of Intimacy

Just because you can come up with a reason for acting like a jerk doesn't justify your behavior—or make it easy for anyone else to deal with.

Your family members might know you're only lashing out at them because you trust that they'll love you no matter what, but there will be an eventual price to pay: the loss of intimacy. "The more anger you express, the less effective your anger becomes, the less you are listened to, and the more cut off you may begin to feel," says psychologist Matthew McKay, Ph.D., clinical director at Haight-Ashbury Psychological Services in San Francisco, in his book *When Anger Hurts: Quieting the Storm Within.*

Over time, the people closest to you will grow tired of being tied to your whipping post. They'll distance themselves, slap on their emotional armor to shield themselves from your ire, and tip-toe around your moods, trying not to set you off. Your relationships will become defined not by love, respect, or commitment, but by your anger and their reaction to it. Worst of all, your family will begin to resent you for your uncontrollable temper—and resentment is one of the most powerful killers of love and trust.

times not to do something, and he still turns around and does it, is frustrating. And that feeling that I'm not being heard, that I'm not making a dent, not making a difference ... it is really frustrating and can put me over the edge pretty quickly.

"I think about this a lot. I feel a lot of guilt and remorse when I lose my temper with my kids. I try to use that as a spur to get better, but in the moment, I flip out. I get angry so fast that those good intentions don't work and then I say I'll do it the next time. Right now, I really don't have the energy to work on myself, so I'm just kind of living day to day with it."

When couples argue, they can create a pattern that is especially corrosive to intimacy. They fight. It doesn't matter over what. One person blames the other for something; the other gets defensive and angrier. They start lobbing insults, pushing buttons; the closer you are to someone, the better you know how to hurt them.

Soon the discussion becomes more about damaging the other person than resolving anything. "There is really no communication going on anymore. There is a lot of noise directed at one another. People wanting to be right, wanting to get the last word," says Susyn Reeve, a personal development consultant, author, and interfaith minister in San Francisco. Even if you get past this particular argument, you fall into a pattern where you respond in this way to every conflict.

Constant Anger Corrodes Your Sense of Self

The irony is that even though it sometimes seems like a justifiable reaction, the angry person isn't helping himself or herself by lashing out. After all, most of us don't like to be angry all the time. It can feel rotten. Some of that is physiological—constant anger puts our bodies under stress, which, over time, can actually make us sick. But beyond the physical aspects, by being angry all the time, we're also undermining ourselves emotionally.

Constantly being furious, always losing your temper, and always snapping at your kids can be confusing. You don't *want* to be that way, you never wanted to be that way, and yet you can't seem to stop.

In his book *When Anger Hurts*, Matthew McKay points out several ways that anger can erode our sense of well-being. We feel helpless and dissatisfied because we're using anger to try and fix problems—and to try to make ourselves feel better—and that anger is met with resistance and rejection by others. We feel less satisfied in our lives because our close relationships, which should provide us with warmth and nurturing, have become distant and closed off. We feel increasingly lonely and isolated.

Worse, we feel ashamed because we're not living up to our own standards of behavior. It's normal to feel guilty after losing your temper—but guilt is a temporary feeling, one that urges you to correct your behavior by apologizing or making amends. Shame is a much more powerful and destructive force. It attacks your sense of self and makes you feel that you didn't just do something bad—you are actually a bad person. Constant anger fosters shame, which chips away at your identity and your self-respect.

"Another piece of the pattern is that people who strike out in anger will apologize and swear to never do it again, which is really unrealistic," says Susyn Reeve. When you do that, you set yourself up for failure, because everybody eventually gets angry. That only contributes to the frustration—and to your negative feelings about yourself.

The Legacy of Anger

My husband's once-frightening temper, thanks to medication for his bipolar disorder and therapy, has improved dramatically. Gone are the daily blowups, the irrational fits, the unpredictable rages. He still gets mad, but it's a normal kind of mad—something we can deal with and talk about.

Still, I worry that his fury will return. There is always a brief moment when he starts to lose his temper when I ask myself if he might go too far, if he might lose control again. It's like an echo in my head from his past behavior. I might carry that—and my own anger, sadness, and fear—with me for a long time.

Q&A

How long will it take me to unlearn the patterns I picked up from my parents?

"The environment that we grow up in stays with us for a very long time. Changing can take a long time, but it doesn't have to stay forever. It does, however, take the same type of commitment as if you were running a marathon—you have to want to change. Overcoming anger is like undoing programming. It requires upgrading the software, thinking a lot about what our anger really means, figuring out what it is that is getting us so angry. Often it is unmet expectations, or the feeling that another person doesn't really care about us. Or we take everything personally—thinking what our partner or our parents or our kids do is about 'me.'" —*Susyn Reeve, personal development consultant, author, and interfaith minister*

That's one thing that anger does: linger. Even past the argument or outburst, anger stays in the air. It also leaks *everywhere*. If you blow up at your wife before she heads off to work, she'll wear your anger like an albatross around her neck for the rest of the day. Your son, who saw the fight, will carry it around with him at school. Her job performance may suffer. His school work may suffer. And you? You feel lousy for being such a jerk. People can't just shut off their emotions when they're inconvenient.

If it's repeated often enough, anger can linger for a lifetime. You risk losing out on a future with your kids when they grow up and build their own lives. Foster emotional distance in your children, and it might grow into a chasm you can't cross.

GET PSYCHED

"The more times you don't reinforce another person's rage—by not engaging them, not talking to them when they're angry—the more you're putting it back in their face so hopefully they'll eventually say, 'Hmm … what is wrong with this picture?'" —*Wendi Fischer, Ph.D., clinical psychologist in private practice in West Islip, New York*

Verbal and Emotional Abuse

Yelling at your wife doesn't necessarily constitute verbal or emotional abuse, but the line can get fuzzy, depending on what you say. If, in the midst of your tirade, you launch into insults or ridicule, or if you degrade or threaten or intimidate her, then you're being verbally and emotionally abusive. If you tell your child that you are going to leave or that you wish that he would, if you reject him, or if you consistently fail to show affection, that's also emotional abuse. *Any* treatment, whether it's in the middle of an argument or spoken in a whisper, that results in severe emotional harm or impairs another person's emotional development or sense of self-worth, is abusive behavior.

Emotional and verbal abuse can lead to serious emotional, cognitive, behavioral, and mental problems in both kids and adults. That's bad enough. But it often doesn't stop there. Psychologists view this type of aggression as a warning sign that the abuser could take the next step and get physical.

Domestic Violence

According to statistics from the U.S. Department of Justice, roughly 1 million to 4 million incidents of physical violence perpetrated by a current or former intimate partner occur every year. Nearly one-third of American women have reported being physically or sexually abused by a husband or boyfriend at some point in their lives.

Does Anger Drive Abuse? Domestic violence is disturbingly common, but does it have anything to do with anger? Certainly, anger can be a factor in abuse—but quite frequently, it's driven more by a desire to control than by a short fuse. In fact, some abusers actually become calmer—physiologically as well as emotionally—as they begin beating their spouse. Their blood pressure and heart rate drop; their breathing slows. Psychologist John Gottman of the University of Washington calls this type of batterer a *cobra*. Cobras constitute about 20 percent of abusers. (The other 80 percent are *pit bulls*, abusers who grow more aggressive and physiologically aroused as they attack.)

An abuser will lash out when he (or she, although women are more often victims than perpetrators) feels his control is being threatened. They may have discovered in the past that the most effective path to asserting control is through violence. Perhaps they have seen it in their childhood; perhaps they experimented with it themselves. They found it worked, and the pattern got set.

Intimate Terrorism Sociologist Michael Johnson, Ph.D., of Pennsylvania State University, lumps cobra types of abuser into a class he calls "intimate terrorists"—that's the prototypical spousal abuser or wife beater. These men (again, they are often men) use a variety of techniques to exert their control. They might isolate their spouse from others, cut them off from their own source of money (by sabotaging their job, for example), threaten them, dominate and intimidate them, and inflict emotional abuse. Underscoring all of these control tactics is the threat of harm: their partner knows they will be physically abusive because they have been before.

Does this type of abuse have anything to do with anger? It certainly can. An abusive person may be more likely to fly into rages and be violent than someone who doesn't beat his wife and children. But anger is not usually the primary motivator. Other complex psychological dynamics are in play. In addition to asserting control, a batterer might be motivated by jealousy or fear of abandonment, for example. For these people, anger management does little to solve the problem. Some courts have instituted special programs that address domestic violence. For Gottman's "cobras," a combination of counseling plus arrest, prosecution, and fines is most effective—although not always.

If you are in an abusive situation and are in imminent danger, call 911. To find an organization near you that can provide assistance, support, and other resources—counseling, shelter, financial services, medical care, legal advice, and more—go to the National Coalition Against Domestic Violence site, www.ncadv.org/resources/Resources_59.html.

WEB TALK: Visit the National Domestic Violence Hotline website at: **www.ndvh.org**

Situational Couple Violence Not all family violence fits that pattern, sociologists and domestic violence experts are now realizing. Michael Johnson distinguishes that abuse from another type of intimate partner violence he calls "situational couple violence," also known as "common couple violence." Situational couple violence is not an effort by one partner to control the other, and it really can involve anger.

As the name implies, situational couple violence occurs in the middle of a heated argument or another time when both partners are feeling high levels of stress, and it often culminates in violence. These couples may not normally get physical when they fight, but if a particular argument spirals out of control, the conflict might lead to assault. Or they might always escalate to that point, but neither party is using violence to assert control.

Situational couple violence doesn't fit the pattern of a classical abuser, but it is no less dangerous. Although a physical altercation might go no further than pushing and shoving (still not good), it can also lead to profound violence, even homicide.

How do you tell the difference between the two types of violence? It isn't always easy, but there are a few clear signs. If both parties are violent, and if the violence only crops up in the midst of a conflict, it is probably situational couple violence. If one partner is clearly dominant and inflicting all the abuse, it's likely a case of classic spousal abuse. Other warning signs of this type of abuse—even if it hasn't led there yet—include unrealistic expectations, a quickness to place blame on other people for problems or emotions, hypersensitivity, and cruelty to animals or children.

Does Treatment Work? In situational couple violence, there's a good chance. The participants in this dangerous dynamic can benefit from counseling that teaches them problem-solving skills, conflict resolution, and anger management. For them, anger can very often be the fuse that sets off an altercation, so anger control tactics can be helpful.

In intimate terrorism, however, anger management can fail miserably (as can many domestic batterers' programs). Couples counseling, Johnson says, can in fact be extremely dangerous for the victim in these relationships. If they disclose the details of their abuse, they risk the retaliation of their abuser.

Child Abuse

As is the case with domestic violence, anger *may* play a part in child abuse, although that is not necessarily true. Child abuse can take many forms—verbal and emotional abuse, neglect, sexual molestation, and physical battery.

In 77 percent of confirmed cases of child abuse in the United States, the parents were the abusers. They are usually not crazy, nor do they have criminal personalities. Instead, they are commonly both poor and poorly educated, with little knowledge of child development and unrealistic expectations about how their kids should act; they might also be lonely, overwhelmed, and unhappy. They might have grown up in an abusive home. (Abused children may have pent-up anger and rage or problems with impulse control that persist into adulthood.) Add all of those factors to a momentary loss of emotional control—a burst of rage—and the result might be abusive.

> **WEB TALK:** Visit the National Clearinghouse on Child Abuse and Neglect Information at: **nccanch.acf.hhs.gov**

Effects of Abuse Being abused, whether once or repeatedly, can have profound effects on a child. Maltreated children are more likely than other kids to become antisocial and withdrawn, passive, aggressive, or hyperactive. They often have trouble concentrating in school and perform poorly, and more frequently fall into drug and alcohol abuse, promiscuity, and other self-destructive behavior. They might suffer extreme anxiety, anticipating another beating or demanding perfection from themselves to avoid one; guilt that they can't prevent from happening; and low self-esteem.

Adults who were abused as children bear lasting scars. They might have trouble establishing intimate relationships because they have no experience with healthy ones, or they might develop substance abuse problems or choose an addicted partner. They might suffer from anxiety, post-traumatic stress, depression, eating disorders, gastrointestinal problems, chronic pain, and more.

Anger Breeds Anger

And abused children might, of course, be angry—*furious*—even if they don't immediately recognize the emotion in themselves.

Many abused children are not allowed to express anger; if it flares, their parents quickly squash it. So they learn to suppress their anger.

Many other children begin to lash out with anger and aggression, particularly those who have been most violently abused. Who are their targets? Smaller kids. They've learned that bigger people hurt smaller people, and they fall into the cycle.

Hypersensitivity to Anger Children who have been abused will react strongly to anger—even if it is not necessarily there. That's the conclusion of Seth Pollak, Ph.D., a psychologist at the University of Wisconsin at Madison. Pollak showed abused and nonabused children computer-generated faces that blended together a couple of emotions—anger and fear, for example, or happiness and sadness. The abused children reacted like the other kids when they were shown faces without any anger mixed in. But when anger was added, it overwhelmed other emotions. A picture that was mostly fearful with some anger was considered angry. The kids who hadn't been abused didn't notice the anger in the same images.

Abuse and the psychological trauma it causes may actually be rewiring the children's brains. In a sense, it's a survival skill: they are able to recognize and respond to anger quickly. But it can also impair the child's ability to form healthy relationships. They might misread the faces of other children, seeing hostility and threat when there is none.

The Future? Will abused children grow up to abuse their own children? It happens. Although the evidence is a bit conflicting, the best guess is that anywhere from 10 to 40 percent of abused children become abusive themselves. (And when they do, their anger over their own victimization can sometimes drive their behavior.) However, that means that most abused kids *don't* walk in their parent's footsteps. Some abused children resolve to never so much as spank their own child. Others, unfortunately, repeat the patterns they know best.

A variety of resources are available to children (and their parents) to help stop the cycle of abuse. Counseling can help children cope with what happened to them and learn better skills to deal with their own aggression and anger, for example, or their sense of betrayal. The adult survivors of abuse can ensure that they won't repeat the same patterns by first recognizing that their treatment was unacceptable and abusive, resolving to not do the same, and then taking active steps to learn other, nonviolent methods of parenting. (A parenting class is always a good idea.)

If you're concerned that a partner or spouse who was abused will act the same way with your future children, you might want to ask them to see a therapist or to join a support group. Also, because abuse can sometimes arise from unrealistic expectations about children's behavior, it can be helpful to take child development classes to learn what you should expect from your children. And what of anger? Again, adults who were abused as children can go a couple of ways. They might continue to be afraid of anger and refuse to let themselves experience or express it—they show no anger at all. Or because they learned that it was not only acceptable but normal to be angry and yelling all the time— because that's what they saw their parents do—they follow in that mold.

Jealous Anger

Jealousy may well be the first form of anger any of us experience— the jealousy that wells up when a parent pays attention to someone else. Kids can feel jealous anger about the time their parents

PsychSpeak

The emotion of **jealousy** occurs when we believe that another person is getting something that we want or believe belongs to us.

spend with a new baby, or about a toy they can't have that other kids do. And when we get older, anger motivated by jealousy can take other forms—a boyfriend might blow up because his girlfriend is flirting with another man at a party. In men, some experts say, jealousy has its evolutionary roots in sexual competition.

His girlfriend, on the other hand, might be jealous because he's spent the party chatting with the cute female bartender. At the end of the night, they're both angry with each other.

The unfortunate thing about jealous anger is that you're often getting out of sorts over something that may not actually be going on. Jealousy is driven by perception—that flirting will lead to an affair, that chatting with someone else means they find the other person more attractive than you. Is it true? Maybe not. But that truth might not become clear until after the blowup, and after the damage is done.

Anger in Divorce

Your husband cheated on you. You want a divorce. But not just a divorce: you want annihilation, to take the house, his car, the kids, and every dime you can get your hands on.

Anger is incredibly common in divorce. "I would say that most people experience some anger in their divorce experience," says divorce counselor Jennifer Coleman, N.C.C., who consults couples and their children at a divorce law firm in Raleigh, North Carolina. Sometimes, says Coleman, divorcing couples—or one or both spouses—are simply angry because the relationship has failed. "But more often than that, people are angry at certain events—marital misconduct. People feel pretty justified in their anger."

In the short term, that's fine. Over time, though, that anger can become more destructive than helpful. It can hurt the kids, drag out the split, and consume your good nature. "I try to get clients to use their anger as a springboard to something positive, to find the most constructive solution, where they want to go with their life."

"**M**y children are mad because they are helpless," says Paula, a mother of two from Tulsa, Oklahoma, now going through a divorce from her husband of 23 years. During her marriage, Paula never realized that her husband's obsessive renovations to their house and re-landscaping of their yard were his way of channeling his anger. "When he finally got the house he wanted and the yard he wanted, that was no longer enough. So he decided to move on to the next thing, which was a girlfriend and another life.

"All this 'mad' is now coming out of him, and it comes in these huge waves that are amazing to me. I come from a big Lebanese family. There were always blowups, it was very emotional, but then you pretty much got over it. You didn't have to talk it to death, massage it," she says. "It was over, you moved on.

"What concerns me is how this anger passes on to the kids. That's how they're learning to cope. My 9-year-old daughter will be really, really ugly to my 12-year-old and then she'll just fall apart in tears and say 'I don't mean to be mean to him, Mom. I'm just so mad and I don't know what to do.'

"My son is the stereotypical first child, in that he tries to make everything right, to 'fix it,' which of course he cannot do. I think he's angry but in a different way. It's not those quick bursts of anger that my daughter has. It's more that he's sad because his dad is not home anymore.

"Both of the kids are angry about broken promises. They can't trust what their dad says because he always told them this would never happen."

Anger from Illness and Loss

When you first learn that you or a loved one have a serious illness—cancer, heart disease, a mental disorder, whatever—you might experience a range of emotions. You might deny that it is happening; you might get depressed. Or you might leap straight to furious, at the unfairness of the situation, at your body for betraying you, or at your loved one because they are sick and that means they will leave you—or because they already have. You might be angry at people who are not sick or suffering because your situation is just so unfair.

Illness, like death, represents a tremendous and traumatic loss, and with loss comes anger. "Not only is your present changed, but you are basically losing the future as you thought you were going to have it," says Susan Romanelli, LCSW, Ph.D., the director of the Hope Adult Program at the Menninger Clinic in Houston. "That anger can be very intense. But you can move off of that after a while. You start to accept and then adapt."

What You Can Do

You love your wife. You adore your husband. Your children mean everything to you. So how do you accept that you've been hurting them, that your rage is driving them away? You must accept it. Because until you do, until you accept the pain that you've inflicted and the bridges you've burned, they can't be healed and rebuilt.

By the same token, you won't be able to pass beyond your anger—from a loss, from an illness, from whatever—until you understand and deal with it. Here are some suggestions to help you get through:

☐ Talk to your family members, and find out how they feel about your behavior. You might already know, but hearing about the pain of the people you've hurt can push you toward change.

☐ Learn to communicate, to fight fairly, to seek resolution in a discussion, and not to go for the jugular.

☐ If you've been abusive, find help. See a therapist or your doctor, lawyer, or spiritual adviser. Remove yourself from the situation if that's what it takes to protect your loved ones.

☐ If you have been or are being abused in your relationship, get support; get help. Get out if you're not safe. The National Domestic Violence Hotline (www.ndvh.org, 1-800-799-7233) can direct you to resources in your area.

☐ There is no excuse for abusing a child—ever. If you've been abusive in any way to your children, talk to someone. Find help. If you know of or suspect that a child is being abused, report it immediately.

☐ You might find yourself overwhelmingly angry during your divorce. Validate that feeling—let yourself be mad without destroying your family with your rage. It's normal.

☐ Give yourself time to get past the rage you're feeling before you make any important decisions. As satisfying as it might be to get ugly, the best thing you can do for yourself and your family is to make rational decisions, not emotional ones.

☐ Do work to get past your anger. Seek the advice of a therapist or divorce counselor, if necessary. And get your kids involved. They need to heal, too.

Anger in the Workplace and in the World

Anger isn't just in the home. Angry behavior crops up everywhere—in quiet snippiness, passive-aggressive insolence, one-upmanship, confrontations at work, yelling matches on the football field, and fights over empty spaces in the parking lot. Perfectly mild-mannered PTA moms turn into vicious barracudas behind the wheel of their SUV. What the heck is going on? Have we collectively gone nuts?

Social psychologists and other scientists have unearthed some clues to explain our uncivil behavior. By understanding the motivations behind our public temper tantrums, we can take the first step to taming them.

Desk Rage

Other than our home, there's no place where professional folk spend more time than at work. For some people, the job can consume more hours than home life. Add frustration, competition, pressure, and other workplace stressors, and it's no wonder that anger bubbles up at the workplace. Heated discussions and even arguments aren't unexpected. But when it turns ugly or gets out of control or violent—call it desk rage or office rage or cubicle rage—it is a problem.

The problem isn't just obvious rage. In fact, overt anger is much less likely to infiltrate the workplace than more invisible acts of aggression. Sniping about co-workers or complaining about the boss might seem socially acceptable, but it can tear at the fabric of the workplace, potentially damaging morale and relationships.

Is Workplace Anger Really on the Rise? But is it increasing? Some evidence suggests that it is. For example, in a 2001 desk rage survey of more than 1,200 working adults, 42 percent reported yelling and verbal abuse—which can be a manifestation of anger but also can take the form of quiet but stinging insults, threats, and constant criticisms—in their workplace, and 29 percent said they had yelled at their co-workers because of stress. In the same poll, nearly 1 in 4 said they'd been driven to tears from stress, while 12 percent said they'd vented their workplace rage by trashing machinery or equipment. A separate study found that employees get annoyed at work at least 10 times a day.

WEB TALK: Visit the National Institute for the Prevention of Workplace Violence at:

🔺 www.workplaceviolence911.com

Provocations Some jobs have always been stressful. It didn't suddenly become tougher to be a cop on the beat, or a commodities trader on Wall Street. But economic down-turns and corporate downsizing can cause formerly secure employees to worry about job security, a frustration that can con-tribute to anger. Also, companies are constantly looking to increase their productivity—and because they're not hiring more hands, that means more work for the current employees.

And if you're in a job you don't like, you've got fewer options. "There aren't a lot of other jobs available," says conflict management expert Andra Medea. "The usual safety valve is that if you are un-happy, you go somewhere else, but that isn't doing very well right now, so you tend to have a higher level of anger and frustration."

More Stressed Than Ever Stress in general, because it is so tightly linked with anger, can contribute to office rage. Your body reacts very similarly when you're in a stressful situation and when you're angry—your blood pressure goes up, your stomach is in a knot, your senses are on edge. When you're in a perpet-ual state of stress, a slight provocation is much more likely to push you over the edge and cause your temper to flare. Your baseline level of arousal is high, so you're less flexible and toler-ant when things don't go your way.

American workers are certainly feeling more and more under the gun. A poll by the Princeton Survey Research Associates found that three-fourths of employees believe workers have more on-the-job stress than they did a generation ago, while one-fourth of employees in a Northwestern National Life survey said that their job was the biggest stressor in their lives.

Q&A

I hate my job, but I can't leave right now. What can I do?

"Problem-solving is a healthy kind of conflict, so I like to give people another kind of problem to solve instead of just being in their job and being frustrated. If this isn't the job of your dreams, what is? What in this job could prepare you for the next one—the one where you want to be? For example, if you're in customer service and you really want to have your own company some day, then being able to deal with problematic customer situations is a skill that can travel anywhere. If what keeps people healthy is a problem-solving focus, and part of that is a sense of their own power, then this is a very good route. They become more capable, better workers, and they are preparing a future for themselves." –Andra Medea, M.A., *conflict management expert and author of* Conflict Unraveled: Fixing Problems at Work and in Families

When Getting Mad Is Motivation Use your on-the-job anger in useful ways; it's really the best way to cope, psychologists say. Negative energy is still energy, after all, and it can propel you toward better things. If you're furious at a co-worker, that's probably not the time to hash out your differences in a screaming tirade. Leave the situation, take a walk, clear your head, and then take the time to distill what is upsetting you into a few clear points that you can discuss—calmly. It can help to write down your thoughts. Even better, come up with viable solutions to the problem. If you need to, involve other people. Talk to your boss about what's bugging you; seek help for unacceptable circumstances (if you're suffering harassment of some sort, for example); or update your resumé, make some phone calls, and get yourself out of your bad situation. If you convince yourself that you're without options, you might just need to look at your situation in a different way. It's hard, but it doesn't have to be impossible.

Deb, a 43-year-old nurse from the Philadelphia area, was raised in a family of yellers. "It was very loud, with everyone expressing their anger," she recalls, "and I have continued that mode of operating, unfortunately, as I've grown to have a family of my own."

She didn't realize that there was anything wrong with her very vocal expression of anger until she reached college. "I saw other people keeping their temper in check, discussing things. That is still extremely hard for me to do. I'm the person who gets the work evaluations that say, 'Deb is so passionate about her causes,' and I am. I get so emotive about it—I don't like the word *explosive*—because if things are not being done in a way that I feel is proper, it is difficult for me to express that in a quiet, positive kind of way.

"I've really had to learn to control it in my professional life, and I think that's why sometimes I come home and the smallest thing will set me off. All day I've kept it inside. I'm a professional. I can't yell. Then I come home and I'm screaming.

"What people don't realize is how physically exhausting it is to be a person who 'emotes' anger and yet has to try and keep that in and talk to the person you are angry with, in that calm, assertive manner that you are supposed to use. Sometimes I have to sleep it off because I'm so exhausted from trying to keep myself under control."

Road Rage

Studies by the American Automobile Association show that the most severe cases of road rage—drivers running others off the road, shootings, smashing someone's window—increased by about 7 percent per year from 1990 through 1995. From that data, it looks like drivers really are getting angrier and angrier.

Jerry Deffenbacher, Ph.D., a psychologist at Colorado State University who has been studying driving anger for nearly two decades, isn't so sure: "Have angry drivers or road rage in the most extreme cases really increased, or has our awareness and reporting of it increased?" Deffenbacher suspects that both are true: we talk about and hear about road rage incidents more often than, say 30 or 40 years ago, but, also, the sheer number of incidents has gone up—but that is also because there are more drivers, more cars, more miles driven, and more traffic than ever before.

WEB TALK: For news reports, research, and other road rage information, visit Leon James's "Dr. Driving" site at:

➤ www.drdriving.org

"It *has* to go up. If the distribution of people prone to anger doesn't change but you add a million drivers, you are going to have that many more angry drivers," he says.

Contributing Factors What's behind the rage? Psychologist Leon James, Ph.D., of the University of Hawaii, who has been studying road rage for more than 20 years, says that Americans have a culture of entitlement and of basic disrespect. "I think that it is also biological," James says. "When you put more bodies, more organisms in a particular space, there is more competition, and in our case, competition and anger go together."

GET PSYCHED

"You're stuck in traffic. The kids are in the backseat screaming, punching each other. This is the last thing you need: to be trapped in a small box with two screaming children. Instead of losing it and yelling at the kids, I have parents start singing really loudly. It dissolves the tension."
–Andra Medea, M.A., conflict management expert

Jerry Deffenbacher also suspects that biology may be at play, but in a different way. "If you are more irritable, have a more difficult temperament"—which studies have shown can be present from birth—"then you may be more biologically vulnerable to anger behind the wheel," he says.

Add to that increasing congestion, other grouchy drivers, and drivers who aren't paying attention because they're on their cell phone, and you've got more reasons to be mad. "We also know that being in a hurry facilitates anger, and if you are in a crummy and angry mood when you're in the car, that also makes a difference," Deffenbacher says.

Influence of Road-Racing Video Games Can playing a violent driving video game make you more aggressive and angry on the road? The jury is still out. "I am aware of no data that says aggressive driving games are related to aggressive driving," says Jerry Deffenbacher. But Deffenbacher says violent video games in general have been linked to an increase in aggressive behavior, and that could spill over to driving. The effect—if it exists—would be small, he says, but it would make sense that if you're more likely to be aggressive in your pretend driving in a game, "you're more likely to also do it on the road."

It's the Other Guy's Fault The funny thing about bad drivers is that they're always the other guy. People don't think of themselves as the "idiot" whose mistakes tick everybody off, or as someone needlessly aggressive on the road. We're all perfect drivers—in our own minds.

The chance of getting angry in general goes up if you have a habit of blaming other people for your problems. The same thing happens when we're driving, says Deffenbacher. "'I'm angry because you're slow in my lane. I'm angry because you cut me off.' Then they'll use it as justification for their behavior: 'I cut him off because he cut me off.' Identifying the other person as the enemy is part of the process with angry drivers."

Q & A

How can I change my behavior in the car so that I'm not yelling or flipping people off?

"One useful intervention for driving anger focuses on the person's behavior—what they do when they are angry. We find that engaging in two different but related kinds of behavior can be very helpful. Let's suppose I'm a screamer when I get frustrated on the road. What if I had to put my tongue between my teeth and just very gently hold it there? Or suppose I am a person who is a finger-flipper or a fist-waver. What if I locked my thumbs on the steering wheel at the 10 and 2 positions and instead gave a covert peace sign with my index finger and middle finger? If I have the urge to run up on a bumper, I might instruct myself to instead back off one car length. Distracting behaviors—listening to music, planning a grocery list in your head—can pull your attention away from being angry but still leave you a calm, safe driver."
—*Jerry Deffenbacher, Ph.D., psychologist at Colorado State University*

Air Rage

We aren't just angry on the road. The Association of Flight Attendants has reported a steady increase in abusive passenger behavior over the last few years, as has the Federal Aviation Administration. The causes, as with everything to do with anger, vary. There are some patterns, though: less space per passenger as airlines push in more seats per plane, anxiety and a fear of flying, flight delays, cancellations, high fares, boredom, nicotine withdrawal if you're a smoker, turbulence—even sitting next to a person who won't let you use the armrest.

If you find yourself getting anxious and irritable when you fly, take precautions. Give yourself plenty of time to get to the airport (and to make connections) so you're not feeling rushed and stressed. Bring snacks so your blood sugar doesn't drop, and consider nicotine gum if you are a frequent smoker. Boredom often breeds frustration, so bring books, music, or small toys, games, and coloring books for restless kids. Stretch in your seat to invigorate tired and tense muscles. Drink plenty of water so you don't get dehydrated—which can cause a killer headache. Try to avoid alcohol, which can make people who are already in a bad mood more disruptive as well as dehydrated, which in turn makes them feel physically worse—and that leads to crankiness.

Sports Rage

In sports such as hockey, football, boxing, and others, aggression is part and parcel of the game. And in sports, unlike most areas of our life, aggression is encouraged—with anger always waiting in the wings. Players—adults and children alike—are told to be tough, to fight hard, to not get walked on. The fans egg on the violence. Great players, in any sport, may learn to control and channel their anger, but in the casual player, emotion can quickly take center stage.

The Players "I think anger is built into professional sports," says clinical psychologist and certified sports psychologist Darrell Burnett, Ph.D. "The problem you also have in professional sports is that you've got some thugs playing. They are coming in maybe with an anger problem, and when they are hired to play a violent sport, I think you are also going to see a lot of anger there."

Burnett says that at the professional level, anger and violence in players are reinforced because there are so few consequences for bad behavior. "You get in trouble for harassment in the workplace, and you get in trouble for road rage, but in sports there hasn't been much done," Burnett says. To a player who makes $10 million a year, a $25,000 fine for throwing a punch is a drop in an overflowing bucket. And when kids watching professional sports see that kind of behavior, they're going to imitate it. "You have to explain to your kids that it is a business. Just because they do it, doesn't mean you do it. It is very difficult," he says.

The Fans Of course, belligerent fans only make the situation worse. It's not just crazed fans at European soccer matches and fanatic supporters of pro football teams. The rage is trickling— or perhaps flooding—down to youth sports. We're now seeing parents who get into screaming matches at Little League games and fistfights at football games. In July 2001, one parent beat another to death in a fight after their sons' hockey game. The kids aren't immune: in April 2005, a Pony League baseball player who'd just pitched a losing game beat another boy to death with a bat.

That's extreme, of course, but youth sports experts such as Burnett say that the anger among parents and players is steadily rising. One study found a 15 percent surge in physical assaults in youth sports over the past 10 years.

The reasons are hard to pin down. Parents are getting more involved in their children's activities and more serious about their kids being successful. The focus on having fun and building skills is often lost, replaced by a desire to be first, to be best. "There is so much emphasis on the brass ring, the talk of scholarships and all that, rather than the fun of the game," Burnett says. And some parents are doing whatever they can to push their children toward that ring. They might have their kids in club teams so they can play a sport all year long, or hire a professional to train their child—all at a cost. "Parents spend a lot of money. I think that is where the anger comes from. If they are investing a lot of money, they expect results," he says. Angry parents make for stressed, angry, and unhappy kids.

WEB TALK: For guidance on youth sports issues, visit the Institute for International Sport's Center for Sport Parenting at:

www.internationalsport.com/csp/

The other girls on my daughter's softball team are giving her a hard time when she doesn't do well, and she's getting very frustrated. What can I do?

When more emphasis is placed on performance than on fun, kids feel the pressure. They start to feel bad about their abilities, or they might turn nasty because they're so worried about winning. Make it known that it's not acceptable. "First go to the coach," says clinical psychologist Darrell Burnett, Ph.D., a certified sports psychologist with a specialization in youth sports. "Say 'this is a recreational sport, and our expectation is that our child won't be humiliated. You are the adult in charge, and if you don't do anything about it, you're allowing abuse to happen.' The coach needs to make sure that nobody makes fun of anyone, because sportsmanship requires encouragement. If you don't get a response, go to the next level–the league's board. Verbalize your concerns. Let them know something has to be done. If it continues, go to the media. The philosophy should be fun first and then skill development, not 'we're going to make professionals out of these kids.'"

Shopping Rage, Parking Rage, E-Mail Rage, and Other Unpleasantries

Angry behavior is cropping up in other areas of our lives, too, due to that same culture of disrespect that leads to road rage. Shoppers are fighting with other shoppers in mall parking lots and over parking spots at the grocery store—big SUVs that hog more than one spot frequently incite parking rage—and then battle it out inside the stores to grab the best deals. There are also news reports of surf rage and boating rage.

Computer rage—getting pissed off when your computer breaks down or won't do what you need it to—is causing users to swear at or even assault their uncooperative machines. The information superhighway has its own form of road rage: e-mail rage. (Ever sent a withering e-mail message without thinking? Flamed someone in a chat room?)

Cute labels aside, is there any difference between this kind of behavior and plain old anger? Not really. The words in a blistering e-mail message are no less hurtful, or no less likely to cause a fight, than if you'd said them in person.

Anger and Crime

Not every criminal act is rooted in anger. Many really are emotionless acts—the banker who embezzles money, for example, may not be acting out of rage or repressed emotions. He may just want the money. And certainly not every angry person will ever commit an illegal act. Indeed, the majority of us angry folk never do.

But the emotion lurks around many crimes. A child who grows up in an angry home is more likely to break the law than one who does not; his illegal acts might be a form of acting out against his tortured childhood, or they might just be a spur-of-the-moment product of rage. Either way, anger is involved. Even violence against property—setting a fire, say, or vandalizing a car—has been viewed as displaced anger. (Ever smash a plate because you were ticked off?)

Link Between Anger and Violent Crime Hundreds of experimental psychology studies have found a clear relationship between annoyance and anger and the likelihood of aggression. When people get angry, they're more likely to get violent. They might smash a window; they might throw a punch. Some violent offenders say they find anger satisfying. They enjoy the rush—and might actually put themselves in situations that are likely to make them mad. The more violent the crime, the more likely anger is involved. Murderers often report that an intense fury preceded their actions.

you're not alone

"I've got a fairly classic anger story on myself. This took place while I was teaching. It was the first cold, rainy day of the season. I had just broken my right collar bone—one of those very painful injuries because you can't set it—and I had my arm taped to my body to take some of the pressure off my shoulder. So I only had my left arm, and with it I was carrying everything I needed for class: my attaché, books, papers, and my umbrella and raincoat.

"I went to the library because I needed to do some photocopying, but as I was trying to get in the building, I kept dropping things. Then I'd bend over to pick up whatever I'd dropped, and I'd wrench my shoulder. It hurt terribly. The copy room was on the other side of this huge ornamental door. I couldn't open it with one hand and realized I was killing myself at this rate, so I ferried my stuff over to a clerk sitting behind a desk, explained my situation, and asked if I could leave my stuff behind his desk. He said no—and then I felt the top of my head just lift off like Vesuvius. I thought 'I know how to handle this: I'll kill him and drag his body the length of the library.' This made perfect sense.

"I'm an expert in conflict management, and with the top of my head lifting off, I had a clue that I might not have been at my best. So I thought of the conflict chart that I've developed, which maps healthy and unhealthy and abusive anger—'Am I on track, am I not?' Everything was blank. I finally managed to bring up one phrase: 'How can we work this out?'

"So I thought, 'Okay, I will say this to this guy, he'll say something officious, and *then* I can kill him.' I have no idea how long this took. I could have been standing there for five minutes. I managed to be civil, and I said 'What would you suggest?' He thought about it and offered to carry my things for me to the copy room. He explained that he just wasn't allowed to hold anything behind the desk. And this perfectly nice, courteous, pleasant guy, who I was about to kill, picks up all my things and walks with me. I couldn't get through the door. He opened it for me. I couldn't manage the copier. He helped me with that. Everything dissipated.

"I could make a lot of excuses to myself—I was in pain, I was under a lot of stress. That doesn't matter. I was very out of control and I needed a way to get a grip on myself again. Most people don't have the training to deal with it, and they might have made a complete mess of it. But the only skill I *really* needed was to know that when the top of my head lifted off, that was not the time to say something. It was the time to step backward and regroup."
—Andra Medea, consultant, conflict management expert, and author of Conflict Unraveled: Fixing Problems at Work and in Families

Does that mean that as anger and rage increase in society, we are also becoming more violent? Not necessarily. In fact, among adults, violent crime rates have dropped precipitously over the past decade or two. Experts don't think we've become calmer and more passive; the drop, while still a mystery, has been variously explained through stricter gun laws, stabilization in the drug trade, more prisons (and, therefore, more violent offenders incarcerated), more policing, and better education. Some researchers say that as demographics change and the average age of the population rises, violent crimes will decrease—simply because older people are less likely to be violent than teenagers and young adults.

Sexual Violence At least 40 percent of rapes—crimes of control and violence rather than sex—are thought to be associated with anger, researchers say. The numbers may be higher. The most violent and dangerous rapists, say psychologists, are motivated by intense anger—deep, seething, festering resentment, especially toward women. Their sexual attacks on women, which are usually not committed during a moment of rage, are their way of acting out that anger. Anger can also fuel sexual obsessions, *perversions*, and other unhealthy sexual behavior, psychologists say.

PsychSpeak

A **perversion** is an abnormal or deviant sexual practice, preferred in place of normal sexual behavior.

More Anger in the World

Anger can be a motivator behind every bias we have or rush to judgment we make (that's prejudice—prejudging without facts). Anger, hatred, and fear may drive terrorism and our outrage against terrorists; it can inspire acts of violence against people we don't know and who are different from us.

What You Can Do

Nobody likes to look like a fool in front of the world—but that's what anger can make happen. If you're shrieking at and flipping off other drivers, losing your cool on an airplane, or constantly arguing with colleagues at work, your anger has gotten the better of you, and it's time for you to get back the upper hand. Here are some suggestions that can help you take control:

- ☐ Try to shift the focus of your fury at work to problem-solving. Yes, the situation is bad. What can you do to make it better? Brainstorm. Talk to friends. Use your angry energy to find your way out.

- ☐ Feeling frustrated and infuriated because your freeway is always packed? Try to work around the problem. Find another route. If you can't, see if you can shift your hours. Sometimes just leaving a half hour earlier or later can push you past the bulk of rush-hour traffic.

- ☐ Remember that being angry in the car doesn't do anyone any good—least of all you. The other drivers usually can't hear your ranting, but your body will feel the effects of that constant stress. Think of it this way: if you commute 2 hours each workday and are upset the entire time, over a year, that's about *500 hours* of anger you've inflicted on your poor body.

- ☐ If you're thinking of putting your kids in a sports league, learn the league's philosophy first. Do they have rules in place against parental tirades? Is there an emphasis on sportsmanship, fun, and skill development rather than scores and standings?

☐ Spend time with your kids when they're watching sporting events on TV, and discuss with them the violence and aggression they see.

☐ Think twice before you send off that flaming e-mail message. Is it really what you want to say? Is it going to cause more harm than the instant of satisfaction you'll feel from sending it? Remember that after you hit Send, there's no getting it back.

Part 3
Taking Charge

Think you have an anger problem? It's time to own up to it and make a commitment to change your ways. A variety of tactics can help you tackle your temper. In Part 3, you learn how to get motivated, what you can do on your own, and, if you need more help, what an anger management program might do for you.

Making the Decision to Change

With some people, anger problems are in-your-face obvious: the woman who smacks her kid for mouthing off; she obviously needs to tame her temper. That guy who rams the car that cut him off in traffic; he clearly has issues.

In most of us, however, the effects of inappropriate anger can brew slowly, insidiously—which can make them harder to spot. But the signs are in your life, if you're willing to take a closer look. Maybe there's a distance between you and your wife. She's avoiding you, and the intimacy is fizzling. No problem ever seems to get settled except with a fight. Maybe your kids have stopped asking you for help on their homework because their questions make you impatient and mad. Or maybe your anger just flat-out has them scared.

After you've read the writing on the wall, what you need to do next is make the decision to change—not an easy thing. Deciding to make your life different—and then motivating yourself to actually *do it*—can be as hard as the work that makes it happen. Sometimes it's harder, because it means you have to take a deep, hard look at yourself to discover why you're acting the way you are and figure out how to not do it anymore.

Just remember that change is a long, often challenging process that can't be accomplished with a snap of the fingers. In the long run, though, learning new ways to reduce stress or express your bottled-up feelings will only improve your life, your health, and your relationships.

Ruling Out a Physiological Cause for Your Anger

As always, it is important to keep in mind that anger is a perfectly normal, and necessary, emotion. Anger helps us notice and respond to dangerous situations; it prods us to modify our circumstances in positive ways. Normally an anger problem doesn't have an unnatural cause: a malfunctioning brain, for example, a hormone imbalance, or even low blood sugar. (I discussed these and other health problems that could lead to unusual or extreme anger in Chapter 6.)

But because it *can* happen, you might want to first be sure an underlying physical condition isn't undermining your emotional well-being before you embark on a path to change.

How do you do that? Simple: get to a physician or a psychiatrist. Talk to a therapist. Tell him or her what is troubling you and don't leave out *any* symptoms. Be sure to mention any brain-related symptoms (blinding headaches or memory loss, for example) if you have experienced these problems in conjunction with a sudden increase in your anger and rage. Yes, it can be embarrassing to admit that you punched your fist through a wall because you were mad that your dog ripped up the newspaper, but your doctor

WEB TALK: Find a therapist in your area through *Psychology Today*'s therapy directory:

therapists.psychologytoday.com/rms/ prof_search.php

does need to know all the grisly details—especially if what happened is out of character for you.

PsychSpeak

Phytoestrogens are trace substances in plants such as soybeans that are said to mimic the effects of estrogen in women's bodies.

Women who suspect that their moods might be related to premenstrual syndrome or menopause should talk to their gynecologist. Hormone replacement therapy (HRT) can help, although there is compelling evidence that it can also increase cancer risk. Herbal medicine practitioners tout *phytoestrogens* as an alternative to HRT, but there has not been much scientific evidence showing that these food-based hormones have much effect.

Deciding to Make a Change

After you've ruled out any medical reason for your troubled temper or unruly rage, it's time for the tough part: doing something about it. You can tame a bad temper, and you can learn to healthfully express your pent-up anger, but you have to decide that you need to change your ways, and that's no picnic.

"It really is the hardest part, because it requires taking a straightforward, honest look at yourself. We all have a lot of positive illusions and denial and defenses that protect us from looking at ourselves with total objectivity," says Mitchel D. Rose, Ph.D., a licensed clinical psychologist in private practice in Boston and a lecturer in the department of psychology at Tufts University.

A "positive illusion" sounds like a pretty nice thing to have, but it can crush any chances you have at seeing yourself clearly because you're merely putting a nice spin on a bad situation.

GET PSYCHED

"When I instruct patients, I say, look, it is almost impossible to change someone else. Your best bet is to do what you can to change the situation unilaterally. You can try to change another person coercively, but that always rebounds badly sooner or later." —*Mitchel D. Rose, Ph.D., licensed clinical psychologist*

"In terms of anger," Rose says "you may have a sense that the locus of control and the locus of irritation is with everyone else." In other words, everyone else is to blame for whatever it is that is pissing you off. You're responding to their flawed behavior, but you don't have any control.

To reign in your rage or learn to express it in better ways, you have to first accept that you are, in fact, in complete control—*of your own behavior*. What anyone else does is their problem. It starts with you; it ends with you. It's all about *you*.

Is Your Anger Hurting You and Those Around You?

That's not to say that other people aren't involved. We all drag around the emotional debris of our childhoods. Perhaps you grew up in an abusive home with more tantrums than talking, or perhaps the only good emotions in your family were those left buried and repressed. Accepting that you drew a short straw in the nurturing-childhood department—and that it may have left you poorly equipped to deal with your emotions in adulthood—can help you decide now to fix the damage.

Or maybe people in your life are telling you that you have anger issues. If they say your anger and your outbursts are causing them pain, you have to be receptive to that. If they tell you that your temper is hurting you—personally, professionally, or otherwise—listen to them. It probably took a lot of courage to even mention that your anger is doing damage. When someone in your life is hot-tempered and always boiling over, you end up walking on eggshells all the time to keep things cool, to avoid upsetting them. Telling an angry person they have a problem may enrage them more, and for that reason, it can be an incredibly hard step.

Another problem your anger may cause is that it creates distance. Between you and the people you care about is a chasm carved by your out-of-control temper. With excess anger comes isolation, loneliness, depression, and anxiety.

Q&A

How do I know that my anger is out of control?

"One, if it is repetitive and consistent. Are you angry from the time you wake up in the morning until the time you go to sleep? Two, if it is causing stress to your family and yourself. Three, if it is causing impairment to your functioning. You are in trouble with the law, or are in trouble with office mates. Those are all signs that your anger is getting out of hand."
—Michael Rayel, psychiatrist and author of First Aid to Mental Illness

The Steps of the Decision Process It'll be easier to accept and digest what your loved ones tell you if you also resist the temptation to punish yourself for not being perfect. Nobody is, after all. The key is introspection—with a heavy dose of cutting yourself a break. Even if you're the one making harsh judgments about your own behavior, "you might respond in your typically terroristic way, which is to bark back," Rose says. If you can recognize yourself as you are, warts and all, without kicking yourself or being critical, however, you have more freedom to change.

Is the work done yet? Not by a long shot. You still have to change your ways. You might try breaking it down into steps.

Acknowledge the problem. This is a crucial first step if you're going to make any change, whether it is losing weight, quitting smoking, or getting your anger under control. If you've done some soul searching and really heard what your friends and family have tried to tell you, you're already at the point where you can admit the problem.

Try to visualize your life *without* anger—after you've made the change. What would it be like if your home were calm? How would you feel if you weren't steaming over something all the time? If you grew up in an angry home, it can be quite difficult to imagine a life without strife. If that's your situation, you might take a more creative approach: imagine someone whose life is now happier and healthier because he got his anger in check.

Alternatively, you can take the Ebenezer Scrooge approach: picture what the consequences might be if you don't change your ways. Where will you end up? Sick from stress? Divorced? In jail? Seeing a less-than-rosy future might be what you need to get motivated to make some changes.

Make a goal for yourself. It can be as simple as "I will go a week without screaming." Don't go overboard: if your goal is to never get angry again, you're being completely unrealistic and setting yourself up for a failure that can derail you from further progress.

Break up the goal into less-daunting baby steps. For example, your week without screaming might be more feasible if you cut it roughly in half: "I will go three days without screaming." Some psychologists recommend a 24-hour anger plan: commit to 24 hours of calm behavior. (You don't have to actually *feel* calm the whole time, but the goal is to act that way.)

Recruit a friend to help you. Ask them to be your emotional barometer and tell you if you're getting too upset and to be available if you need to talk about a problem that's getting your temper going. They can't control your temper or express your buried emotions, but having that support can make the process less daunting.

Q & A

My boyfriend is always angry over something, and it's turning into a big problem. How can I get him to change?

"That's a tough one. One thing that potentially works is to say, 'I'm not going to be in your life anymore if you continue that way.' Sometimes, people will then seek a solution. But you could also get into the loop that battered women often fall into, where they accept their partner's pledges to work on their anger and not be hostile and aggressive. It might be successful for a month or so, and the partner gets rewarded by getting the other person back, but then the same behaviors start to happen again. What you can do is encourage them to change, perhaps encourage them to get professional help or go into therapy, and provide a supportive and nonpunitive environment. Sometimes if you can give a person a reason for their anger–if you think they might be depressed, for example–they're less likely to take it as a character assassination. Also, whatever you can do to encourage empathy in the person who is angry–to make them see what you are going through–is important. The problem is that a lack of empathy is often the problem in someone who is angry." *–Mitchel D. Rose, Ph.D., licensed clinical psychologist, Tufts University*

Following Through on Your Decision After you've decided to change your ways, nothing is going to happen unless you actually *do* it. If you don't feel you're emotionally ready to start, make an appointment with yourself. Set a date (not too far in the future) and stick with it. This is something your partner in change can help a lot with, by reminding you of the target date or giving you some gentle prodding.

And after you've taken the giant leap and have committed to changing your ways, embrace that decision. Recognize that it will make you a better person and improve your life and the lives of the people you love.

Tactics to Temper Your Temper

You've seen the light; the decision has been made; you're ready to change. Now what? For many people, therapy or a formal anger management class isn't necessary. You just need a better handle on dealing with stress and daily annoyances; you need to learn to be assertive and expressive without boiling over. Keep in mind that what's best for someone else might not work for you, so you might have to try a few things, or a combination of tactics, to learn the best way to keep your cool.

Reducing Arousal When we get angry, we are in a highly aroused state (both emotionally and physically), and that means we are also highly impulsive. We don't do the best thing but jump toward the response that quickly comes to mind—even if it's the worst possible solution.

That's why social psychologist Brad Bushman, Ph.D., of the University of Michigan recommends a number of tactics to reduce arousal. The idea is to call on these methods when you feel yourself starting to get hot under the collar. You might try counting to 10 or 100 if you're really mad. Or you might distract yourself by thinking of something else. Deep breaths and listening to soothing music can also help you relax and reduce your arousal, as can doing something incompatible with the angry feelings you are having. Kiss your lover. Watch a funny movie.

Reducing Stress Easier said than done, you say? Well, true, but the benefits are tremendous. Stress and anger are intimately linked; if you're constantly stressed out, you're much more likely to blow. But there are other, less-damaging ways to burn it off.

"I always desperately wanted children and I had had a number of miscarriages. In 1996 when I was about 46, I had my last miscarriage. I just felt horrible. I felt like nothing could live in me.

"The way I expressed that anger was overeating, abusing substances, and, on a daily basis, by being angry at my stepkids. I raised my voice. I pouted. Everybody started walking around me on eggshells. They didn't know what was going to happen next.

"The truth is that while I certainly made it uncomfortable for them, I was suffering, and I just couldn't shake it. No matter what I did, no matter what promises I made, no matter how terrible I felt, I could not shake it. It resulted in a big argument one day, something small to do with my step-kids. I didn't feel supported by my husband at the time. We had a major argument, a lot of screaming and hysterics, and then I left and went to a friend's house. When I spoke to him on the phone a few days later, he said he had filed for divorce.

"I was, first of all, brokenhearted. This was my worst fear. I believe that we get our wake-up calls in the language that speaks to us. Some people get physically ill, but for me it was another failed marriage, another thing I'd screwed up.

"So I made a commitment to myself to change from the inside out. I saw a psychiatrist and took antidepressants for six months. That opened up a space of hope for me. I saw a regular therapist. I was in group therapy every week. I did energy work every week. Every day I did inspirational reading. I wrote in my journal, I prayed, I mediated. I went to Al-Anon meetings four days a week even though alcoholism wasn't an issue. I just got constant support. I changed the story of my life. Now when I start getting angry, I recognize the feeling. I've had enough practice to know to call someone and say 'I'm angry, help me get back on track.'" *—Susyn Reeve, management consultant, interfaith minister, and author of* Choose Peace and Happiness: A 52 Week Guide

Exercise is a great way to release negative energy. Vigorous exercise causes the brain to release endorphins, natural tranquilizers that can help reduce stress. (Sex does the same thing.) Or if you're of a more contemplative bent, meditation, yoga, progressive muscle relaxation, and deep breathing can help ease both mind and body. Some people find that music relieves their stress, or watching a string of horror movies on TV; other people write in a journal or do jigsaw puzzles.

Learn What Sets You Off We all have our sore spots. Psychologists call them "anger triggers," and if you're going to stay calm, you'll need to identify yours. Maybe nothing gets you mad quicker than standing in a long line at the grocery store. There's not much you can do about the line after you're there, but you could try flipping your schedule to shop very early or quite late to avoid the rush. Find out what is most likely to set you off and then figure out a way to keep yourself out of the situation.

Sometimes our anger triggers mask other, more deep-seated feelings. Maybe it's not really the line that's bugging you, but the fact that you always have to do the shopping after work, while your husband goes home and takes a jog. That's the issue you'll need to tackle if you want to tame your temper.

Walk Away Often the best way to defuse a potentially explosive situation is just to get the heck out. Excuse yourself from a heated discussion; leave the room if your children's bickering is pushing you to the breaking point. A five-minute walk or a breath of fresh air can be soothing and rejuvenating.

If you're walking away from someone in the middle of an argument, be sure they know you're just calming down and not trying to duck the issue. Set a time for when you'll resume the conversation—in a hour, perhaps, or later that evening, when you can both be calm. And stick to it. The time-out tactic won't work if there's never a "time in" when you can resolve your differences.

Unfortunately, the situation doesn't always end there. Sometimes, the person you're arguing with doesn't want the fight to end. They might follow you, confront you, demand that you continue the argument, and that can intensify your emotions. Your heart is pumping; your breathing is fast. You're already in a state of arousal. Now you've got someone stalking you, and that can lead to fear, sometimes, or rage. What do you do then?

"I'd suggest for the person who is being followed to just sit down, maybe close their eyes. Try to calm down, even if the other person is hovering over you," says Susan Romanelli, LCSW, Ph.D., the director of the Hope Adult Program at the Menninger Clinic in Houston. "It may make the other person angrier, but a lot of times if one person calms down, the other one will, too." Tell them you're not ignoring them—you just need some time to pull yourself together.

Think Positive Psychologists call them "coping thoughts"—the phrases you can say to yourself to keep a clear head. The idea is to create and memorize a mental inventory of helpful statements ("Getting mad won't solve anything," or simply, "Stay cool") that you can pull out when you start getting frustrated or mad. They will remind you that your anger, and your behavior, is under *your* control.

Coping thoughts are especially useful if you're prone to *catastrophising*. Say your husband forgets to pick up the dry cleaning. Your best suit is still at the cleaners, which means you can't wear it to the presentation you're giving at work tomorrow. You won't look your best, you'll feel self-conscious, and you'll do a bad job. And

PsychSpeak

Catastrophising is a type of irrational thinking in which the consequences of an action are exaggerated or seen in the worst possible light. This mindset can set the stage for anger.

that means your boss will be upset—and *that* means you'll lose your job.

GET PSYCHED

"… you have every right to express your needs. Other people have that same right …. By using assertiveness, you can work toward a settlement without anger and seek a solution where both parties get at least some of what they want. You can protect yourself without blame. You can set limits without turning other people off …. Assertiveness is the antidote for anger." *–Matthew McKay, Peter D. Rogers, and Judith McKay in* When Anger Hurts *(New Harbinger, 2003)*

No wonder you're screaming at your husband! However, with a ready index of coping thoughts, you can remind yourself that the situation really isn't that bad. "Getting upset won't help." "I can find a solution." "It was just a mistake."

Rumination Anger ignored doesn't just disappear. It festers, brews, and builds. Some people, especially women, obsessively stew over their problems, a style of thinking called rumination. The ruminator doesn't come up with solutions to her problems. Instead, she runs it over and over in her mind, becoming increasingly anxious, and often angry. One way to stop endlessly chewing over an issue is to simply time yourself; tell yourself that you have five minutes to think about it and then you stop. Use a timer if necessary.

Assertiveness and Expression, Not Suppression

Although blowing up over every little thing is hardly healthy, suppressing your angry feelings can be just as damaging to your body and mind. What you want to do is express your feelings— calmly, rationally, and respectfully. In other words: be assertive. If something is bothering you, say so; if there's something you want, ask for it. Don't expect people to read your mind.

It's a good idea to take your own mental inventory if you're starting to get frustrated and mad. If you're in an increasingly caustic discussion, for example, you should ask yourself if you've really made your point clear, and if you've really tried to understand the other guy's view. If any of those answers are no, state your case again—and be just as willing to listen.

Sometimes there is no good moment to express your feelings. At work, for example, there might be no positive way of telling your boss that he is being a jerk. Give yourself another outlet for the feelings. Karin Bruckner, co-author of *The Anger Advantage*, and a licensed professional counselor in private practice in the Dallas area, calls the technique a "think tank."

you're not alone

"When I was pregnant I was terrified that I'd turn into my mother. My brother and I swore when we were younger that we'd never touch our kids the way we were getting beat, and yet he wound up abusing his kids. He was arrested for brutally beating up his 14-year-old son. So I was scared.

"I did have a moment when my son was 18 months old, and he was really out of control. He was naked and I was trying to get him into the bathtub, but he was defiantly saying no and looking me in the eye. Just being a toddler. If you did that to my mother you couldn't walk for a week. I felt the anger seethe. It goes right through my veins. I reached out and swatted him on his behind.

"I left a red mark. My hand was stained. And that wasn't what hurt. It was the look on his face. He looked at me with such horror—'I trust you to love me, and you're hurting me'—that I never touched him again. But that doesn't mean that I don't feel angry. I handle it differently now.

"If it gets bad, that's when I use my husband. I say, you have to take over, I'm feeling it. And I'll leave the room, or leave the house, whatever I have to do. I'll even go into the bathroom and put the fan on so the sound, the white noise, will calm me down." *—Jenny Moran, child abuse survivor and author of* Jenny's Monster: A True Story of Grace

"Take it up later—a couple of minutes or a few hours or whatever—with a friend or colleague," she says. And then don't just complain about how rotten your boss is, but reexamine why you're mad, discuss it with your friend, and see what you can learn from the emotions. He or she might have some insight that will help you cope.

What You Can Do

Nothing is ever simple when it comes to emotions, and especially not anger. Even after you've recognized that you (or a loved one) have a problem with an appropriate and healthy expression of anger, things can get tricky if there's an underlying medical condition you need to deal with. The best thing to do is find out exactly where you stand. With that knowledge in hand, you can begin to make changes.

- ☐ If you think your anger might have a biological basis, be sure to mention to your doctor any unusual headaches, blurred vision, or other possibly neurological problems. Your emotional changes can be as crucial as physical symptoms in diagnosing a possible problem.

- ☐ That said, biological causes of anger are rare. Don't immediately assume that if you're having headaches and your temper is flaring, you've got a brain tumor or some other ailment. You might just be in a bad mood because you have a headache—or your headache and angry outbursts are both due to too much stress!

- ☐ Stop blaming everyone else for your anger. Yes, people can be annoying. Yes, situations can make you mad. But other people and situations do not control how you respond. That's up to you.

☐ Beating yourself up for your angry actions won't help you change. Be honest with yourself, but be kind to yourself, too.

☐ Remember that you're absolutely entitled to feel what you feel and want what you want, and to express those feelings and needs in an assertive, but respectful, manner. Also remember that there's no guarantee you'll get what you want, because other people are just as entitled to disagree.

☐ Stress reduction is crucial if you've got anger issues. Choose your poison: go for a run, read a book, practice deep breathing. Whatever makes you feel most comfortable is what you're most likely to stick with.

10

When You Can't Do It Alone

f you find you have difficulty with anger, and if the self-help tactics discussed in Chapter 9 aren't cutting it for you, it's time to seek some outside help. A spiritual adviser or a therapist can teach you techniques to take the most destructive edge off your anger. For others, a more structured anger management class might be the answer. Although researchers still aren't sold on the effectiveness of some of the programs, there's no shortage of courses to choose from, and you may find them to be of some benefit. In this chapter, I discuss where you might locate one, what you might find when you get there, and in what circumstances you could be required to attend.

The General Principle of Anger Management

At the most basic level, anger management represents a series of techniques that teach people how to keep themselves from getting angry and how to prevent anger from spiraling out of control with relaxation and calming techniques. The concept appears to date at least as far back as the ancient Greek and Roman philosophers. Aristotle, for example, wrote about anger that stems from our sense that we've been done some injustice.

In 1975, psychologist Raymond W. Novaco, Ph.D., of the University of California at Irvine, coined the term *anger management* to refer to methods that address an individual's thoughts, feelings, and actions, and how they conspire to trigger anger.

Thirty years ago, only people with severe rage accompanied by other mental disorders such as paranoid schizophrenia, major depressive disorder, and bipolar disease received anger treatment. These days, the attendees of anger management classes number in the millions and range from violent felons and mentally disturbed patients in long-term care to hot-under-the-collar employees to kids needing some help in conquering their confusing emotions.

Is anger management effective? The scientific jury is still out. Perhaps the best studied and most successful of the programs are those first devised by Novaco and based in cognitive-behavioral therapy, which places an emphasis on modifying both anger-causing thoughts and our behavioral responses to them. For the most part, however, very little rigorous scientific study has been done on the long-term benefits of most anger interventions. We really know very little about what works and what doesn't.

What does seem to be clear is that the people who are helped the most by anger management classes are highly motivated to change. The courses may not be able to "fix" somebody who is stubborn and determined to maintain an angry, rageful outlook on the world. But a person who attends the class with an open mind and a strong desire to learn a new way of behaving may find the courses extremely useful.

you're not alone

"**I**'m a down-to-earth guy, likeable, easy to get along with," says John, a 35-year-old event producer from Manhattan. "That's why it surprises me how mad I can get, and how quickly. My anger can go from 0 to 60. It gets uncontrollable."

As is the case with many people, John's anger is most easily triggered by his close relationships—including his dog. But just as with humans, John's connection to his dog isn't always under his control. When the dog was young and untrained, she pushed him to the edge. "On the night before Easter, I was in a dog park with my puppy. At the time, she wouldn't come to me, and I could only catch her when there were other dogs around. It was 10:30 P.M., raining, dark. All the dogs were leaving the park as I bent down to tie my shoe. When I looked up, we were all alone—and my puppy would not come to me.

"I tried to catch her until 1:30 in the morning. My knees were bloody from diving, my hands were bloody. The park officials came to shut down the park, and they said they were going to call the police if I didn't leave. I said 'Call them. Tell them to bring a canine unit.' Instead, they left a door open for me and left. Then I tried to find someone on the street with a dog—because she'll come for any dog—and I was running around like a madman, furious, with bloody hands, saying please come to this deserted park with me to help me find my puppy. I looked like the typical serial murderer."

Eventually, John caught his frightened and dirty pup. By then, his anger was through the roof. "I threw the leash at her, I was screaming. I have never been that frustrated in my life, because she is the only thing that I've ever had depend on me and there was no one but me to fix the situation. I'm responsible, on so many levels—to the world, to her. So my anger went where it has never been. I literally wanted to kill her. I could imagine myself twisting her head off. It has made me see how you could get so mad that you'd do something physical on an impulse, not meaning to, and have it do irrevocable damage. I've thought of that. I know I need to keep my cool, be cognizant of that."

Finding a Program

If you think an anger management program may be helpful, the first step is finding the right one. With so many anger management courses available, you'd think it would be a snap to find a program that's perfect for you—in your area, for the right cost, with a philosophy that suits you. Think again.

Sure, there has been a surge in the number of anger management programs over the past few years—particularly since September 11, says anger management pioneer George Anderson, MSW, founder of Anderson & Anderson, the country's largest provider of anger management services. The tricky part is knowing whether a particular class is any good. There are no federal, state, or local standards for anger management curricula; even courts that order anger management often have no specific requirements. Anderson recommends searching the Internet, where there is no shortage of providers with websites and listings. As with any Internet search, you'll have to muddle through a lot of garbage, but it's a good stepping-off point for more research. Some providers offer online courses—although experts are divided on how effective they are.

Ask any potential provider where they got their training and what their credentials are. An anger management provider who is also a trained therapist or licensed clinical social worker likely has the professional training to help you. Someone trained and certified through a well-established program such as Anderson & Anderson also has completed a minimum amount of coursework in anger management. Remember that there is no official degree that makes someone an anger management expert—so if someone says they have one, walk away.

WEB TALK: The American Association for Anger Management Providers offers a directory of its members at:

angermanagementproviders.com/directory.php

Through Your Health-Care Provider Because anger is not an officially diagnosable mental disorder (according to the psychiatrist's bible, the *DSM-IV*), don't expect your insurance company or health-care provider to foot the bill for anger management courses. Anger is not considered an illness, so a psychiatrist likely won't treat you for an anger problem alone; although if your anger is caused by another condition—bipolar disorder or depression, for example—anger control might be part of your therapy.

Managed health-care companies such as Kaiser Permanente often *do* offer in-house anger management classes as part of their behavioral health-care programs. Other managed care providers, such as Pacific Care, don't offer classes per se, but provide counseling for an anger problem as part of their therapy services. Other private insurance companies help cover the cost of anger management classes. Check your policy or contact your health-care representative to find out what your coverage is. (Even if you're not covered, your doctor may be able to give you a referral to a therapist or a counselor.)

In the Workplace Companies faced with rising numbers of tense and irritable employees often offer classes to help employees reduce stress, improve their communication skills, and lower their anger levels. Some contract the work out to therapists and anger management programs (the top dogs at big companies might find themselves enrolled in "executive coaching" rather than anger management); others offer their own on-site courses. Your boss may know what's available to you, or if you're not comfortable talking to him or her, talk to your human resources department.

> **GET PSYCHED**
>
> "Yelling 'you jerk!' is rarely cathartic because it pumps up your blood pressure while doing nothing about the jerk who is bothering you." —*Carol Tavris, Ph.D., social psychologist and anger expert, in* Anger: The Misunderstood Emotion

School, Religious, and Other Community Programs

There are also courses available in your local community. Many large churches, synagogues, mosques, and other religious organizations now provide training in stress reduction and anger management. Expect the curriculum to have a spiritual bent—which may be just what suits you. Be aware, however, that the teacher of a religiously affiliated course may not have any training in psychology or anger management. Furthermore, if you need to go to anger management because of a court order, these classes might not satisfy the judge.

If your child is having trouble controlling his temper, talk to his or her teacher, the guidance counselor at school, or even the school nurse to get suggestions for an appropriate program. If none can provide the information you need, talk to a vice principal or the principal, or contact the school district. Many YMCA and YWCA chapters also offer classes for angry adolescents and young adults. Your phone book should list the nearest affiliate, or try an Internet search.

Other national and state organizations such as the member agencies of the United Way may offer programs. Many are free or low cost, often on a sliding scale appropriate to your income. Contact your local office for more information. Alternatively, you can get recommendations from nearby mental health agencies, women's centers and shelters, and family violence centers.

WEB TALK: Find your local United Way chapter at:

national.unitedway.org

What to Expect

The curriculum of your class or anger treatment can vary in duration as well as in content. Some programs claim to cure anger problems in an intensive weekend session, while others require

10 or 20 sessions or as much as a year of weekly meetings. One program might place more emphasis on stress and arousal reduction—how to relax, how not to let things get your goat. Another might focus on changing the cognitive processes that lead to anger: avoiding those "shoulds"—"he should have watched where he was going" or "she should have thought about my feelings more"—and blaming thoughts that can set you off.

Your provider might also train you to be more empathetic or teach effective communication and listening skills, along with problem-solving, impulse control, and positive *self-talk*. Still other programs might put emphasis on what the Bible, for example, has to say about anger and keeping it in check.

Before you sign on the dotted line and fork over a payment, ask any potential provider exactly what they're going to cover and what their emphasis will be. Find out if they use a particular book or written curriculum, and ask if you can review it. That way you'll have a better sense of whether the class will work for you (or meet the requirements of a court order or your employer).

PsychSpeak

Self-talk is your normal internal dialogue (as opposed to hearing external voices). Anger management might train you to avoid self-defeating negative talk, such as "I'm a loser," or "I screwed up again."

What's Best for Your Anger Problem

We all handle anger differently. A good anger management program should ideally address your particular needs. Before any treatment gets started, many of the larger (or better) anger management programs first do a psychological assessment to determine your level of anger, how well you communicate, how you handle stress, how empathetic you are, and other factors.

"The assessment is not a test, but more of a map that lets you and your provider know what your functioning level is, what your deficits are, so you can improve your skills in those areas," Anderson says. For example, you might be a good communicator but be terrible at managing your stress, or you might be good at managing stress but awful at speaking your mind and listening to others. Or you might be great at communicating and handle stress well but be completely lacking in empathy. Ideally, your curriculum will be tailored to address your needs—although this is more likely in a one-on-one setting, with a therapist or a counselor, than in a large group format.

Employer-Mandated Treatment

Much of the increase in anger management treatment is due to large numbers of employers seeking help—or requiring it—for their stressed-out, temperamental employees. Most anger experts agree that workplace anger is on the rise due to a number of factors (more work, fewer available jobs, less job security, and so on). Being angry on the job isn't just bad for the employee; it's bad for business. It can reduce productivity, hasten the departure of other valuable workers, and tarnish the reputation of the institution. If you're increasingly irritable, annoyed, and aggressive on the job, your boss—or, more likely, your human resources department— may encourage you to enroll in anger management.

In most cases, the curriculum is much the same as if you'd walked in off the street for a class. Some employees don't have the time to take off days of work (and some employers simply cannot take their workers off the clock for prolonged periods of time), so you might be enrolled in an accelerated course. If you work for a big company or are a bigwig on the job, your employer likely will foot the bill for the classes, although other employers will make their troubled workers get help on their own dime, or get the boot. Costs can range from a couple hundred dollars to several thousand, for individual, one-on-one sessions.

Q&A

Are group classes or one-on-one type anger management programs more effective?

In some respects, it depends on whom you ask. Some psychologists argue that the members of a group tend to reinforce each other's angry, aggressive, and antisocial attitudes, negating the positive effects of the training. They recommend individual counseling and treatment. Others, such as anger management guru George Anderson, Ph.D., of Anderson & Anderson anger management services, say that the group approach is the way to go. Anger problems are generally interpersonal in nature, so "they are best addressed in a group setting, because the whole purpose is to learn how to relate to other people. A group is also more effective because you get feedback not just from the teacher but from the other people in the group who are in the same or a similar situation, and that can be powerful and easier to take."

Court-Ordered Anger Management Programs

More and more, people convicted of relatively minor crimes are being sentenced to an anger management course in lieu of jail time; others attend during their incarceration or after their release as a condition of parole. In many cases, these classes also follow the same game plan as an employer-mandated program or one you sign up for on your own—although you might have to stick it out for much longer. In California, for example, classes average 26 weeks but might be as long as 52 weeks.

The requirements for court-required programs vary from state to state and even county to county, so it's impossible to make generalizations about what to expect. Although the California Superior Court system requires enrollment in a course using the Anderson protocol, other states have their own criteria. The court, or your lawyer, will be able to guide you. The court will likely give you a list of providers from whom you can take classes. Family and domestic relations courts can be a good source for information on anger management programs even if you're not under a court order to attend. Ask the clerk for a list.

Certain courts offer their own in-house anger management programs. Again, the court will let you know where you stand and what's available.

Types of Crime Generally, judges order anger management for crimes such as misdemeanor assault, disorderly conduct, vandalism, bar fights, and other aggressive acts. "Road rage could require anger management," says clinical psychologist Ari Novick, MS, who runs an anger management program in Laguna Beach, California, "or a domestic situation that didn't escalate to the point of violence. Someone using very abusive language might be told to go to anger management."

Anger Management for Batterers? A person convicted of spousal abuse also may *not* have to attend an anger management course. For these offenses, judges require a program that is specific to domestic violence. The reason is simple: anger is only a small part of spousal abuse—and some batterers are not particularly angry at all. Problems with control, power, and empathy are more fundamental.

"Domestic violence is violence that occurs in intimate rela-tionships, and really only there," says George Anderson. "It has nothing to do with road rage, nothing to do with people in-volved in bar-room brawls. The perpetrator of domestic violence does not have to be angry. He or she will do whatever it is they do as a way of frightening the victim into permitting themselves to be controlled."

you're not alone

Mike, a cameraman living in the Los Angeles area, never realized that he had any problems with his temper until a judge ordered him to take an anger management class.

"In August 2003, I was arrested for misdemeanor battery, and part of the sentencing was a year of anger management classes. I had never been arrested before—my lifestyle is a churchgoer, I go to charity events—and the incident was convoluted to say the least. I was guilty of what they charged me with, but in my opinion, anger only played a secondary role in the offense. In general, I'd never thought of myself as an angry person. I try to be upbeat. I don't beat the kids, I don't beat the wife. I either try to resolve issues or I walk away from them. You'd be hard-pressed to find people who would suggest that I was an angry person.

"But because I had to go every week, I tried to not make it painful. I would do the reading, the assignments. I was good with that. After three or four months, something finally cracked and I realized that I had anger-related issues that I hadn't been facing. For example, I would frequently get angry while I was driving. I'd get angry at someone who had cut me off or was acting like a knucklehead. What I realized was that this driving thing is stupid. Reacting in that manner is just not called for. I'm 46 years old. Why am I acting like an 18-year-old?

"Now, I make the decision not to go in that direction at all. I'll back off, slow down, avoid the situation in a good way. Instead of flipping someone off or saying, 'You dummy,' I make the decision to act in a polite manner, to get out of the way, or to disengage completely.

"I don't know how you *don't* get angry, but learning to decide what I am going to do with it and how it is going to affect me was huge. It was momentous."

Q & A

What is the difference between a certified and a noncertified anger management program?

There is no official group that can "certify" an anger management course, so if a provider tells you that they are certified, don't take it at face value. Ask them who is doing the certifying. For example, Anderson & Anderson have trained hundreds of practitioners in its own curriculum and considers providers who have taken their courses to be "certified" in their program. In some states, only certain types of anger management courses are accepted for court-ordered therapy. Programs that meet the court's criteria may be labeled certified. Other programs are noncertified but may suit your needs best.

What You Can Do

Many therapists and scientists remain skeptical of anger management as a means to combat rage, arguing that the classes haven't been proven to be effective for many people. Nevertheless, you may be required to attend a program to fulfill a court order or to salvage your job—or you may just decide that you need the help to conquer your temper. There are many programs and protocols to choose from. Here are some tips to help you sort through them.

- ☐ Be a cautious consumer when looking for an anger management program. At present, there are no state or federal guidelines for anger management courses and no regulation, licensing, or certification. Ask if the program you're considering has a written curriculum, and ask to see it. Get references, and find out where the provider got his or her training.

- ☐ You might also check a potential program with the Better Business Bureau. If they've had complaints from disgruntled clients, you should know about them.

☐ One way to find a program is through the American Association of Anger Management Providers' website at angermanagementproviders.com/directory.php. The organization is new and its listing is by no means comprehensive, but it is a start.

☐ Courts often (but not always) require particular coursework. If you're ordered to go, your lawyer or the court clerk can tell you what those requirements are and often provide a list of approved classes.

☐ Anger is not a recognized psychiatric disorder, so don't be surprised if you have to foot the full bill for an anger management course without help from your health insurance company.

☐ That said, your health insurance provider may offer their own anger prevention or stress reduction classes, especially if you have managed care. Ask your patient representative what your options are.

☐ If you *have* to go to anger management, do try to make the best of it. You might not have chosen to go on your own, but you're there now. Let yourself learn something.

11

Learning to Stay Calm: Part 1

There's no single obvious path to gaining control over an anger problem. If you need to learn to express yourself more assertively or to squash a cantankerous temper and think that anger management is right for you, you can learn the techniques of a host of different programs. Some emphasize changing the thought processes that generate our rage; others focus on reducing stress and arousal and the physical manifestations of anger. Others teach you how to modify your behavior, to either avoid the situations that make you mad or calm yourself down when you're in them. Many offer a combination of tactics.

In the following two chapters, I discuss the major types of anger management philosophies, both mainstream methods and those slightly off the traditional path. Use this overview to learn your options so you can select what's best for you.

What Is Cognitive-Behavior Therapy?

Remember the last time you got angry at a fellow shopper for cutting you off in line? Maybe you decided she thought she was better than you, and therefore entitled to go ahead of you. Is that really the case? Only the rude shopper knows. But you were *convinced*, and therefore enraged.

Psychologists call that sort of mind-reading *distorted thinking*. Cognitive-behavioral therapists say that these thinking errors are to blame for a host of emotional problems, from anxiety and depression to, of course, anger. They argue that uncovering the errors, practicing new thought patterns, and combining that with behavioral change can overcome problem anger.

Although it's "therapy," it's nothing like old-fashioned psychoanalysis. You don't lie on a couch, you don't talk about your mother, and your therapist is actively involved in helping you change yourself. Also, unlike traditional talk therapies, cognitive-behavior programs tend to have clients make logs, lists, and practice exercises—so expect homework.

The first psychologist to use cognitive-behavior therapy for anger control was Raymond Novaco, Ph.D., of the University of California at Irvine, in 1975. Novaco, in fact, coined the term *anger management*—although his clients were patients with extreme anger issues wrapped up in other problems such as post-traumatic stress disorder, substance abuse, and mental illness.

In Novaco's view, cognitive-behavioral therapy needs to be a multi-layered approach. Anger doesn't come from out of the blue. It's connected to a particular environmental context; it relates to an individual's cognitive style and their emotional patterns. In his view, successful treatment needs to address all these

aspects of a person's life. Novaco
uses graded exposure to anger
triggers (I discuss that later in
this chapter), to help people
cope with what incites them.

WEB TALK: Learn more about cognitive-behavior
therapy and its historical origins at:
↑ www.cognitivetherapy.com

Many anger management programs follow a general cognitive-
behavioral protocol, Novaco says, but they don't incorporate all
the techniques that he might use to treat a seriously angry person
who also has other psychological problems.

There are a few variants of cognitive-behavioral therapy. One
popular method is rational-emotive therapy, first developed in
1955. The concept behind rational-emotive therapy (sometimes
also called rational-emotive behavior therapy) is that our views,
thoughts, and beliefs determine how we interpret a situation,
which in turn determines how we respond to it emotionally. Our
thoughts, then, determine our feelings. When those thoughts are
irrational—for example, that we should always be successful, or
that we have no hand in any bad thing that ever happens to us—
we're setting ourselves up for piles of bad stuff: disappointment,
frustration, anxiety, anger. Learning to recognize and change this
disordered thinking is the first step in controlling anger.

In cognitive therapy, the emphasis is strictly on faulty thinking
as the root of our misery and emotional dysfunction. More commonly, though, says Novaco, cognitive therapy interventions
involve behavioral therapy—blurring the official distinctions.

Changing How You Think

Anger experts have developed numerous techniques to change
how we think in anger-invoking situations. If you take an anger
management course, or just work on anger control on a one-on-
one basis with a counselor or adviser, you might be introduced to

GET PSYCHED

"If you can talk about what you are feeling rather than what the other person is doing wrong, you are in control of what you can control. You can't control how the other person is going to respond, if they are going to change, but you can control how you express yourself and if you are true to yourself. That's constructive anger."
—*Karin Bruckner,*
co-author of The Anger Advantage *and a licensed professional counselor in private practice in the Dallas area*

several of these skills, from identifying your negative thinking patterns, to problem-solving, to role playing, and more.

Identifying the Sore Spots Just about any anger management protocol requires clients to create an anger log, or anger journal. This is no teenage girl's diary; it won't be filled with puppy love, but pain and real-world unpleasantness. But the log has a vital purpose: to help you discover what sets you off, gets you boiling, and pushes you to scream, so that you might learn to avoid or better cope with anger-inciting thoughts, behaviors, and situations in the future.

Most anger journals have several components. You'll have to record every "angry" event over a predetermined time period (say, a week). You'll note when and where each happened and who was involved. Then you'll rate just how angry or aroused you were, what your physiological responses were, and how aggressive your behavior became. And you'll have to note what stressors might have been in play (Were you tired? Worried about work? Stuck in traffic?), and what your trigger thoughts were. Finally, you'll have to describe the outcome of your anger. And, yes, that might be ugly.

After several entries, some predictable trends should pop out. You may see common circumstances or identify what was going on in your head or your surroundings in those times when you're most likely to blow. Those are the areas that you'll then want to work on. You'll also become more attuned to the physical cues your body is sending you when you're ramping up into a rage so you can learn to recognize them early on and put the brakes on before things get out of control.

Negative Thinking Patterns Do you often think in terms of "shoulds"? ("He should remember to feed the dog." "She needs to stop nagging me all the time.") Engage in blaming? ("It's his fault that I forgot my appointment, because he distracted me.") These are negative thinking patterns. There are more, including the following:

- **Catastrophising.** Exaggerating the impact of a situation— believing that if something has gone wrong, it can never be righted.
- **Mind reading.** Believing you know what another person is thinking, how they feel, or what their motivations are.
- **Dichotomizing.** Breaking everything down into good or bad, black or white, so you fail to see the gray areas.
- **Global labeling.** Using a single, usually pejorative, label to define a person.
- **Magnifying.** Making things worse by overgeneralizing— saying someone is "always late," or "never polite," for example.
- **Fortune-telling.** Making assumptions—usually bad—about what will happen in the future or how something will turn out.

Do any of these sound familiar? If so, it's time to start replacing them with positive patterns.

A New Way of Thinking When you have a better idea of what your thought patterns are, you can begin to change them, a process psychologists call *cognitive restructuring*. One way to start is by eliminating "you" statements from your thoughts and conversations: "You are making me mad" attaches blame to another person and puts them in charge of the situation. It also won't help you deal with the problem, because it'll put them on the defensive. "I am starting to feel mad because ..." is less confrontational and nonblaming and forces you to analyze your own feelings.

It is also helpful to remind yourself of the futility of flying into a rage and to learn to use hard logic to assess your feelings and your situation. Anger experts speak of replacing "hot thoughts"—those that get your temper burning—with "cold thoughts," or "coping thoughts"—set phrases you say to yourself as a reminder to stay calm, not get angry, and so on, which calm you down and help you deal.

In many courses, you'll learn to assess your self-talk, the inner dialogue most of us have with ourselves: "I need to get moving," if you're running behind on your errands, or "I'm going to ace this test." This internal discourse is perfectly normal and not to be confused with hearing hallucinatory voices. However, angry people are often prone to negative self-talk—"I'm going to be late again," "I'm going to fail this test," "I'm a loser"—and it can both be self-destructive and lead to a generally bad frame of mind. Becoming aware of how you talk to yourself and beginning to change it may help you talk to and respond to others in a healthier way.

Consequences, Consequences Although it can be painful, realizing the effect of your anger on those around you and on other parts of your life is a key step on the path to change. Resist the temptation to wallow in guilt over past bad acts; instead, try to take a clear-headed, impartial look at what you did and where it led. Did losing your temper at your son over his failed math test actually make him study harder and ace the next one, or did he just seem deflated, defeated, and sad? What would have been the outcome had you tried another, perhaps kinder, tactic?

Seeing the potential consequences of your angry acts can also help in the heat of the moment. This is a skill that anger and aggression programs focus on. Before you yell at your husband for coming home late, do a quick analysis of where blowing up might get you. Will he feel bad and apologize? Snap back? Turn around and leave?

Look at the short-term effects, the long-term effects, the consequences to you, and the consequences to others around you. It may seem like a lot of thinking to do in a heated moment, but pushing yourself into a more logical frame of mind can reduce your impulse to anger in the same way that counting to 10 can serve as an emotional breather that cools you down.

> **GET PSYCHED**
>
> "Sometimes the situation just becomes so unbearable that the pain you are experiencing becomes the gateway to your saying 'this is not working, I am not going to do this anymore' or the kids saying 'you are fighting so much.' There is a wake up." —*Susyn Reeve, management consultant, author, and interfaith minister*

Seeing the Other Side We like to think that we always consider other people first, but when we get mad, we mostly see things only from our side and we make the other person the enemy—their actions didn't just happen to anger you, they were *intended* to do so.

PsychSpeak

Empathy is the insightful awareness of another person's thoughts and feelings.

This mind-set is bound to get you in trouble—and make you lose your temper. The way around it, anger experts say, is *empathy*.

Empathy training teaches you that when a situation has you fuming, you should stop and ask yourself why the person making you mad might be acting that way—and, more important, how they feel.

It's the classic case of putting yourself in the other person's shoes. Maybe you are on the freeway, and another car is weaving around like a maniac, cutting cars off, putting you all in danger.

He could just be a selfish jerk. Or maybe his pregnant wife is in the car, about to give birth, and he's panicked. (Okay, that's not so likely, but thinking it might calm you down.) Even in the midst of a heated argument, it's helpful to step back and think about what the other person might feel and what the situation is like for them. Try to understand their motives, accept their failings, and be forgiving.

Problem-Solving It's not enough to just put yourself in the other guy's shoes. That may defuse your annoyance temporarily, but if the same thing continually upsets you, you'll be hard pressed to stay calm. What you need to do is figure out how to stop the situation from happening in the first place—or, after it starts, how to resolve the conflict in a rational way. That's where problem-solving comes in.

Don't decide that your problem is getting another person to change. It won't work. Also don't conclude that your best solution is to ignore the situation or do nothing. Being proactive is always a better path.

Psychologists have devised a systematic method you might try. First, identify any areas of your life that are giving you grief and making you grumpy. Have a bad relationship with your mother? Want a new job? After you have your list, decide what is the most pressing problem or the one you're most able to fix for now, and focus just on that. Then brainstorm like crazy and come up with ideas and alternatives. Decide which idea seems most promising, and then develop a plan to get it done. It's a good idea to evaluate your progress down the road. If your solution hasn't worked, try something else.

Remember, though, that not every anger-provoking situation *has* a solution. Say you're angry because your candidate lost an election. Can you change *that* outcome? No way. You have to accept it. In that case, figure out how to cope with your disappointment or channel your energies into making the outcome of the next election more to your liking.

Role Playing One of the benefits of the group format of many anger management classes is that it provides ample opportunity for role playing, a skill that helps clients practice handling troublesome and temper-flaring situations.

The idea is simple: you and another person act out a scenario. For example, you can experiment with ways to state your mind without losing your cool, or respond to anger in a more positive, less-confrontational way. Not an actor? Don't worry. It's the practice that matters.

GET PSYCHED

"I'm convinced more and more that we all have the ability to calmly express our anger. You have to practice—like playing tennis, like playing the piano—you have to practice working on your anger. If someone has a short fuse, they have to deliberately and consciously practice making that change. It takes time, and it is challenging, but it is very rewarding when the change comes."
—*Rachel Greene Baldino, MSW, LCSW, therapist in Worcester, Massachusetts*

By practicing your responses in circumstances that routinely set you off—and perhaps stepping into the other person's role to really see things from their side—you'll start to think about the situation differently and train yourself to respond more appropriately.

Facing the Forces A key element of cognitive-behavioral therapies is *inoculation* to anger-provoking situations, a procedure akin to the desensitizing methods used on people with phobias. Deathly afraid of spiders? You might be helped through that fear during a series of sessions in which you gradually get closer and closer to one. First you might be shown lots of pictures of spiders. Then you'll have one put in the same room as you. Then you'll have to touch it. Finally, you'll have to let it crawl all over you.

PsychSpeak

Inoculation, or graded exposure, involves subjecting a patient or client to increasingly difficult or upsetting situations, from mild to extremely anger-inciting, so they may rehearse and practice their coping thoughts and relaxation skills.

Raymond Novaco, who pioneered the use of cognitive-behavioral methods for anger problems, considers inoculation "crucial, because you are building up the person's capacity to deal with increased doses of provocation." Studies have shown inoculation to be quite effective, but some cognitive-behavioral programs don't emphasize this technique. You might inquire with the anger management programs you're considering to see if it is part of their curriculum.

you're not alone

"I've always had issues with anger of one sort or another," says Michele, an editor from New York. "Part of the problem is that I'm scared of people who are angry, and particularly of angry men. I tend to want to run in the other direction. My father wasn't a particularly angry person, but we didn't have that much of a relationship so I tried to curry favor with him whenever I saw him. During those infrequent times when he was angry, I guess it was more significant for me because I don't think I was really sure of his love.

"I also tend to be a people-pleaser, and if I'm angry, I don't tell the person I'm angry with because I want them to like me. What happens is that by the time it comes out, I'm really upset. Because of that I have difficulty dealing with angry feelings on the job. I'd like to be able to express how I feel in a calm, controlled way, but it is very hard for me. I don't know what to do with very strong feelings. A couple of times I've instead lost control and yelled at people, although I've been trying to learn to express my anger more appropriately.

"It has, however, gotten easier for me to express anger when I'm not in a position where I really care—when I know I'm never going to see the person again. Then I let it fly. I recently did it with somebody that I will see again: my super. He is a very sweet man, but he gets paid so little that he has to take other jobs. He's basically out all day doing these jobs and not taking care of the building. It's frustrating. One day I tried to get out the front door and it was locked from the outside. I started to panic. Another tenant came down. She tried to get out with a credit card. It didn't work, but thankfully I had my cell phone, and I called him. While we were waiting for him, the neighbor said that this had happened before.

"Something about that made me snap. I was fairly calm, but when the door opened and I saw him, I absolutely lost control. I screamed at him, 'When are you going to fix this? I heard this was broken before! If this building had been on fire, we would have burned to death!'

"He's a very sweet man, not the kind of person who would hurt anyone, and he's been very good to me. That had always made it hard for me to get angry with him about not doing his job. I don't know if this outburst was a matter of me holding in all this anger toward him, or whether it really was just sheer panic and fear on my part from that specific episode. It probably was a combination of both. All the anger I'd kept in every time he didn't show up, the broken promises when he said he'd do something and then he didn't.

"It was really frightening to me. Later, I apologized, and he was great. He said, 'I understand, we'll fix it, it will be okay.' I said 'I'm so sorry, that's not me'—but I guess that *is* me. It's a part of me that comes out every so often."

Changing Behavior

Changing the way we think about things often isn't quite good enough. We also have to change what we *do*—how we respond in a frustrating situation, how we deal with pressure, how we state our feelings. Remember—effective anger management isn't just about stifling your feelings, but about expressing them constructively. Experts have developed several methods to modify that behavior, including a number of arousal reduction and relaxation techniques, which are discussed in the next chapter. As with anything, these take practice and a good bit of patience to learn.

Assertiveness Training Often, a large part of the training you get in anger control involves learning to be assertive about your thoughts, feelings, and needs. That means firmly but tactfully and respectfully saying what's on your mind. If your tendency is to suppress your angry feelings, you might have the most to gain from assertiveness training. The tactics can also benefit you if you're an exploder—you'll learn how to express yourself in a more positive way, before you get angry enough to lose your temper.

GET PSYCHED

"Good-humored laughter at oneself may really be the best antidote to anger." *–Carol Tavris, Ph.D., social psychologist, in* Anger: The Misunderstood Emotion

De-Escalation If you find yourself building up to the boiling point, the outcome doesn't inevitably have to be rage. There are ways to control the escalation of anger. One of the most effective, and most likely to be taught in anger management, is a variant of the toddler's "time-out."

It's as simple as it sounds: if you feel yourself losing your cool, you call a time-out and leave the scene for a previously agreed-upon length of time. This obviously works better with family, because you can explain in advance what you're doing. During the break, reduce your physical arousal by taking a walk or doing deep-breathing exercises or anything else that relaxes you. When you revisit the issue—which you do have to do, or the time-out will be pointless—you'll be in a better frame of mind to resolve the problem.

If you can't leave, you might try more immediate tricks to simmer down. Mentally repeat some of your coping thoughts. Wait several seconds before you respond to slow down the conversation, or take a long drink of water. Sit down to talk (it's less threatening than standing). Change the direction of the discussion.

WEB TALK: Learn more about de-escalation at the International Online Training Program on Intractable Conflict at:

 www.colorado.edu/conflict/peace/ !overlay_problems.htm#escalation

Avoidance Try to avoid situations that needle you or send your fury flaring. No need to hide from the world; avoidance can be a simple matter of taking an alternate route to work— maybe the long way around, but with less traffic, if road rage is your problem—or shutting the door to your messy teen's room because you know the squalor routinely gets you raging.

Of course, you'll have to make some level-headed decisions about what battles you can afford to desert. Ditching your wife or your boss, for example, probably isn't advisable. Your therapist or anger management facilitator can help you in those choices.

What You Can Do

The dual approach of changing anger-inducing thoughts and introducing calming, stress-reducing behaviors is thought to be the most effective form of anger management. If you find yourself in a program that takes this path, you can enhance your odds of success. Here are some tips.

☐ Keep an anger log. You may be required to do so in your class, but if not, do it for yourself. The basic idea is to keep track of those times you lost your temper, what provoked you, and why. Reflecting on those lapses can help you understand the causes of your anger and how to avert it in the future.

☐ Keep track also of your successes, those times when you kept your cool, especially if it was a situation that previously might have pushed you past the brink.

☐ Reward yourself for your achievement. Positive reinforcement always works better than beating yourself up.

☐ Cut yourself some slack if you slip. Promise yourself that you'll just try harder next time, and remember that angry emotions are perfectly natural. You don't want to never get angry—you just don't want to go overboard.

☐ Try to avoid negative thinking patterns such as mind-reading. Don't assume you know what people are thinking or feeling, or what their motivations are. *Ask them*. And don't always expect that things will turn out as badly as you imagine they might (that's catastrophising). Sometimes, stuff actually turns out okay.

☐ Strive to come up with constructive solutions to your problems. Ask friends or co-workers for advice. Think things through before you blow up, and see if there's another alternative. The more logical you can be, the less likely it is that your emotions will take over.

☐ If you do find yourself getting worked up, turn down the heat. Leave the room, count to 10, or repeat in your mind, "It's not that bad, I won't lose control," or other coping thoughts you've practiced in advance.

12

Learning to Stay Calm: Part 2

There is more to healthy anger than just retraining the mind. Anger is innately physiological, akin at the deepest level to our physical response to stress. For that reason, relaxation, meditation, deep breathing, exercise, and other techniques that help clear the mind and body of tension can also combat anger.

There are other routes to getting a handle on anger: conventional psychotherapy can uncover the deep psychological roots of our negative emotions and anger response, for example, while alternative methods such as homeopathy and acupuncture are said to promote emotional stability by integrating the mind, body, and spirit.

Are all these techniques proven anger-busters? Not in every case, but they may appeal to you. In this chapter, you learn a little bit more about some of them.

What Is Arousal Reduction?

Anger is a heightened state of arousal. The body goes through profound changes when you're mad: your heart races, your blood pressure climbs, your face gets flushed, your muscles get tense, and more. Because those changes run in lockstep with emotions, psychologists and other scientists have found that controlling the physical response can have a calming effect on mood. Cool down the body, and you also mellow the mind.

Relaxation, meditation, exercise, and other stress-reduction tactics may help at the moment of anger, but they can also lower your body's everyday level of what scientists call "activation." Basically, that's how revved our stress engines are and how close we are to kicking into anger overdrive. Decreasing the activation level is kind of like lowering your idle speed. It reduces your threshold for anger so you're less likely to blow your top and more likely to let small problems or frustrations roll off your back.

These techniques, usually part of a daily or weekly routine, plus the tricks you might use in the heat of the moment to chill yourself out (counting to 10, taking a time-out, cracking a joke), all fall under the mantle of *arousal reduction*.

Techniques and Tactics

There are dozens of arousal reduction techniques. You may want to experiment with a few and combine them. Find something you feel comfortable doing and will keep up with—especially when your anger starts spiraling out of control.

you're not alone

For Cheryl, a 35-year-old divorced mother of three from Colorado, the hour of reckoning came after she quit her job to become a high school math teacher. The stress of teaching and the unruly, disrespectful kids she had to cope with on a daily basis were her undoing. "I stopped eating and lost 15 pounds. I cracked up a little, sat down, and cried for a few days. It was all that anger that I was swallowing."

Cheryl eventually quit her job and went back to her former career as a staff engineer for a computer tech company. She started seeing a therapist, "to see why I have such an aversion to negative emotions. I realized that as a child, I'd been socialized not to get angry—'good girls don't do that'—and I learned to not be aware of it and not express it. In my marriage, it was never okay for me to express my anger because my husband was a bully.

"I've learned a lot. Now I've found that anger can be a useful thing. Expressing anger if you really mean it can be very powerful. It's like using cusswords. If you never use them, they have a lot of power when you do."

Word Power It is virtually impossible to be both relaxed and furious at the same time, which is why therapists and anger control consultants teach relaxation methods. Many advocate a beguilingly simple but successful relaxation technique devised more than 30 years ago by Harvard University physician Herbert Benson, now president of the university's Mind/Body Medical Institute.

Benson's Relaxation Response method involves just a few easy steps: find a comfortable and quiet place to sit and get settled in—but don't doze off! Relax your muscles. Then breathe slowly and steadily through your nose. Next, either out loud or in your head, repeat a single word or a short phrase—"relax," for example. A religious saying or a prayer could also be used.

Continue to repeat the word as you relax and breathe regularly. Practicing the exercise for 20 minutes twice a day, experts say, can help keep you less stressed.

Q & A

What is progressive muscle relaxation?

In progressive muscle relaxation, you focus not on your entire body at once but instead concentrate your attention on individual muscles or sets of muscles you learn to loosen up in succession by first tensing and then relaxing them. For example, you might start by clenching your fists for 10 seconds or so and then releasing them, while you imagine the tightness and stress flowing out of you. Then you move to your elbows and biceps, and then to your head, neck, and shoulders, down to your stomach, back, and buttocks, and finally to your legs and feet.

The premise behind the exercise is that physical tension causes stress, which makes you more likely to get angry—which, in turn, causes more tension in your body. Relieving muscle tension may lower your likelihood of losing your temper.

Meditate Quieting the mind can work wonders for the emotions, which is the premise behind using meditation to dissipate anger. (Ever seen a furious monk? Didn't think so.) There are scores of different techniques—transcendental meditation, holistic integration meditation, mindfulness meditation, samatha meditation, Vispassana meditation, walking meditation, and so on. The details vary, but the goal is the same: to cut off the racing thoughts that preoccupy your mind so you can reach a place of both pure awareness and mental stillness.

Sound impossible? Think of the extraordinary benefits. Research shows that meditation reduces anxiety and stress, lowers blood pressure, and enhances the ability to concentrate. Studies by scientists at the University of Wisconsin at Madison have shown that meditation can actually shift brain activity so a person is less likely to fly into a flight or fight response (the reaction that launches us into anger). In June 2005, neuroscientists from the University of Queensland in Australia revealed evidence that meditation actually helps Tibetan monks linger longer in a "happy" frame of mind.

Breathe! Sometimes the best way to chill out is just to breathe—but not just any old breathing, and especially not the stifled breaths into the chest most adults have grown accustomed to using. If you've ever watched a baby or a child breathe, you'll notice that their belly, not their chest, rises with each inhalation. These deep breaths use the *diaphragm* to completely expand the lungs and send richly oxygenated blood throughout the body. The effect can be profoundly relaxing.

> ## PsychSpeak
>
> The **diaphragm** is a thick, dome-shaped sheet of muscle that separates the abdominal and chest cavities. It contracts and flattens with each inhaled breath, allowing the lungs to expand.

Next time you're feeling hot under the collar or simply stressed out, try this simple breathing exercise: put one hand on your stomach so you'll know you're using your diaphragm. Take a deep, long breath for a count of three seconds, hold it for three seconds, and release it slowly for three seconds. Repeat a few times. "This nine-second breathing exercise starts to immediately create a sensation of calmness," says Yvonne L. Thomas, Ph.D., a psychologist in private practice in Los Angeles. "I have my clients do this in the office, and you can see them relax. The tension leaves their shoulders. It helps people break through their tension and rage, both emotionally and physically."

Other breathing exercises are said to be just as effective, although they might require more practice. For example, in alternate nostril breathing, practiced in yoga, you inhale through the right nostril, out through the left, in through the left, then out through the right, and then repeat. Alternatively, breathing through a tube you make with your tongue (if you can manage that) and into your belly, holding for 30 seconds, and then exhaling through the nose is also said by yogis to dissipate anger.

Exercise Just as effective as deep, relaxing breathing is burning off energy and stress with physical activity. Countless scientific studies have proven how well exercise works to release anger, partly because it simply takes your mind off whatever is eating at you, and partly because the energy you burn off makes it easier to settle down and relax. You might take a brisk walk, run, dance, ride a stationary bicycle—or even do some jumping jacks next to your desk if you can't escape your office. Even pulling weeds or mowing the lawn can help. For best results, try something that raises your heart rate for 20 minutes or more.

Another benefit of very vigorous exercise: your brain may release a rush of pain-relieving endorphins, your body's natural happy hormone. Also, exercise helps offset the damage to your body—particularly your cardiovascular system—caused by your previous overwrought anger.

GET PSYCHED

"People who are angry don't want to pet a puppy; they want to pound on a wall or kick a trash can. They will do what comes naturally unless they know otherwise, are aware of other options. Education is a big key." –*Brad Bushman, Ph.D., social psychologist, University of Michigan*

Perfecting Your Posture You don't have to run and sweat to cool down. You can also induce a calmer state of mind with nonstrenuous activity such as stretching and practicing the postures of yoga, a Hindu discipline that uses physical, mental, and spiritual exercises to achieve tranquility and insight.

The postures of yoga are called *asanas*, and yogis say that when asanas are properly done, energy flows freely in and out of the body, and the body functions in perfect harmony. Modern

Western scientists might not agree with that interpretation, but there's no doubt that this practice stretches the muscles and limbers up the joints. Yoga relaxes the body and releases tension—in itself a great stress-buster—while increasing strength and stamina.

WEB TALK: To learn more about yoga and other natural and traditional calming methods, go to:

🡵 **www.mothernature.com**

Creating Calmness You can also use your imagination to cool a rising rage. One dramatic way is to close your eyes and simply picture what you look like when you're enraged. (Easy enough to do if you've ever seen someone else's face contorted with fury.) Just the thought of that ugliness—especially if you're losing your temper with your children—can give you enough distance from your boiling feelings to calm down, or at least pause before you lash out.

You might also try visualizing a soothing place: a cool, shady forest glen, a beach at sunset, a hot bubble bath. It can be someplace you've been, or somewhere you'd like to go. Concentrate on the details: what it would smell and look like, the sounds you'd hear. The more vividly you imagine and experience this serene place, the more you will relax and forget what's needling you. After you calm down, you can think and act more clearly.

Other tricks you might try include imagining how someone else—a far more level-headed person—would handle the situation that has you seething, or mentally putting yourself outside the action,

GET PSYCHED

"People describe feeling a 'wave of anger' because the emotion tends to rise and fall. It crashes over you. It may knock you off your feet for a moment, but it will ebb and recede and you can get your bearings again …. You have the choice of how to respond to your anger …. This is the challenge, this is the moment of truth."
—Matthew McKay, Ph.D., et al., psychologist, in When Anger Hurts

as if you were watching it unfold. It sounds kind of nutty, but it allows you to emotionally dissociate yourself from the action and to think more rationally.

Hypnotherapy Anyone who has witnessed a Las Vegas hypnosis act would rightfully be suspicious of using the tactic to understand and manage anger. But countless clients claim that *hypnotherapy*—a treatment that combines hypnosis with conventional talk therapy—has helped their anger problems.

In a hypnotherapy session, the client concentrates fully on the hypnotherapist's monotonous voice, which relaxes him into a trancelike state. The client won't be asleep, but in an enhanced state of internal awareness said to reveal the subconscious mind. When the client is fully hypnotized, the hypnotherapist begins to probe the subconscious for information about the psychological roots of anger, anxiety, fear, or other issues. The hypnotherapist then introduces suggestions that are supposed to counteract those feelings or experiences.

A word of caution: hypnotherapy, like most alternative therapies, is not well regulated. Many "certified hypnotherapists" get their degrees after little or no training through online courses. Check carefully the training, credentials, and references of any hypnotherapist or alternative medicine practitioner you're thinking of seeing.

Heeding the Feedback The better we understand our bodily reaction to stress or provocations, the better equipped we are to change that response. In biofeedback, electrodes attached to the skin measure skin temperature, blood pressure, heart rate, muscle tension, and other functions. Fluctuations in those readings are transmitted back to the client, maybe through a tone that rises and falls in volume in response to muscle tension. Heeding the feedback and learning to direct it—perhaps by slowing breathing rate or relaxing tense muscles—teaches the patient to master biological activities that would normally be beyond conscious control.

In the case of anger, biofeedback can help a client learn to reduce the physical manifestations of stress and anger—racing heart, elevated blood pressure, muscle tension, and so on. Without those reactions barreling the body toward a blowup, anger becomes less likely. Patients don't have to stay strapped to a machine to benefit; with training, the client learns to recognize and control these changes without external feedback.

Insight Therapy

Talk therapy, insight therapy, psychotherapy, psychodynamic therapy—all these terms describe the same fundamental approach to mental health. Insight therapists believe that our behavior, emotions, and feelings in the present are motivated by unresolved issues and unconscious thoughts, usually arising from our past that can be uncovered through intensive, one-on-one sessions with an experienced professional.

"If somebody has an anger problem, they probably have many years' worth of feelings that they have never dealt with," says psychologist Yvonne L. Thomas, Ph.D. Those feelings—maybe hurt, maybe fear, or the residue of some other unpleasant experience, linger for years without being recognized or understood as the cause of a perpetually bad mood or short temper. Because their anger has grown so much, "it starts being spewed out almost randomly," Thomas says.

GET PSYCHED

"We have a privilege as human beings to feel, for good or bad. We can't arbitrarily decide to feel only the positive things. If you mute out and don't let yourself feel the negative, uncomfortable things, you numb out all of them." –*Yvonne L. Thomas, Ph.D., psychologist in private practice in Los Angeles*

Jeff, a contractor from Venice Beach, California, used to release his frustration and anger by blowing up. "I'd scream it out and then usually I'd be all right." It seemed normal to him, because that was how the emotion was expressed in his family. "I grew up around people who were pretty angry. They weren't very grounded or content with their lives. But I never thought of it, or of myself as an angry person.

"But recently I found that I'd stopped expressing it at all. I was around people who were pretty nice, and it didn't feel right to be angry in those particular situations, around certain people. So it kind of built up." He didn't realize that the pent-up anger was taking a toll until he started having heart palpitations and problems in a relationship. "I had no comprehension of it, why it was a problem, because anger seemed to me to be very natural. Everybody has anger. And I never thought it was something that you could get rid of— not get rid of entirely, but that you could release the unexpressed stuff that was stacked up from the past."

To soothe his anger, Jeff tried hypnotherapy. "It was radical. We went back to the very first time I could ever recall experiencing anger and then looked at it, tried to understand what was happening in that situation. It was really simple then to see that the people who were involved were really doing the best that they could, and they didn't know any better. Making that recognition instantly released and relieved the resentment, the blaming, and my thinking that someone had done me wrong intentionally. Then I learned to make a picture in my head with a little hook in the bottom right corner, and I could just unhook it and release that anger. I did it for other situations in my life. It was pretty awesome. Within the next day or two, whenever I was experiencing situations where in the past I'd have felt the anger welling up, I didn't have as much reaction in my body. I was lighter. I could deal with it. Now, within a minute or two of experiencing that frustrated or angry feeling, it is gone. I don't go to sleep with it or carry it around. It is a beautiful thing."

Often, she says, "the person who is angry doesn't know why they are angry. They just feel wounded; they don't recognize that their anger, and their sense of being hurt or done wrong, is a collection of unresolved experiences. Old things, old rifts, old interactions with other people," Thomas says. "You can go back years, to childhood, especially if the person is from a family where you aren't allowed to feel emotion. Then anger is really scary, and so they'll suppress it." The impact is just as damaging: "If you feel you can't express anger because anger is a horrible thing, it is not like out of sight, out of mind," Thomas says. "It is there, it is building. It starts to eat at one's self-esteem and can turn into self-loathing or self-hate."

The solution, says Thomas and other psychotherapists, is to discover the roots of the anger—the hurt feelings, the disappointment, the bad relationships. Uncovering and dealing with those feelings also removes the source of the person's rage. It takes time—sometimes years—but, Thomas and other experts say, the result is a more thorough resolution to the anger problem than a relatively short anger management class provides.

Emotion-Focused Therapy (EFT)

In emotion-focused therapy, developed by psychologist Leslie Greenberg of York University in Canada, negative emotions such as anger and anxiety or fear are identified, accepted, and then systematically replaced with other, usually opposite, emotions. The idea is that the best way to deal with a dysfunctional emotion is by identifying it and replacing it with another emotion; cognition—thoughts and logic— is taken out of the picture.

WEB TALK: Learn more about emotion-focused therapy at:

🏹 www.emotionfocusedtherapy.org

Complementary and Alternative Medicine

Complementary and alternative medicine (or CAM) practitioners believe that the secret to health, healing, and happiness is to harmonize the body, mind, and spirit. Twenty years ago, CAM methods were practiced mainly on the distant fringes of conventional medicine. These days, some techniques are creeping into the mainstream, bolstered by scientific studies that support their effectiveness at treating certain conditions—acupuncture, for instance, is a proven pain-buster. Use caution: most CAM interventions aren't backed by solid evidence, and some may not do anything for your anger, despite what you might read or hear from proponents.

Diet Some natural medicine practitioners believe the right diet can tame a terrible temper. According to the ancient traditions of Ayurvedic medicine, for example, anger can by cured by consuming simple, bland foods instead of hot, spicy dishes. Other practitioners say hot-tempered folk should consume milk, fruits, spinach, barley, and curd and avoid carrots, onions, garlic, and cauliflower.

Still other naturopaths say sugar is the root of a seething soul because it causes swings in blood sugar that have a big influence on mood: we're happy when we're on a sugar high but cranky when the levels crash. Overindulgence in general has been blamed for bursts of anger. Eat a lot, and the resulting bloat makes you uncomfortable, agitated, and prone to peevish behavior.

There's absolutely no scientific evidence proving that food makes you cranky or prone to anger, or that changing your diet improves your mood. But if you want to try it, it probably won't hurt you.

Massage It's hard *not* to feel calmer after a massage that unkinks knotted muscles and soothes tension. Practitioners of this ancient art, part of virtually every traditional form of medicine, believe that when the body is relaxed, so is the mind.

Traditional Eastern methods of massage include Shiatsu, acupressure, rolfing, and reflexology; contemporary Western forms include Esalen, Swedish, deep-tissue, and neuromuscular massage.

Acupuncture The ancient art of acupuncture, practiced for more than 3,000 years in China, supposes that health and the harmony of the body and mind are dependent on the flow of the life energy, Qi, through channels that crisscross the body. If Qi cannot flow freely, the result is mental or physical illness. Backed-up Qi causes muscle tension and stress—making a person more prone to anger. The channels can be unblocked by the insertion of fine needles into particular spots, or acupoints, along the channels.

So far, there's no evidence that acupuncture can actually alter your mood or help with emotional difficulties. Some people do find the procedure relaxing, however, and that might help keep you calmer.

I've heard about acupuncture, acupressure, electropuncture, and even reflexology. What's the difference?

In acupuncture, thin needles are inserted into acupoints and then the needles are gently twirled, stimulating the points. In acupressure, deep but gentle pressure is exerted on the points with the fingers or thumbs or with small round beads; in electropuncture, the points are stimulated with a tiny electric current that is sent through electrodes attached to needles. Reflexology is like acupressure, except the focus is only on points in the hands, feet, and sometimes the ears.

Hot for Herbs Practitioners of homeopathic medicine believe that natural herbs can relieve a variety of ailments—including oversensitivity, irritability, and rage. Two herbs are often prescribed for anger problems. The most common is Nux vomica, which comes from the seeds of the *Strychnos nux-vomica* tree (a source of deadly strychnine poison). Folks needing Nux vomica, say homeopaths, are picky and competitive, intolerant, and overly critical. They're also prone to explosive fits of temper.

On the other hand, the insecure, angry person who flies off the handle because of his or her own fear of failure and lack of confidence is treated with an herb called lycopodium, which derives from the powdery yellow spores of the common club moss (*Lycopodium clavatum*).

When properly used and given in small doses, these herbs are not dangerous. Do remember, however, that Nux vomica is derived from a poisonous plant and it can cause serious illness or even death if taken in too high of a dose. Don't self-medicate—and, as with any alternative or unconventional therapy, it's a good idea to seek the advice of your physician first.

WEB TALK: Learn more about Nux vomica, lycopodium, and a host of other herbs at: ↑ www.botanical.com

What You Can Do

Anger reduction concerns the body as much as it does the mind. By relaxing, reducing stress, and burning off extra energy, you can help avert an anger attack.

Is that the only way to train yourself in healthy anger expression? Far from it. From traditional talk therapies to the controversial and sometimes unusual tactics used in complementary and alternative medicine, scores of methods are at your disposal.

☐ Meditate. You don't need to be a Buddhist monk to meditate. Find a quiet place to sit; relax your body; take deep, slow breaths; and try to still your thoughts. Be patient.

This takes some practice. Classes or audiotapes may help you learn this technique.

☐ Next time you're feeling irate, try deep, slow breathing using your diaphragm (the sheet of muscle separating your chest cavity from your abdomen) to completely fill your lungs. The effect can be quite calming.

☐ Exercise—whether strenuous sprints or soothing stretches—can release tension from taut muscles and pent-up stress. When you're mad, it can also take your mind off what's bugging you and help you cool down.

☐ Often troubles from the past can affect your current emotional state. Talk therapy can help uncover those issues. Find a qualified therapist from *Psychology Today*'s online therapist finder: therapists.psychologytoday.com/rms/prof_search.php.

☐ If you decide to go for an outside-the-mainstream approach such as hypnotherapy or homeopathy, just remember that in most states, these treatments are poorly regulated. Ask for credentials, find out exactly what the treatment can (and cannot) do for you, and get references. And if you have (or suspect you have) a health problem of any kind—physical or mental—seek the advice of your regular doctor first.

13

Helping the Angry Child

Dealing with—and helping—an angry child can be one of the most frustrating, heartbreaking, and enraging challenges a parent or caregiver ever faces. We love our children, and want them to be safe and successful and filled with joy. Seeing our kids battling anger—dangerously stifling it up or boiling over—is not what we hope for. Nor do most parents know how to cope when their formerly sweet and loving babies turn into seething monsters.

Rest assured, there is help—and plenty of hope—for angry children and their beleaguered parents. Experts on anger and aggression in children say that no child is a lost cause; even the angriest kid can be cooled down.

Children Are Different

Kids aren't just adults in small packages. They are growing—physically, intellectually, and emotionally. And while the physical differences are manifest, we sometimes forget about the emotional ones. Children are emotionally immature, and that doesn't just mean they throw tantrums. They lack a fundamental understanding of what their emotions are and what they mean. A seven-year-old boy getting enraged because his brother is using his things won't necessarily even know what he is feeling, much less how to better express it.

"With kids, it is really about teaching them the language of the emotion; of anger," says clinical psychologist Eva Feindler, Ph.D., of Long Island University in Brookville, New York, who in 1979 developed the Anger Control program, a protocol for anger management geared toward children and adolescents. "They need to learn what an appropriate expression of anger is, what is inappropriate—when it harms other people—and how to differentiate anger from aggressive behavior."

Q&A *How do I know that my child has a problem with anger and that I'm not just blowing normal kid behavior out of proportion?*

"A child's behavior within the home is always different than their behavior in another forum. So you need some kind of reality check or a basis for comparison. For the most part, parents who should get help for their children have gotten some kind of feedback—whether it's from a Scout leader or a teacher, a neighbor—that their child is difficult, oppositional, has difficulty following rules, and is more aggressive than is normal for a child. That isn't to say that you should ignore behavior within the home. If your child is inconsistent, so that at times they can control their own temper and they are able to verbalize what they are upset about as opposed to acting it out, then it shows they do have the skill but something—usually some emotional dilemma—is in the way. Then you might need to deconstruct whatever is in that situation that is making them unable to control themselves." —*Eva Feindler, Ph.D., psychologist, Long Island University, Brookville, New York*

Helping Children Understand and Manage Anger

Children may not know very much about their emotions, but they are immensely receptive to information. They absorb new skills quickly and willingly. That means anger in a child can sometimes be much easier to get past than anger in an adult, who has issues and baggage and years of bad habits to unlearn.

Over the past few decades, psychologists have perfected some very successful programs to help children with anger, many of them with *emotion coaching* at the core.

PsychSpeak

Emotion coaching is a technique that helps kids recognize, describe, and self-soothe their emotions.

Building a Safe Emotional Climate Kids need to know that it's okay for them to feel and express any feeling, good or bad, as long as they do it in a respectful way. Expressing feelings by being physical, for example, is not acceptable. You can't simply tell your kids this and expect it to sink in—you also need to create a nurturing and comfortable environment for them at home, so they know they are loved and will be taken care of no matter what.

One way to help that happen is by setting rules that are clear, consistent, fair, and enforced. Let them know what is acceptable and what is not. Let them know what the consequences are if they cross the line. And if they screw up, enforce the rules and then move on and help them learn from their mistakes.

Labeling Feelings Compared to adults, children have a limited vocabulary. That can make it frustrating for them to express themselves. Because they don't know how to describe what they're feeling, they might instead just act it out—maybe by throwing a toy or by hitting.

Caregivers can help kids by letting them know that those actions really represent something they are feeling. To a child throwing toys, you can say, "I think something is bothering you, and that is why you are throwing things," and try to get them to talk about it. Offer suggestions for words they might use to describe what's going on inside, including *frustrated, annoyed, mad, upset, irritated, angry*. Perhaps work with your child to make a chart with those words, or have your child draw faces to represent them. The idea is for your child to know that there are lots of ways to feel things and lots of words to use to talk about them.

Awareness of Anger-Causing Situations Just because kids learn words to explain their anger does not mean anger is inevitable. Kids, like adults, tend to get mad over the same things—they have anger triggers, too. Avoiding those things can prevent an outburst.

If you don't know your child's triggers, watch your child to see if you can pick up on the problems. Does your daughter lose control when she sees you paying lots of attention to the new baby? Or does she predictably throw a tantrum when it's time for math homework? In the first case, her anger might arise from her fear of being replaced; in the second, she might be feeling frustrated because she can't quite grasp the new math skills she's supposed to know.

Then talk with your child about why it's upsetting and see if together you can come up with problem-solving strategies. Scheduling special time with you and your daughter—and no new baby—might alleviate her fears. And a math tutor might be helpful to get her over algebra anxiety. Even running interference between bickering kids—distracting them, keeping them separated when you know they're cranky—can avoid meltdowns.

Older kids often know the circumstances that get them fuming (when their sibling takes their stuff, for example, or when they're being bullied at school). You can't always help them avoid those situations, but you might sit down with your child and discuss strategies so they can get through them with less strife.

Also, be mindful that your own actions might be setting up your kids for a meltdown. "If you know that your child has a temper tantrum every time you lug them around to the dry cleaners, the drugstore, the supermarket, and the bank, maybe you don't do all that," says Wendi Fischer, Ph.D. "Maybe you go to one place, or maybe you bring a toy, or say, 'After we do this, we'll take a break and go play.'"

Teenagers, Fischer says, often get set up in entirely different ways. Ever promise your daughter you'd take her to the mall "later," and then "later" becomes tomorrow, the next day, then next week? "One of the biggest causes of anger in teenagers is neglect. That is the only way they can get their parents' attention," she says. Instead of saying "I'll get to it later," tell your child when you can. Set an appointment: Thursday at 4 P.M. And follow through. "That would prevent a lot of problems. Instead of thinking, 'They're grown up, they can handle it,' parents need to look at their own behavior and what they are doing to their kid, or what their kids are expressing and why they are getting angry. It is the key to prevention."

Books, Songs, and Other Tools Books, songs, and stories can be a great way to help kids understand what it means to be angry and how to handle it (assuming, that is, anger is presented responsibly in the story). It can also show kids that it is, indeed, acceptable to get mad and to say what they feel.

you're not alone

"My son was always such a happy baby. He almost never cried, always laughed and smiled. That's why it has been so hard to see the birth of what I hope won't turn out to be a terrible temper. It breaks my heart to see my once joyful little boy sad and angry.

"I know why he is upset. It started with his constantly worrying about his father's health, through various illnesses and injuries and infections and heart problems and then the brain surgeries. If my husband left the house for any reason, J. would wonder where his dad was, if he was at the doctor, going back in the hospital, if he was okay. He was stressed—but he also wouldn't talk about it. I'd see this stricken, worried look on his face, but he'd say he was fine. He'd grind his teeth in his sleep, though.

"My husband had been irritable and moody for years before his first brain surgery. We argued too much, and that affected J. But everything escalated horribly after my husband's brain surgeries in 2003, and his mental problems. (He was diagnosed in 2004 with bipolar disorder.) Brain trauma, I now know, can lead to extreme anger, especially when the trauma is, as was my husband's, to the frontal lobe, behind the forehead. My husband seemed to be angry *all* the time. He'd fly into terrible rages.

"J. was confused. One moment he'd be furious at his dad for being so mean; the next, he'd be defending his dad's behavior, saying it wasn't his fault. It wasn't, but an eight-year-old shouldn't have to make excuses for his dad screaming at him without cause. Then J.'s temper started to flare, too. He become angry over not being allowed to do something, or not getting a toy that he wanted, and he would just explode. He'd blow up—almost never at his dad and almost always at me—he'd curse, he'd throw things, he'd hit. He once kicked a hole in the wall. Afterward, he'd say that he didn't know why he couldn't control his anger, that it overtook him. He'd feel awful. Then it would happen again.

"Things are, thankfully, getting better. His father has a better handle on his anger, his bipolar mood swings are under control, and he's no longer constantly at the doctor, so J. has less reason to worry. J. is seeing a counselor, who is teaching him to recognize the signs of his anger coming on and ways to calm down. We're trying to get him to open up more about his feelings, we're trying to let him know that it's okay to be mad or sad or worried, but he has to talk to someone about it and not just yell or lash out.

"And he decided he wanted to take karate. You might think that would be a bad idea for a kid with a temper, but it's teaching him self-discipline and making him feel good about himself again. I watch him at practice and sometimes he will just break out in a beautiful, spontaneous smile—the smile I remember from when he was a toddler. We still have some bad days, but he is healing, I think. I'm keeping my fingers crossed." —*Kathy Svitil, author of this book*

"Bibliotherapy is very important in our program and in many others," says psychologist and former school superintendent Sara Salmon, Ph.D., executive director of the Center for Safe Schools and Communities based in Denver, Colorado, which has developed the Peace4Kids anger and aggression control program.

You can't just plop your child down with a book and expect everything to click, however. "Just writing or listening to a story is not going to cut it," Salmon says.

Instead, discuss the situations presented in the book with your children. Ask them what the characters did and why; ask them how they might have responded differently, or if they've ever encountered something similar in their own life. In Salmon's program, books are woven into lessons on anger control and in the context of skills development, done through extensive role play.

For a bibliography of useful children's books, go to the Center for Safe Schools and Communities website at groups.msn.com/CenterforSafeSchoolsandCommunities. You have to join the group to access the list, which is under "documents."

Aggression Replacement Training

One successful program to help kids who have become violent (or are on the verge) because of their aggression and anger is called Aggression Replacement Training. The protocol has three parts.

Structured Learning Training As adults we sometimes have a hard time knowing how to respond to a given situation. Say we're accused of doing something we didn't do. How do we respond? Get defensive? Get mad? But for kids, it's even tougher, because they have no experiences to draw from for those decisions.

The idea of Structured Learning Training is to teach the social skills that will help them get through. Skills include starting a conversation, apologizing, dealing with someone else's anger, dealing with group pressure, dealing with an accusation, negotiating, solving problems, making decisions, learning to read facial expressions and other social cues, and so on. They are taught and reinforced through role playing.

Anger Control Training Kids can benefit from anger management skills as much as adults. The ART program uses a version of psychologist Eva Feindler's Anger Control protocol. Kids might learn to recognize that they are getting mad and then learn what to do to reduce the anger after it sets in (saying phrases that promote calm or practicing deep breathing). They also learn to think about the consequences of their actions should they actually blow up.

Moral Reasoning Moral reasoning has nothing to do with a particular religious belief. Rather, the point is to give kids a sense of why they should keep their anger in control.

Kids don't instinctively know to think of others, so the aim of the moral reasoning component is to give them a solid base of ethics, a sense of fairness, an awareness of the global good, and concern for mankind. Some programs put special focus on empathy—the awareness of another person's thoughts and feelings. Moral reasoning skills will then inform the decisions children make about how to respond to a given situation.

WEB TALK: The International Center for Aggression Replacement Training is at:
www.aggressionreplacementtraining.org

Role of Caregivers

You can't just expect to drop off your kid at the therapist's office or in an anger class and have the problem solved for you. As the caregiver of a child with anger difficulties, expect some work of your own. At the very least, says Eva Feindler, "you need to understand what approach is being taken with your child and then really support that in the home environment."

In some programs, the parents get the same information and learn the same skills as the kids. "It is extremely important," says psychologist Sara Salmon, Ph.D. "We have about an 85 percent success rate with kids in alternative programs, but when you get the parents involved, it rises to 97 percent. Parents will say 'I don't yell at the kids now, I use my anger reducers; I can manage my anger better, be a better parent.'"

My son's teacher and the counselors at his school are recommending that we start giving him medication to control his anger. Is that a good idea?

"It is a big question mark. Some kids with developmental delays or psychotic-based disorder who are aggressive or particularly self-injurious may need to be medicated so that they don't harm themselves or others. It's like a tranquilizer. But other children with an explosive temperament or aggressive behavior suffer instead from attention deficit/hyperactivity disorder (ADHD), and although there are specific medications that have been indicated, the jury is still out on how good they are. In general, I think medication in young children is not a good idea. Parents are right to resist the recommendation. I would exhaust other methods—learning anger management or aggression control in the family, as well as working with the school to enact some kind of behavior management plan in the school." *—Eva Feindler, Ph.D., clinical psychologist and child anger expert of Long Island University, Brookville, New York*

Leading by Example Kids often pick up the patterns of their parents, so even though some kids can handle their tempers even when their parents are out of control, it's more likely that they'll struggle with the same problems.

If you have a child who is getting overly angry, it's time to step back and take a cold, hard look at your own behavior. It does no good to tell your children that they must use their words to talk about why they're mad if when *you* get ticked off, you scream and throw things. Also, if your children are getting help for their anger, it will take them longer to acquire healthy habits if there is no reinforcement at home.

If your kids are blowing up at you, you need to stay as calm as possible. "Let them know there is no way, no how, you are addressing what they're mad about until they can talk to you in a civil tone," says clinical psychologist Wendi Fischer, Ph.D.

Let Them Get Mad: Allowing Good Anger Think your kids should not get angry? Think again. "Anger isn't the problem. The problem is how it is expressed. Anger has to be channeled and controlled," says Feindler. "We should advise our children to be angry and to express it, because it is a part of everyday life and a part of relationships. Anger is a very intimate emotion—90 percent is evoked and directed toward someone you love—so you have to give it a language, variation; you have to teach kids how to say it."

Say your child comes to you and says "I hate Daddy." Your gut instinct might be to tell him that he does not mean that, and that it's not nice. "But then," Feindler says, "you are missing the opportunity to give the child a different word to describe his feelings, or to explain why they are feeling angry at Dad."

The key, though, is to insist that your kids be appropriate and respectful. "So as a mother you can say to your child, 'If you want to tell me that you are angry with me, fine, tell me that. Use your words. You can use an angry tone, say, 'I'm really angry,' and explain why, but you cannot curse at me; you cannot say 'shut up' to me. It is unacceptable behavior because I am your mother."

The Importance of Respect Just as you expect your children to respect you, your authority, and your feelings, you also have to offer the same to them. Let them have their feelings, and don't tell them their feelings aren't valid or real—even when what they're upset about seems irrational or unwarranted. Kids often act out inappropriately because they are struggling to understand what they're feeling. You won't help them learn to do that if you don't respect those emotions.

Part of that respect is listening to what they're telling you, even if it's that they are mad at you. If you're not sure what they mean, which can happen when younger kids can't explain or even understand their thoughts, probe a little. Try active listening—in which you repeat back what the other person has said to you so they know you've heard them. Attach feelings to their words, and ask them if that's right: "Are you feeling sad that Daddy didn't come home and play with you?" Your child may not be able to immediately articulate what they're feeling, but if you poke around a little, you might uncover it.

What You Can Do

Anger in children can be upsetting and frustrating, but there is hope for all of you. The key thing to remember is that kids are emotionally immature. They often simply don't know what they are feeling or why, and they don't know how to describe those feelings. You—or a trained professional—need to be there to guide them.

- ☐ Not every child who gets mad has an anger "problem." Remember that kids almost always act worse at home and around you than they do at school or with friends. If no one else is telling you there is a problem, it might not be severe.

- ☐ That said, you shouldn't ignore anger in your child. If he or she is sometimes unable to stay in control, something is up.

- ☐ Be sure your children know that their emotions—whatever they are—are valid. They are entitled to get mad as much as they are entitled to feel love, happiness, and fear.

☐ Help your children learn the language of anger. Explain that there are many words they can use to describe how they feel. And encourage them to use those words—not actions—to get it out.

☐ Look at your own behavior to see if you're contributing to your child's anger problem. Do you and your spouse argue instead of discuss things? Do you throw things? You're providing a model for how your children will act—and it may not be one you want.

Part 4

Managing Anger in Your Life

You've admitted your problem with anger, and you've learned how to use anger wisely and constructively—to assert your feelings without rage. The hard work isn't over. Now you have to maintain those changes. In Part 4, you learn how to keep cool—and cope with and repair the damage your anger has caused to your life and your relationships.

14

Keeping Your Cool

You've recognized that you have some difficulty with anger. Maybe you bottle it up; maybe you blow it out; maybe you stew about it and then take it out on people in underhanded ways.

You've taken some steps to change, either on your own or with the help of a counselor, an adviser, or an anger management program. Now the tricky part: staying on track. It's not enough to modify your behavior for a few weeks or months, or with the guiding hand of an anger control expert. You eventually have to go it alone—and for the long haul—and that can be tough when you're faced with the same stresses, the same provocations, and the same chaos that set you off before. Changing an ingrained reaction is always difficult, but with focus and persistence, it can be done.

Accepting Anger in Your Life

No anger management program or self-help method you've practiced on your own can completely eliminate anger from your life. If that's your aim, you're setting yourself up for big-time disappointment. We all lose our temper at some point. Anger can also be a valid signal that something is not right, should be paid attention to, or should be changed.

One secret to controlling anger, then, is accepting that it exists. You may sometimes get angry, but with tools to manage it, understand it, properly express it, and use it to your benefit, you'll be okay.

Self-Awareness

Accepting and embracing your anger is a huge step, but it's not the only one. You also have to analyze it. Figuring out why you get mad and learning to recognize your anger early enough to take evasive action are both critical tools for keeping cool—but they might take some very deep soul-searching, and sometimes the assistance of a therapist.

Q&A

I've learned anger control techniques, and they seem to be helping—but how long do I have to keep doing them?

Possibly a very long time. "These are patterns of dealing with anger that we've often unconsciously learned in our families," says Susyn Reeve, a management consultant and interfaith minister based in San Francisco. But the benefits are lifelong. "I think it takes the same type of personal commitment, the desire to make the change, as if you were running a marathon. But it doesn't have to be forever. And what is underneath that: it simply feels better," Reeve says. After you begin to reap the benefits of a healthy anger style—happier relationships, calmer on the job, angst-free driving—you won't find it such a chore. Furthermore, looking back on the misery your rage used to cause in your life will give you ample incentive to stay the course.

Know Your Anger Triggers What gets you mad? If you've been attending a class or seeing a counselor to help with your anger, you may already have taken inventory of your anger triggers—those thoughts or situations that repeatedly and reliably start you on the path to blowing up. By recognizing what makes you mad, you can (at least sometimes) avoid those situations or learn to deal with them without rage.

Now that you're out of treatment, you need to stay mindful of the triggers and keep an eye peeled for new ones. When you find yourself getting mad, even if it doesn't progress to full-on fury, ask yourself what about the incident is upsetting you.

Psychologist Yvonne L. Thomas, Ph.D., who has a private practice in Los Angeles, recommends a bit of emotional detective work: "When you're feeling angry, first remove yourself from the situation, do some deep breathing, and then ask yourself, 'What am I feeling?' The answer will probably be 'angry.' Then ask yourself why? 'I didn't like the way my husband talked to me. He was being dismissive of my feelings.' Next, ask yourself what else you are feeling—anger very often is a messenger of other feelings that a person doesn't want to feel. 'I am sad.' Why? 'It hurts me when my husband treats me like that, because it seems he doesn't love me as much anymore.' In this way you can sort yourself and your feelings."

If you can't easily come up with other feelings behind your anger, or if you're feeling more jumbled than clear, spoon-feed yourself feelings to see if they're there, Thomas says. "Am I sad?" "Am I frustrated?" "Am I anxious?" After you've sifted through your emotions, she says, write them down, perhaps as part of an anger log or in a journal devoted to anger.

Know Your Body's Anger Cues Stay attuned to your body, especially when it's tipping you off that you're about to lose your cool. We all experience a range of physical changes when we're getting angry. You may clench your fists or your jaw, and your muscles may tighten. Or you might feel your face get flushed, your heart rate increase, or get a sick feeling in your stomach. Your exact suite of signs will differ from the next guy's, but they'll be distinctive and noticeable. Make mental notes or write a list and keep it handy.

Heeding the Anger Alarm When you're in an intense situation and start to notice physical changes, that's a clanging alarm bell: you are revving up into a rage. Don't ignore it. It's at that moment—before you say or do something you'll regret—that you can change course. Remember that the goal is to acknowledge your anger, understand it, and express it properly, not to squash it down or bury it. Anger ultimately comes out in some form or another, and by internalizing it, you're raising the chance that your health will suffer or that you'll become depressed—or quite likely, blow over something else later on.

What you *should* do is take a mental step back, take some deep breaths, and try to clear your head. Then take inventory of how you feel and why. Look for another way to deal with the problem without blowing up. If you have to, walk away, count to 10, call a friend, visualize yourself in a soothing place, or repeat some of your coping thoughts ("this is no big deal," or "I'm not going to lose control")—whatever keeps you on top of your temper. If you can, try to think of something funny; humor is an excellent antidote to anger.

The Anger Log If you had to keep an anger log as part of an anger management course, it's not a bad idea to keep it up after the class has ended. It's a self-check that you're staying the course.

you're not alone

"It is the cat that's going to drive me nuts. I would never hurt an animal, but I'll be honest, I look forward to the natural demise of this particular animal. Yowling for its food like it is starving to death at 5:30 in the morning, and again at 6 P.M. every evening—every morning, every evening—it's like fingernails on a chalkboard. It makes me crazy with anger. Not a good way to start the day. And don't get me started on how I feel when the cat uses the furniture as a scratching post.

"It is, I have found, the little things in life that drive me nuts. Give me a crisis— a death in the family, my son falling and breaking his arm—and I'm okay, reasonably calm and focused. I get annoyed with people, my co-worker drives me crazy, I argue with my wife. But my anger in those situations, I think, isn't out of the ordinary. If I hit my head on a cabinet or crack my toe against a desk or chair, however, I go berserk—to the point where I'll hit the thing back, knowing full well that it is an inanimate object I'm raging against, and of course, usually hurting myself all over again.

"I've never hit another person, and never will, but one Mother's Day, when I couldn't find a restaurant in town that had an available reservation, I actually smacked myself in the head out of frustration. Stupid? Of course it is. Now. But at the time it was just, so, so, annoying." —*Mark, a writer in southern California*

Even if you've never enrolled in a formal program, there's nothing to stop you from creating a log on your own. Record incidents when you lost your temper, what set you off, and what your physical anger cues were. Also make note of other events in your life that might have been stressing you out at the time. Describe—honestly, of course—the outcome of your rage.

Hopefully, after you take steps to ease the outbursts and learn to express your feelings assertively and respectfully, you'll rarely have angry incidents to enter. But if you do, writing them out will give you a chance to reflect on and learn from what happened.

Psychologist Yvonne L. Thomas suggests that after you write down your anger incidents, you put the log or your journal aside.

Later you can review the incidents. Maybe you'll uncover some behavior patterns that will help you understand what motivates your actions. Don't think of the log as some kind of "shame sheet"—you will always have anger in your life, and you will undoubtedly lose your temper now and then. It's *normal*. The key is to try to learn from each event so you handle things better next time.

Also, write about times when you successfully kept your anger in check. If you stayed cool in a situation that would have previously had you in fits, pat yourself on the back!

Success on the Front Lines

Self-awareness is vitally important, but it isn't going to get you through every difficult situation. Sometimes, a heated discussion dissolves into an argument, or the kids begin to drive you crazy, or a co-worker behaves badly. With the right tools, you can get through without losing your cool.

Communication One of the biggest problems in relationships is that we don't communicate well with each other. We don't know how to speak our mind respectfully and assertively—or *really* listen. Unfortunately, whatever communication problems that exist in relationships in their good moments are magnified when things get heated. When we're angry, the gloves are thrown off—and healthy dialogue gets tossed aside along with them.

WEB TALK: Psychologist Lynne Namka, Ed.D., offers a long list of rules for fighting fairly, for both adults and kids, at:

members.aol.com/AngriesOut/fairfigh.htm

You can learn skills to communicate effectively, even when angry. Most anger management courses—and traditional therapists and counselors (especially relationship therapists) teach communication skills. The tactics may keep many disagreements from escalating into an ugly and unproductive shouting match.

PsychSpeak

"I" messages are a means of expressing your thoughts or feelings in a nonhostile, nonconfrontational manner.

Learning to use *"I" messages* is an important skill. "I" messages don't push the other person onto the defensive or make them feel as if you're blaming them for your issues. There's a big difference between saying "You don't care about being on time, and your constant lateness is making me furious!" and saying, "It upsets me when you are late, and I feel like you don't care about being on time."

Remember, too, that you are the expert only on your own feelings, not anyone else's. "A lot of people, when they get into arguments, think they know what the other person is thinking— and very often they are wrong," says Susan Romanelli, LCSW, Ph.D., director of the Hope Adult Program at the Menninger Clinic in Houston. "If they would have asked the other person what they meant, they could have avoided walking around angry."

This is critical in the midst of a discussion as well. When the other person tells you what they think or feel, parrot it back to them. Psychologists call this process *active listening*.

Suppose your spouse tells you "You're not spending enough time with the family." Repeat it back to be sure you've heard them correctly: "So you're saying that you think I'm not home enough?"—and then make a guess as to how it makes them feel—"and that is making you frustrated?" You might guess wrong, but they'll know you're not just listening to what they say but also thinking about their feelings and trying to understand them. That can reduce a lot of tension in a conversation.

By the same token, be sure that you are assertive—that you clearly state what you feel, what you think, and what you want. And be sure the other person understands; they're no better at reading your mind than you are at penetrating theirs. Remember, though, that just because they hear and understand what you're saying, they don't have to agree with you or want to do things your way.

Also be sure to keep your conversation focused on the topic at hand. "Try not putting the entire kitchen sink—every problem in the entire relationship—into the discussion. That will escalate an argument," Romanelli says.

Other communication tips include being willing to negotiate and compromise (even if it means you don't get exactly what you want), learning to use positive reinforcement or, when necessary, enforcing sanctions, which could be specific steps you'll take if the other person doesn't follow through with what you've agreed on. Otherwise, you could very well end up getting walked on, which will likely lead to frustration and possibly rage. Also, it's a good idea to schedule potentially heated discussions for a particular time on neutral ground, so neither party feels defensive or ambushed.

Giving Yourself Personal Time As much as human beings crave social contact, having too much can drive anyone batty. We occasionally need time on our own, without other people constantly around us and making demands.

It can feel horribly selfish to demand personal time, especially if you're the parent of small children, but experts say it can be critical for both stress relief and anger control. Take a walk by yourself for an hour or go to the movies. The important thing is to promise yourself the time and follow through.

Picking Your Battles You can't always control your temper—nor should you. Part of having the upper hand on your anger is having the ability to use it wisely, when it is warranted by the situation.

Make a habit of weighing each situation and deciding if it is really worth your effort and energy to take a stand. Should you blow up when a co-worker takes your sandwich out of the office refrigerator? Not unless you want a reputation as the lunchroom loon. But what if that colleague repeatedly harasses you and makes your work environment unpleasant and uncomfortable? Anger, in that case, is understandable and, indeed, necessary. Don't just seethe and stagnate; use the tremendous power of the emotion to stick up for yourself and get changes made.

Reward Yourself Anyone with kids knows that positive reinforcement is much better at encouraging good behavior than criticism is at dissuading misbehavior. For adults—and for adults with anger problems—it works the same way. Rewarding yourself for your successes *feels* much better and keeps you trying harder than beating yourself up when you fall short.

Have you gone a week without yelling at anyone? Did you handle a difficult situation with angerless aplomb? Give yourself a prize. It doesn't have to be elaborate; you might treat yourself to a manicure or a new CD. It doesn't even have to be a thing. Saying "I'm proud of myself" can be a great emotional boost.

"I let my mother-in-law Bernice destroy my psyche for 15 years, but everything changed one January when my family and I visited her in Florida. I was bored one afternoon and came across a stack of holiday cards on her living room table. Figuring they were there to be looked at, I opened them. Only the top few cards were from the holidays. Others were notes from Diane, my brother-in-law's ex-girlfriend.

"In the notes, she told Bernice how much she missed her, worried about her, loved her. By this time, Diane and my brother-in-law had been separated for two years. I was shocked that Diane and Bernice were still so close. In one card, Diane thanked Bernice for the 'generous check' for her birthday—enough for Diane to buy a floor-length wool coat. I was enraged. Every year for my birthday, Bernice has sent me inexpensive gifts—even though I am her only daughter-in-law. The year before she'd sent a pair of cheap earrings identical to some she had already given me.

"For the next two days, I spent a lot of time thinking about what I'd read in those cards and what they implied. I thought about all the years that I had spent agonizing over this woman, screaming about her to my husband and my friends and my mom, about how she had always been selfish and uncaring and critical and mean to me. About how she treated me like my husband's maid. I thought of all the time I had wasted being angry at her. The truth is, I had always tried to make her love me. I thought that if I rearranged my house and bought new clothes, lost five pounds, taught our son how to say her name, she would like me more. If I spent $200 on a gift for her, she'd change her opinion of me. It had never mattered. And, I realized, it never would.

"Bernice's behavior and attitude had nothing to do with me personally because she didn't know me, and had never tried to. She had never been kind to me, or spent an hour of her life asking about what I liked to do, what books I read, what I did with my time every day. Her view of me was based on some other girl she'd conjured up who didn't exist. *It wasn't me.*

"It was an astonishing moment. It changed my life. Suddenly, I didn't care about what she said or thought of me. All that mattered was that my husband loved me, and that my son loved me. And just then, for the first time, she appeared pathetic and pitiful to me. Lonely. Angry. Mean. Frustrated. Old. I felt sorry for her, but I didn't care about her. She was just Steve's mother, a woman who had made awful mistakes in her life and caused plenty of pain for everyone, but she wasn't powerful or frightening or intimidating. I separated her from my life.

"It has made all the difference. I no longer hate her. I'm not upset when she calls. I listen to her complaints, her gripes, her criticisms—and it all goes away when I hang up the phone. It isn't relevant to me. It is just her being angry at … I don't even know what. Her life being disappointing? Having her sons move across country and away from her? I don't know, and I don't care to find out. I listen and then go on with my life.

"It took me such a long time to realize that the anger got me nowhere. The hatred didn't change her; it didn't change the way she treated me. It didn't make me feel better. But now it's gone, and I feel better all the time."
—*Roslyn, a novelist from Oregon*

Anger Plans Devising a plan of attack against your anger can also help you stay on track. Say you start to feel the fury building. What will you do? How will you handle it? Develop a strategy that will help you relax and cope with your emotions before they get the better of you (kind of like an earthquake readiness program or a fire safety plan). Maybe your plan will be to leave the room and go for a walk around the block. Maybe you'll do five minutes of deep breathing or briefly meditate. Maybe you will call a friend and talk it out with them.

When you have your anger interventions mapped out, write them down, read them over, and etch them into your memory. The next time you start to lose your cool, you'll know instinctively what to do.

> ## GET PSYCHED
>
> "Life is not meant to be lived unhappily, or feeling unworthy, or unsuccessful, or angry. It is not our birthright. Our birthright is for joy and peace and happiness, and there is no reason we should not have that. We learn all the other stuff." —*John McGrail, clinical hypnotherapist based in Los Angeles, California*

"When someone has anger issues, they have so much reserved anger that they can have a flare-up without warning and they can react very quickly," says Yvonne L. Thomas. "So they need something to help prevent that. If you have built an anger plan into your consciousness, you will hopefully default to that first rather than going straight into anger."

Anger Buddies Your friends know if you have an anger problem, and if you ask, they'll undoubtedly be more than willing to help you through it. Think of two or three people whom you'd feel most comfortable talking to. Ideally, they should be friends or relatives you can reach just about any time, because your anger isn't going to stick to the nights and weekends when they're home. Ask them if they'll lend an ear when you start slipping into your past bad patterns. When you find yourself in temper trouble, *do* call and talk it through.

What You Can Do

After you have a handle on your anger, it can be quite a challenge to stay on track. Your life, after all, probably hasn't changed—the people, the stresses, the triggers for your rage. That means the hard work is still on your shoulders. Here are some suggestions for how to not let it drag you down.

- ☐ Give yourself credit for how far you've come. Admitting you have a problem and striving for change are hard to do, and you're succeeding.
- ☐ Be prepared to forgive yourself if you fall off the anger wagon. Dust off and learn from the mistakes you've made.
- ☐ Be aware of your anger triggers. Make a note—mental or otherwise—and keep it handy. Also keep an eye out for new things that seem to set you off.

☐ Be mindful of your body—how you respond to anger or when you're spiraling toward trouble. When you spot the cues, take immediate action—deep breaths, a brisk walk, a call to a friend. Just heed the alarm.

☐ Be sure you don't move toward the other anger extreme and push inside the rage you would have formerly let fly. Suppressed anger is just as unhealthy as those ugly outbursts.

☐ Learn to communicate with friends, family, business associates—even enemies. Try "I" messages, those non-confrontational statements of how you think and feel, and practice "active listening": repeat back what the other person says so they know you've really heard them.

☐ Have a plan. Know what you'll do if you start to lose it. Will you call a friend? Be sure you have numbers handy, and arrange in advance for them to support you.

15

Coping With the After-Effects

S o you've conquered your anger problems—you're expressing your feelings rationally and respectfully, you're calm in the car, and you've stopped screaming at home. Are you done yet? Not even close.

It's important for you to make amends to those around you for the pain your temper has almost certainly caused. You need to say you're sorry. You need to mean it. You need to rebuild those relationships that can be salvaged and accept those losses that are irreparable. You need to move forward and, maybe, move on. You—and the people you love—need to heal.

In Anger's Wake

"I'm sorry." It's such a simple phrase, and yet for some of us, it can be incredibly difficult to say. For others, it can be incredibly difficult to accept and believe. But if you're going to mend fences and undo the damage Hurricane Anger has left in your life, you *have* to ask for forgiveness. There's no getting around it.

WEB TALK: Read about forgiveness, post your own apology, or read others at the Forgiveness Web at: www.forgivenessweb.com

"Make a list of the people you believe you've caused pain through your issues, and your anger, and your actions," says John McGrail, a clinical hypnotherapist based in Los Angeles. "The people on the list ought to at least be approached. Say, 'Listen, I sense I have caused you a great deal of stress or pain through my actions, and I am sorry. I'm working to change the way I behave, and I hope that you might forgive me for it. I didn't mean it to purposefully hurt you. I was out of control.'"

Accepting the Anger of Others Will they forgive you? Maybe, maybe not. It depends on a number of factors, including the magnitude of the pain you caused, the nature of your relationship, and the intensity of your anger. Some people are, by nature, forgiving; others are inclined to hang on to their grievances or even hold a grudge.

"If it is someone you are very close to, have known for a long time, they might react differently than someone with whom you have a less intense personal relationship," says David Baron, Ph.D., chair of the department of psychiatry and behavioral health at Temple University Hospital and School of Medicine in Philadelphia. "It may be that in your eyes, what you did wasn't that big of a deal, but it was a huge thing to the other person. Or you might think that what you said was absolutely terrible and they didn't make too much out of it. You don't always know how people feel."

The people you have hurt might in fact be *furious* at you. They might resent you, even hate you. And they might be absolutely unwilling to let those feelings go. The most important part for you, though, is to try. You can never get forgiveness, after all, if you don't *ask*. "I think it would work a lot more often than you'd expect," says Rachel Greene Baldino, MSW, LCSW, a therapist in Worcester, Massachusetts. "People admire it when others come around and see the error of their ways. They are willing to give second chances, even more so than people are willing to forgive themselves."

And therein lies another crucial point: you have to forgive yourself. "You have to remember that you learn these behaviors," says John McGrail. "You are not born angry, you learn to be, and when it is ingrained it becomes automatic. You weren't thinking when you went into those rages and had those anger attacks. You weren't consciously thinking about what you were doing and who you were hurting. You were acting out of instinct. Now it's great that you've gotten rid of it, so let it go. Forgive yourself."

> **GET PSYCHED**
>
> "A lot of times when people are feeling angry at someone close to them, it is because the other person did or said something mean. When you love another person and they hurt you, that's more intolerable than the anger. 'If you love me, why would you hurt me like that?'" —*Susan Romanelli, LCSW, Ph.D., director of the Hope Adult Program at the Menninger Clinic in Houston*

Dealing With Grudges Anger can be incredibly destructive, and the pain your anger has caused can cut deeply. If you are genuinely sorry, genuinely changed your ways, and genuinely attempted to make amends, you may indeed be forgiven. Unfortunately, there's no guarantee. Some people might just want to get you back. It may be frustrating and you might feel guilty—or, worse, *angry*—but part of your own healing is recognizing that you can't do anything about another person's grudge.

"The person with the grudge has their own issues," says Yvonne L. Thomas, Ph.D., a psychologist in private practice in

Los Angeles. "They are intractable, they are in their grudge, and they may stay in it for the rest of their life. The person holding on to the grudge is not dealing with their feelings very healthfully. Who is to say that they haven't had grudges against people their whole life and you are just part of the heap? You have to let it go, because otherwise you are beating your head against a wall."

Fixing Damage, Accepting Loss You've offered your sincere apology. Now move forward, keeping up your new, healthy, behavior while cutting yourself slack for slip-ups along the way. "You need to show that you are trustworthy again, and that means not just talking the talk," says Thomas. "Consistency in words and actions are so important. It is evidence that you are reliable again, you can be depended on again, and you can be trusted with the other person's emotional well-being. You have to prove yourself." If you can manage that, your relationships have a chance to heal—and because you have resolved your temper problems, they will probably be healthier and happier.

you're not alone

"When I became an adult, sobered myself up, and got myself together, I realized that I had to let go of all my resentment toward my mother," says Jenny Moran, author of *Jenny's Monster: A True Story of Grace.*

As a child, Moran was abused by her alcoholic mother. The reverberations of the violence led Moran to substance abuse and a series of other abusive relationships. "I put some boundaries down. When she would call me and I knew she was drunk, I would say, 'You know what, I'm not going to talk to you. Because you are going to put me down, you are going to say mean things, and I don't want to talk to you.' I was probably 29 or so. And I did hang up on her. I set a boundary. She didn't talk to me for four or five months, but when she called the next time, she wasn't drunk, and she only had

Accept, however, that it might not work. Sometimes, despite your best efforts to make amends, a relationship simply cannot be fixed. The wounds are too deep, and the other person has suffered too much. They won't forgive you. Or they might forgive you, but for their own emotional health, they've decided to cut you out of their life. That might mean the end of a friendship, severing bonds with a family member, even divorce.

Is it painful? Absolutely. It might also seem terribly unfair, because you have, after all, honestly changed your ways. But that's life, and you can only move forward if you accept the loss.

"It is a loss, but it doesn't have to be a total loss," says Thomas. "The way it becomes that is if you don't learn your lesson and make it count. Do something productive, not destructive, not demeaning, not adding to what you have already lost. If you are beating yourself up, you are adding to the loss pile because now you are losing your self-esteem."

nice things to say, and we really never had a bad moment again. In fact, she walked me down the aisle on my wedding day.

"She didn't change at all, herself. She was still drinking. She was still mean. She was living with a woman who was also an alcoholic, and she beat up on her.

She was still the most violent, miserable, angry person in the world, but I didn't participate any more, and because I changed, our relationship changed.

"We had a couple of good years before she died, which was great for me, because I always wanted a real mother and

didn't have one. Not that she became a real mother, but at least I had some kind of solace before she died. She didn't die with me feeling that all that stuff was unresolved."

I've tried apologizing to the people my anger hurt, but some people just won't forgive me. How can I get them to?

You can't make anyone forgive you. You can sincerely offer your apology and then give them some time and space, says psychologist Yvonne L. Thomas, Ph.D. "When a person feels that they have been so mistreated by another person that they can't forgive them, they must have also felt disrespected. If it is not a grudge, one reparative thing is to tell the person that you are going to respect that they are not ready to let you in. Tell them you respect their boundaries, their feelings, that you are sorry you hurt them and disrespected them and didn't value them, and that now you are going to show them that you do. Tell them you're sorry they're not yet at a place where the two of you can be friends—or family—or a team, and move forward at the same time, but you are going to respectfully let them go at their own pace and have the space they need. Even though you care and want their forgiveness, let them know they have every right to take as much time as they need to decide if they want you back in their life again."

Coping With Other Angry People

You may have made great strides toward conquering your temper, but you still have to deal with other people who haven't. The world is full of unpleasant, irritable, easily annoyed folk, and you're sure to encounter them on a daily basis. What's worse, you may be very close to a lot of angry people, or people who are used to dealing with you with threats and yelling. They're probably more likely than anyone else to set off your alarm bells and pitch you over the edge into fury again. How do you keep their foul mood or short temper from spoiling your newfound equanimity? Practice and patience.

It may be that the angry people you encounter are those you have wronged. They're mad—at you. If that's the case, you really have to respect their resentment. Give it time, and don't force them to forgive you.

Repairing the Angry Legacy You've Created in Your Family

Sadly, the impact of rage can have lasting reverberations within a family. The screaming, the fights, and the suppressed rage that manifested in sarcasm and criticism, can damage your relationships with your spouse and children. And they can leave scars. Children of rageful parents often learn that knee-jerk yelling is the proper first expression of bad feelings. Even if the parents stop their belligerent behavior, the patterns are there. Your spouse and children may find it more natural to shout than to work out differences in a respectful manner.

Other families go the opposite direction and avoid anger at all costs. "If a child has parents who, when they get angry, are verbally abusive or physically violent; if it is disruptive to everything in the entire household; and if the child never sees any resolution, they will learn to be fearful of anger. They suppress it," says Susan Romanelli, LCSW, Ph.D., director of the Hope Adult Program at the Menninger Clinic in Houston. "If you have learned that it is unacceptable to be angry, you will eventually turn that anger toward yourself, which can lead to depression."

In any case, the problems don't have to be permanent. The first step is for you to be consistent, calm, and cool. Set a good example. Impress upon them that emotions, including anger, aren't bad, but they should be expressed without being disrespectful or hurtful to other people.

> ### GET PSYCHED
>
> "Maybe what you did or said was so hurtful that it is not going to turn around overnight—or maybe ever. Then you could consider saying 'I understand how hurt you must be that you can't accept my apology. I accept that,' and then just let it go." —David Baron, Ph.D., psychologist, Temple University Hospital and School of Medicine, Philadelphia

If you sense your kids are in pain, or if their behavior is beyond your capacity to deal with, consider getting them trained help. "The beautiful thing about children is that they are so suggestible," say hypnotherapist John McGrail. "If children start seeing a different paradigm in your actions, it is easy to reverse the patterns because they are so impressionable."

Taking Responsibility for Your Angry Actions

Part of being an adult is owning up to your behavior. Asking for forgiveness goes a long way toward repairing the destruction caused by your rage, but it might not be enough in every area of your life.

Professionally Don't expect your boss to forgive and forget if you lost his best account when you screamed at the client. If your rage didn't already cost you your job, it certainly affected your reputation and credibility. Now you have to build it back.

If your boss or human resources department made you take an anger management course, let them know you've completed it. Let them also know that you're prepared to prove yourself again. Don't grovel, and don't accept any sanctions that seem inappropriate or demeaning. If you've concluded that you'll always have anger problems in your current job, it's time to explore other options. The point of getting control of your temper, after all, is to make your life better—and if it takes a job change to do that, so be it.

Legal For some people, only a brush with the law brings to light an anger problem. Arrested for a bar fight or for overzealous driving during a fit of road rage? The court may require an anger management class. Whether you saw it as a chore to get through or as a cause for deep soul-searching and change, there are still legal repercussions to deal with. You have a record now, with anger stamped all over it.

Consult with a lawyer to find where you can go from here. You may be able to get your record expunged, but to do so, you'll likely have to prove that you've recognized the error of your ways and accepted responsibility for what you've done, and you can never repeat the same actions. Ever.

Creating a Support System

When my husband's rage was at its worst, in the aftermath of the brain surgeries and before his bipolar disorder was diagnosed, I spent many months in an emotional cave, hiding from my friends and family. I didn't tell them what was going on, and I didn't reach out for help and support. Maybe it was embarrassment—who wants to admit that their husband is screaming at them daily? I didn't want people to know I was tolerating that kind of emotional abuse. I was supposed to be stronger than that.

And that was a mistake. When I eventually revealed to family and friends what we were going through, the love and support I received was immediate and profound. People worried; people cared; people tried to help us. Ultimately, that—plus a proper diagnosis and treatment for his mental condition—saved us. Saved me. I still have a bad habit of shutting myself away when things get difficult, but usually not for very long. Having a support system is vital to getting through any kind of problem, and those involving anger are no exception.

If you're recovering from anger—your own or someone else's— talk to people. Let them know the situation. Enlist their help and guidance. If you're worried that you might lapse into old patterns, tell your friends to watch your back and let you know

"When I was young and growing up in my family of origin, there was freedom to express angry feelings, to be aggressive," says Brian, a 46-year-old native New Zealander. "It didn't turn to violence. But early on while working—I came from a rural, farming background—I found that I could use anger to motivate myself to get through a lot of work when the pressure was on. Say I was shearing sheep and the sheep were particularly unhelpful, I'd get angry but use that anger to drive myself to work harder. I wasn't really angry at having to do work. I just tapped into it in some way."

Because of health problems, Brian eventually left agriculture and went back to school, where he took courses to become a counselor. His training gave him a different perspective on his anger. "Now I have a lot more knowledge, a framework to understand my anger. I see anger as an indicator—a red flag waving or a road sign saying, 'Stop, take notice of this, there is something happening that you need to pay attention to.' I'm far more aware of what is happening within me, and that self-awareness means I can think at an earlier stage that I'm getting angry and make sense of what is provoking me and sort it out before the anger hits me.

"And whereas once, if anger was expressed toward somebody, I saw it as unhelpful and 'bad,' now that I have that framework, I don't see it in that light. It is not right or wrong; it is just a normal, natural emotion."

if they see it coming. Be sure your spouse and your children know they are not alone in dealing with this. Tell them it's okay to talk about it and to reach out—you want them enveloped in love and support.

When Is Counseling Appropriate?

Have your spouse, your children, or other family members suffered from your actions? You may want to seek counseling for all of you. Even if you have already seen a therapist, it helps to get the family together to talk things out. The family dynamic brings up issues beyond what you have discussed in one-on-one sessions, and the neutral ground of a therapist's office allows all of you to air grievances and to learn to communicate more effectively with each other. It certainly won't *hurt* to get professional help.

Many insurance companies cover counseling services. There are also free or low-cost services available through churches and other community resources.

What You Can Do

Getting past an explosive temper isn't the end of it. Your past behavior may have damaged your credibility. You may have hurt the people you love. Now it's time to clean up and move forward.

- ☐ Make a list of the people your anger has scarred. Say you're sorry. Mean it.
- ☐ Be sure your actions are consistent with your words. If you say you're sorry you've yelled so much and then start to yell, no one will take you seriously.
- ☐ Give them the freedom to accept your apology, but also room not to. They might not be ready to forgive you. They might not ever forgive you.
- ☐ If, despite your best efforts, you can't get someone to forgive you, let it go. Respect their feelings and their decision.
- ☐ Some people may hold grudges. Accept that it is their issue, not yours.
- ☐ If your family has been hurt by your anger, consider counseling—for all of you. Don't assume your family's not suffering just because you're behaving better.

16

A Guide for Family, Friends, and Caretakers

Relationships—personal, business, or otherwise—are always complex. Add in a volatile and potentially destructive emotion such as anger, and you may be stewing up a toxic brew.

Coping with an angry person can be confusing and frustrating. You may feel responsible or full of your own rage over their behavior. You might just feel helpless and sad. Whatever you're experiencing, know that help is out there—not just for the angry person in your life, but for you as well.

When Someone You Love Is Angry

You'd think it would be easy to see that a loved one is going too far—their rage is out of control or they're suppressing their feelings to the point of being sick. But sometimes it just blindsides you. Nobody willingly enters into a relationship with a person

GET PSYCHED

"If you can change your own behavior—by setting boundaries, for example, that establish what is acceptable and unacceptable behavior toward you— you are not doing it to change the other person, but you'd be amazed at how much they may change. Eventually. It is not a quick fix." –Kiki Weingarten, M.Sc.Ed., MFA, life and career coach, co-founder of Daily Life Counseling in New York City

who is condescending or cruel or who screams at them constantly. If you have that kind of partnership now, it's probably because that behavior has built up over time. Maybe your husband used to occasionally get angry, and only over big things. And then, as his life grew more complicated, his anger became more frequent. Over time, he reached the point where he was mad all the time—and often at you. Did you willingly agree to that? Of course not. And yet, here you are.

When is another person's anger your problem? When it begins to affect your life. Are you frequently upset because of their outbursts? Do you tiptoe around their moods or warn the children to do the same? Are you wondering if the love is gone, feeling distant and disengaged, concerned about their mental stability? All these things should set off alarms, telling you that the situation is not as it should be.

Knowing You Are Not to Blame It's hard living with an angry person, and not just for the obvious reasons. Angry people are often expert blamers. They lose their temper because of what someone else did—another person's mistakes, their stupidity, their disrespect, their rudeness, their actions, reactions, behavior .... If you live with a person who routinely blames others for his or her foul temper, you're most likely the prime target.

Are you to blame? Absolutely not. That angry person is responsible for his or her actions. The only exception would be if the person with rage problems has a physical or mental condition that leads to uncontrollable outbursts—bipolar disorder and psychosis, for example, or brain trauma and brain tumors. And even then, *you* are not the cause. You cannot make someone get angry at you any more than you can make them, by sheer force of your will, shower you with affection and love. We control only our own behavior.

Q & A

My husband's anger is making me crazy. I don't want to leave him, so how can I learn to live with it?

"Sometimes it is a matter of being around the person for too many hours. So in the evening, go for a walk, walk the dog, watch a different show on TV, listen to a book on tape, work on your computer—just physically get yourself out of the situation. The other thing is to really set boundaries. You can tell children, 'Don't raise your voice to me—that is unacceptable.' Do that with your spouse, as well. It sounds weird to tell the other person, 'I cannot accept your yelling at me that way. I cannot talk to you right now, when our emotions are this heightened,' but what you are doing is saying, 'This is what I will be a part of, and this is what I won't.' In a way, it is a very generous thing to do for the other person, because they are out of control." *—Kiki Weingarten, M.Sc.Ed., MFA, life and career coach, co-founder of Daily Life Counseling in New York City*

Raising the Issue How do you tell your friend or loved one that they have a problem? Gingerly. Don't try when the person is in the middle of a rant, because they won't hear anything you say. Wait until a calm moment, maybe after a nice dinner or a relaxed evening at home. "Say, 'I care about you, but you have said some things that were hurtful to me and that I know were hurtful to others,' and then give them an example," says psychologist David Baron.

"It is not as easy for them to deny it if they are confronted with a specific example. You can say that you don't think they were really trying to hurt anyone, but just trying to express their feelings and it came out badly. Tell them that you think they might have an anger issue, and that they might need to figure out how to deal with that," advises Baron.

If you are in an intimate relationship, Baron says, make it clear that you don't love the person any less, but you're concerned about how their anger seems to consume them. "Pose it in a way such as, 'I'm not saying you're a bad person, but I don't think this is helpful in our relationship, and I don't think it reflects who you really are,'" he says.

Can You Change Them? In short—no. Another person's behavior, attitude, and actions are out of your control. "When you are around a person with anger, the first thing that will make a difference is to realize that you *cannot* change them," says career and life coach Kiki Weingarten.

"You cannot get someone to see something they don't want to see. It's almost as though they're blind—they don't want to see their behavior. You need to take that pressure off of yourself. Say to yourself, 'I am stuck in this situation and there's nothing I can do about this person's behavior'—and by 'stuck' I mean that you are choosing to remain in the situation—'So how can I manage myself?' By taking the pressure off yourself, you liberate a tremendous amount of energy, and you are able to put that energy and focus on yourself in a very positive way."

you're not alone

II❙have lived with an angry father for about 20 years now," says Anthony, a student from Missouri. "Ever since I can remember he has had anger problems. I remember him throwing a dish on the floor and breaking it once when he was angry at my mother. This occurred when I was only four, but it left a mark on my developing mind.

"He has been emotionally, mentally, and, at times—although rarely—physically abusive to the family. It is not so taxing on me as I am an adult now and moving on campus to go to college in three weeks, but when I was younger it was hell for me, day in, day out. He didn't blow up every day … but I always walked on eggshells and had to live with that constant fear of him losing his cool. It created an atmosphere of fear and repression of emotions to keep the house peaceful. This obviously was not conducive to a healthy life. He has been to counseling for this, yet he obviously has not learned or at least not incorporated the help into his life. He no longer is much of a problem to me because I avoid him and, although it is unspoken, he knows I dislike him for the way he has treated my family and me. He doesn't really attempt to form a real relationship. To sum it up: living with someone with anger issues is hell. It is a horrible thing to have to go through."

That doesn't mean you are powerless to alter your situation. Remember that you are in total control of yourself. You can choose how you respond to their anger, what you say, and what you do. And sometimes that can make a difference. "One strategy is to totally shut down," says Wendi Fischer, Ph.D., a clinical psychologist in private practice in West Islip, New York. "If someone is ranting and carrying on, remove yourself from the situation. "Or if you can't remove yourself, make sure that it doesn't happen again. A lot of times families are trapped in the car, on their way to visit Grandma, or on vacation, and not able to do something in the moment. But the next time you might say, 'I'm not going with you; we are taking separate cars. I'm not even going to take the chance.' Or you may just want to be quiet and wait until it's over and say, 'If you ever do that again, wherever we're going, when we get there you can stay and I'm taking the car and going home.'"

Whatever your tactic, Fischer says, you have to be firm and show the other person that their behavior is unacceptable and you will not participate. "You can do it with love, and you can do it gently, which is the most effective way," she says. "If you yell back, you are giving the other person justification for their anger."

Where to Turn

Excessive anger is a complicated problem, and it can have many causes. If the anger is severe and completely out of character for the person (for example, if a normally mellow person suddenly turns into a bellowing maniac), it might be a sign of a physical or mental disorder.

Bring up the subject with your loved one, let them know you are worried, and encourage them to see a doctor or therapist for an evaluation. You may feel more comfortable with a family member or friend present to back you up. If you have to, contact their physician or a therapist on your own and get some advice. In cases of dangerous behavior, you might need to call in the police; in some areas of the country, mobile mental health teams can come to your home for an on-site evaluation.

Importance of Support When you are living with, working with, or enduring an angry person, you have to know that you're not alone. Talk to your friends and your family. If they don't know what is going on in your life, *tell them*. Vent to co-workers. Commiserate with friends.

Although you're not likely to find a specific group for the loved ones of angry people (I could find none in researching this book), you should be able to find support from other sources. The Center for Safe Schools and Communities (groups.msn.com/CenterforSafeSchoolsandCommunities) has online resources for the parents, teachers, and caregivers of kids with anger issues, and so on. Or try your local church or community center. Be sure you don't hole yourself up and wallow in your bad situation. Get out; be with people. Just getting involved in something—a yoga class, book club, or softball team—to give you a distraction and an outlet for your energy and connection with people with similar likes is an emotional boost.

> **WEB TALK:** Is your loved one's anger from mental illness? The National Alliance for the Mentally Ill offers support groups and online communities.at:
>
> ↑ www.nami.org/Template.cfm?section =Find_Support

In an Emergency The angry person may not want to get help. That's their choice, but, if you feel that they are endangering themselves or that you or your family or another person are at risk, don't sit by and wait for disaster. Leave the house and go to a friend or neighbor, go to a domestic violence shelter, or call a friend or relative to be with you. Do not be alone with someone who makes you physically afraid. If you can't get out and feel you are in imminent danger, call the police.

When dealing with an out-of-control person, have an emergency plan in place. Develop a strategy, and be sure you can execute it on a moment's notice. Have a bag packed, let your friends know you might show up at their doorstep, or get a key to their house, and so on. Hopefully, you'll never need to put it in motion, but you'll feel more in control if you're prepared.

> **GET PSYCHED**
>
> "One of the things that will dissipate your own anger is when the other person starts to return to the person who you used to know." —Susan Romanelli, LCSW, Ph.D., director of the Hope Adult Program, Menninger Clinic, Houston

Elizabeth, 39, a mother of two from New York and a partner in an ad agency, has been married for 10 years to a man whose anger has grown increasingly out of control. She suspects that he might have bipolar disorder—a mental disease characterized by extreme swings between depression and manic periods that are often characterized by anger and irritability—a diagnosis their marriage counselor agrees with. Her husband admits that his anger can be a problem, but he also believes that he is provoked—that other people, including Elizabeth, are to blame.

"I remember when it first occurred to me that this was bigger than him. I took a poll on bipolar disorder, and checked eight of the ten things on the list. In some way it was freeing for me, because I could identify *something*. Even if he wasn't willing to do anything, I thought, 'Okay, I can't control this. I have to deal with it, but I can't control it.' My therapist has told me that I can't wait for him to get well to make decisions in my life. And it's true.

"It is not that he is physically abusive. He can scream and go crazy, but it is more the 'tone' that he gets, even with the kids. His first reaction is the most punitive. He can be very hostile, takes almost an interrogation approach to communication. But he is very up and down with his anger, so it's never quite clear when it's going to emerge or what is going to set it off. I think there is a manic element to his anger, because there are times when he is very gregarious and sweet.

"For a long time his anger was directed at the outside world, not at me. He was the kind of person you'd see flipping out in the line at a ticket counter. Some of it has been very serious—it's almost like he blacks out. Then his anger started to turn on me, and I started withdrawing more and more, in many ways sort of checking out. Now I feel like the best thing for our kids would be for us not to be together, but I am very concerned about where he will take this. That he would fight me, drag them through court. He is very vindictive. So a real issue for me is feeling safe to leave.

"I think he truly believes that his reactions are a result of external circumstance. He feels that if things didn't happen to upset him, then he wouldn't have to get so angry. I have played into it, too, almost in an adolescent way. I've gone out with my friends and stayed out until midnight and not told him where I was. I've gotten so pissed off that I've acted out. It's a very hard thing not to do. How do you break out of that? Anger is very serious, and I'm not accustomed to it. I don't have any frame of reference.

"It's tough. I'm a very strong person. In any other area of my life I wouldn't let anyone treat me like that. My cousin once very logically asked me, 'Why don't you just leave?' But I have a responsibility to these kids. You hear about how women are abused and wonder why they stay. When you're in the situation, you start to realize, it's really not that simple."

Should You Forgive?

That's entirely up to you. Some people find comfort in forgiveness. They find it eases their own spirit to accept the shortcomings of others and let go of their resentment, sadness, or anger. For others, though, forgiveness is harder to come by, especially when they have been deeply wounded by someone who was supposed to love them or protect them.

You have to decide how badly you've been hurt, if you can ever trust the person again, and if you honestly believe their change and remorse are sincere. You may decide you can't go back and be with the person whose anger hurt you, even though they've changed, and even though you still care or love them. It is your right to move on.

Coping Strategies

You don't have to be a martyr and tough out a bad situation, but if you do decide to keep an angry person in your life, you need to learn to cope. Sometimes it may be the best option.

For the Parents, Teachers, and Caregivers of an Angry Child Overwhelmed by the anger your child or student is displaying? Don't be afraid or ashamed to ask for advice and help. Yes, it may be hard to admit that your child has an anger problem, or that you don't know how to handle a particular pupil. It can feel like you've failed them, or that you're saying they're bad kids. You haven't, and they aren't. The problem is just a bit bigger than you.

PsychSpeak

A **functional behavioral analysis** assesses a person's thoughts, feelings, and actions in their situational context.

The first step is to figure out why the child is getting excessively mad, and to do that, you may need the services of a trained therapist or counselor. Talk to your family doctor for a referral, or ask around at your child's school. Many community-based organizations, such as the member agencies of the United Way, offer quite a number of no- or low-cost programs to troubled kids. (Those groups may also offer support services for you.)

If you see a therapist, they initially may do what is called a *functional behavioral analysis* to uncover the roots of your child's anger. "You want to figure out what happened just before, and just after, their temper problem," says clinical psychologist Wendi Fischer. "Is something setting it up? Is something reinforcing it?"

Also be prepared to take a hard look at your own behavior. Although angry adults have to take responsibility for their actions (unless they have a physical or mental problem that is exerting control), children are shaped by their environment. If the adults in a household are yelling at each other, the kids will learn to do it, too. Are you setting your kids up for an outburst by dragging them out on 15 different errands without feeding them? Are you telling them to *never* get angry, so that their very natural feelings are squashed until they come out in a blowup?

I don't understand why my daughter gets so angry and screams at her brothers. We are a "vocal" family, but we tell her all the time not to yell.

"Children pick up their behavior from their parents, so you really need to look at your own actions. Are you yelling? If so, you need to stop doing that. You may be doing it for perfectly legitimate reasons, but that is not the issue. The issue is that you are teaching a methodology of how to handle something. You are giving your children a model that says when you are upset, even for a good reason, you start yelling and screaming and throwing things, or whatever the temper outburst is. It doesn't matter what you say to a child and tell them to do. If you are not exhibiting that same behavior, it won't matter." *—Wendi Fischer, Ph.D., clinical psychologist in private practice in West Islip, New York*

Options for Employers and Co-Workers

Anger on the job can be a tricky business. A belligerent boss or crabby co-worker can make your day-to-day dealings unpleasant and unproductive. You do have options:

- **Quit.** It's effective, but if you love your job or need the money and don't have something else already lined up, this may be an impractical solution.

- **Stick it out, but be looking.** In the short term, your life might be miserable, but if you put out lots of feelers and channel your energy into finding a new position, you'll be happier in the long run.

- **Complain, and try to force some change.** If a co-worker has you troubled, first talk to your boss and let her know your concerns. Ask that the tantrum-throwing employee get some help, or, perhaps, that one of you be moved to a new position. If your boss doesn't respond, take up your concerns with her boss, or your ombudsman, employee assistance office, or human resources department. If your boss is the person with anger problems, definitely report the situation to your human resources office.

This serves several purposes, says executive coach Steven L. Katz. "First, it is important that you not think of yourself as a human shock absorber, and second, it creates a record of what has been going on," which is vital, Katz says, if you have to take further action (including legal action). "It also kicks the issue up to the radar of the people on top," he says. Katz also advises that you bring a colleague with you when you complain—ideally, an executive on the same level as the offending employee. "It is important to have an ally, simply to be with you, even if they haven't experienced the same behavior."

What You Can Do

Living, working with, or just being around an angry person can tax the emotional resources of even the strongest soul. Maybe you blame yourself. Maybe you're embarrassed. Maybe you're scared. However it affects you, you have to recognize that it *does* affect you. You're allowed to hope for change—and you're allowed to ask for help.

☐ Never blame yourself for an out-of-control person. They choose their course. The only exception to this: a person with a physical or mental condition that predisposes them to irrational, rageful behavior.

☐ If you suspect that a loved one's anger is out-of-character or extreme—suggest that they see a doctor or a therapist to get evaluated. Keep suggesting it until they do so.

☐ If you have to, enlist an ally, a friend or relative who will back you up when you state your concerns.

☐ Never bring up a person's anger problem when they're in a rage. They won't hear you. Choose a moment when they're calm and at ease—and be sure they know you say it because you care.

☐ Don't think you can change anyone's actions. If they choose not to deal with their anger, the next step is yours.

Glossary

abuse   An action that causes harm or injury to one's self or other people. Abuse can be physical, emotional, verbal, or sexual.

adaptive   A behavior or trait that increases the survival or reproductive success of an organism.

adrenal gland   Gland located on top of each kidney that produces cortisol, the body's stress hormone, plus other hormones critical to the physiological state of anger.

adrenalin   *See* epinephrine.

adrenocorticotropic hormone   A hormone secreted by the anterior lobe of the pituitary gland that causes the production of cortisol, the body's stress hormone.

affect   A behavior that expresses a person's emotional state.

affective   Pertaining to emotions, feelings, or the internal state.

aggression   An action or behavior (physical or verbal) performed with the intent to cause harm.

aggression replacement therapy (ART)   A type of therapy, often used for children, that uses cognitive restructuring and teaches problem-solving, social skills, moral reasoning, and anger control.

amygdala   An almond-shaped part of the brain, located on the side of the head above the ear and on each side of the brain, that helps process fear and anger. Known as the seat of emotion.

androgyny   The combination of both male and female personality traits in a single individual.

anger log   A log or journal of anger incidents, their causes, and their consequences. Often used in anger management classes.

anger style   A person's pattern of expressing (or suppressing) their anger.

anger trigger   An anger-provoking thought or event.

anger-in   A type of anger expression in which an emotion is felt but not outwardly displayed or experienced. This is bottled-up anger.

anger-out   An anger pattern in which an emotion is directly outward, toward other persons or things.

arousal reduction   The technique of diminishing a state of physiological or emotional activation.

assertiveness   Expressing thoughts and feelings in a direct, firm, but respectful manner.

attention deficit/hyperactivity disorder (ADHD)   A behavioral pattern usually in a child and not in-synch with typical developmental levels that consists of poor impulse control, restlessness or constant motion, and difficulty paying attention.

autonomic nervous system   The part of the nervous system that controls involuntary function, such as the contraction of the muscles of the heart or the digestive system. It links directly with regions of the brain involved in our emotions and consists of the sympathetic and the parasympathetic nervous systems.

biofeedback   Techniques that use sensory feedback (lights or tones) to relay information about the body's internal state, such as muscle contractions, blood pressure, and temperature.

bipolar disorder   A mental disorder, also known as manic-depression, that is characterized by alternating periods of depression and mania, with periods of normal behavior in between.

borderline personality disorder   A mental illness characterized by unstable moods and instability in interpersonal relationships. The disorder often produces extreme flares of rage.

bruxism   Grinding of the teeth; often caused by psychological stress.

bully victim   A bully whose behavior is in response to rage at their own victimization at the hands of a bully or abuser.

bullying   A type of aggression performed not in response to provocation but with an intent to cause physical or psychological harm to the victim.

c-reactive protein   A compound found to be elevated in the bloodstreams of angry and hostile subjects. This protein may lead to heart disease.

catastrophising   A type of thinking error in which the worst possible situation or outcome is imagined.

catharsis   The violent venting of anger.

central nervous system   The brain and the spinal cord.

cerebellum   The brain region responsible for regulating subconscious activities such as balance and coordination.

cerebral cortex   The brain's "gray matter," responsible for higher thinking functions.

cognitive restructuring   Changing negative or irrational thinking patterns and replacing them with positive, more healthy ones.

cognitive therapy   A type of cognitive-behavior therapy with an emphasis on changing thinking patterns.

cognitive trigger   An anger trigger that originates in one's own thoughts and not from an external event.

cognitive-behavior therapy   Therapy that focuses on irrational thinking patterns as the cause of emotional problems. Behavioral modifications are part of the therapy.

coping thoughts Practiced phrases or statements a person can say to himself when in a stressful or anger-provoking situation to de-escalate his emotions.

cortisol A hormone produced by the adrenal gland in response to stress.

diaphragm A sheet of muscle that separates the chest cavity from the abdomen. In deep breathing, the diaphragm is expanded downward to inflate the lungs.

displacement The transference of emotion from one idea to another, which allows the patient to avoid acknowledging the original source of the emotion.

emotion-focused therapy (EFT) A form of therapy that focuses on emotions as the key to understanding and removing negative emotions such as anger.

empathy The insightful awareness of another person's thoughts and feelings.

endorphin A chemical produced in the brain that acts as a natural opiate and increases the threshold for pain.

epinephrine A hormone produced by the adrenal gland and secreted when the sympathetic nervous system is stimulated. During the body's physiological response to stress, epinephrine is responsible for maintaining blood pressure and cardiac output, keeping airways open, and raising blood sugar levels. All these functions are useful to frightened, traumatized, injured, or sick organisms.

flight or fight response The instinct to respond to danger by either fighting or running away.

frontal lobe Part of the brain, located directly behind the forehead, that is responsible for voluntary movement, thoughts, and feelings.

frontotemporal dementia A type of dementia that attacks the nerve cells of the frontal and temporal lobes of the brain.

Mood changes, such as excess anger, can sometimes be the first symptom.

frustration   The emotional response from being denied or prevented from achieving some goal or desire.

frustration-aggression hypothesis   The idea, developed in 1939, that frustrated desires are the explanation for all anger and aggression.

gene   A segment of DNA that describes the sequence of a particular enzyme or protein. A gene is the basic unit of heredity.

hippocampus   A seahorse-shaped structure, part of the limbic system, that serves as the seat of our emotional memories. It evaluates situations based on those memories.

homocysteine   A chemical that can damage the insides of arteries, promoting heart disease. High levels have been found in chronically angry people.

hormone   A chemical messenger secreted by one part of the body that has an effect on another part of the body.

hostility   An enduring personality trait that predisposes a person to chronic anger.

hydraulic model of anger   Sigmund Freud's idea that repressed anger (or sexual desires) can build up inside the psyche, causing physiological problems. Aggressive behavior or viewing aggression is said to release the pressure.

hypnotherapy   Treatment of a psychological problem through hypnosis.

hypothalamus   Part of the brain's limbic system that is responsible for automatic functions such as appetite and body temperature regulation. The hypothalamus translates sensory information from the amygdala, indicating a possible threat, into a physical response from the body.

inoculation   A gradual desensitization to upsetting stimuli through repeated, increasingly more intense, exposure.

insight therapy   A form of psychotherapy that seeks to uncover the roots of psychological problems through the exploration of unresolved issues and conflict. Also called talk therapy.

instrumental aggression   A form of proactive aggression in which the goal is to acquire a tangible, concrete thing; as opposed to bullying, which is proactive aggression with the intent to cause harm in another person.

intermittent explosive disorder   A mental disorder characterized by unpredictable episodes of extreme, sometimes violent, anger. The anger may be without cause, and it is out of character even for the afflicted person.

intimate terrorism   Prototypical spousal abuse, inflicted not out of anger but because of a need to exert control over another person.

jealousy   An emotion that arises when someone believes another person is getting something he wants or thinks rightfully belongs to him.

limbic system   A more primitive brain region, including the structures of the amygdala and hippocampus, that helps regulate emotion and memory.

magnetic resonance imaging (MRI)   A medical imaging technique that uses a powerful magnetic field to induce changes in the hydrogen atoms in the body, allowing a three-dimensional representation of structures to be generated.

meditation   The process of stilling the mind.

meta-analysis   A research study that compiles and analyzes data from many other studies to provide more comprehensive and accurate results.

myocardial infarction   The loss of living heart muscle as a result of the blockage of a coronary artery.

neural network   A set of interconnected nerve cells in the brain that work in a coordinated way.

neurobiology   The biology of the nervous system.

neurodegenerative disease   A disease characterized by wasting, deterioration, or death of the cells of the nervous system.

neurons   The signal-conducting cells of the brain, consisting of a cell body with branching arms called dendrites on one end—which receive signals from other neurons—and a long axon on the other end—which transmits those signals to other nerve cells.

neurotransmitter   Chemicals that pass from one neuron to another, transmitting messages.

norepinephrine   A hormone produced by the body's adrenal gland, which acts in the brain to alter basic processes such as heart rate and blood pressure. Norepinephrine is a key hormone in the body's fight or flight response.

optic nerves   The nerves that carry sensory information from the eyes to the brain.

parasympathetic nervous system   The branch of the autonomic nervous system that reduces physiological arousal.

passive-aggressive   A type of communication or anger style in which a person masks his anger and aggression under a passive, compliant exterior.

passivity   The condition of being dependent on others, with a reluctance to be assertive or responsible.

personality trait   A stable, consistent pattern of thought, emotion, and behavior.

perversion   A deviation from normal behavior, in terms of intellect, emotions, actions, or reactions.

PET-1   A gene, first discovered in mice and more recently in humans, believed to help regulate anxiety and aggression. Defective PET-1 genes may lead to mental disorders including excess anger.

phytoestrogen   An estrogenlike compound naturally found in some plants.

pituitary gland   A small, gray, rounded gland on the lower surface of the hypothalamus in the brain. It releases a number of hormones involved in emotional responses, including adrenal corticotropic hormone (ACTH).

positive reinforcement   The use of desirable rewards to increase another person's tendency to behave in a particular way.

positron emission tomography (PET)   A medical imaging technique that measures the movement of radioactive tracer dyes through the brain and body to give a visual representation of metabolic activity. PET is used to study the physiology of the emotions.

post-traumatic stress disorder   An anxiety disorder associated with a severely traumatic event or series of events.

prefrontal cortex   The brain's executive decision-making center, located just behind the forehead and between the temples.

prion   A small, foreign protein particle. Prions are the cause of several neurodegenerative disorders, including mad cow disease.

proactive aggression   Aggressive acts or behavior with the intent to achieve a goal. Also called calculated aggression.

progressive muscle relaxation   A relaxation technique in which groups of muscles are sequentially tensed, then relaxed, from head to toe.

psychiatrist   A physician concerned with diagnosing, treating, and preventing mental illness. Psychiatrists are medical doctors and can prescribe medication.

psychologist   A trained counselor and/or therapist with a Ph.D. Unlike psychiatrists, psychologists cannot prescribe medication.

psychotherapy   The treatment of mental illness and psychological problems through verbal—as opposed to pharmacological—means. Includes counseling and psychoanalysis.

rational emotive therapy   A type of cognitive-behavior therapy that assumes that emotional problems stem from faulty thinking patterns, especially unrealistic expectations people set for themselves.

reactive aggression   Aggressive behavior in response to a feeling of threat or provocation. It's the most common form of aggression seen in children.

relaxation response   A simple relaxation technique that uses steady breathing and a repeated word or phrase to create a calm state.

repression   Denying or submerging disturbing or painful ideas and feelings into the subconscious.

self-talk   Our inner dialogue.

serotonin   A neurotransmitter that plays a role in learning, memory, sleep, appetite, and sex drive. Low serotonin levels can cause depression, anxiety, and other disorders and have been linked with irritability and high aggression.

situational couple violence   A type of interpersonal violence that arises as a result of circumstance—in the heat of the moment. Although it can lead to intense violence, it doesn't fit the pattern of spousal abuse because it is not about control. Also called common couple violence.

social skills training   Behavioral therapies that teach people (often children) how to appropriately respond in social situations and improve their interpersonal skills.

State-Trait Anger Expression Inventory   A widely used psychological assessment test of the expression, experience, and control of anger.

stress　An extreme demand on the body or mind.

stress response　Physiological changes in the body in response to stress.

stressor　An uncontrollable, unpredictable, challenging event or situation that causes stress.

stroke　The sudden loss of neurological function, caused by a vascular injury to the body.

suppression　Retaining or bottling up feelings, particularly negative ones.

sympathetic nervous system　The part of the autonomic nervous system that when activated launches the body into an energized state.

temperament　The manner of behaving, reacting, or thinking that is characteristic of a specific individual.

temporal lobe　The lobe of the cerebrum located laterally and below the frontal and parietal lobes. It processes sound and also plays a role in emotions such as anger.

thalamus　An area of the brain that receives all sensory stimuli (except smell) and relays the information to other brain regions.

thyroid gland　An endocrine gland located in the base of the neck.

Type A personality　The personality characterized by extreme ambition, competitiveness, and a sense of time pressure. The hostility of Type A people is believed to contribute to their higher rates of heart disease.

vascular dementia　A type of dementia that can occur when brain cells become deprived of oxygen.

violence　Aggression with the goal of inflicting extreme harm.

visualization　Using the mind to make a mental image of a thing or situation.

Further Reading

Cox, Deborah, Karin H. Bruckner, and Sally Stabb. *The Anger Advantage: The Surprising Benefits of Anger and How It Can Change a Woman's Life*. New York: Broadway, 2003.

Damasio, Antonio. *Descartes' Error: Emotion, Reason, and the Human Brain*. New York: Quill, 1995.

———. *Looking for Spinoza: Joy, Sorrow, and the Feeling Brain*. San Diego: Harcourt Books, 2003.

Darwin, Charles. *The Expression of the Emotions in Man and Animals*. Available in full text online at human-nature.com/Darwin/emotion/contents.html.

Deffenbacher, Jerry L., and Matthew McKay. *Overcoming Situational and General Anger*. Oakland, CA: New Harbinger Publications, Inc., 2000.

Ellis, A., and R. Tafrate. *How to Control Your Anger Before It Controls You*. New York: Carol Publishing Group, 1997.

Engel, Beverly. *Honor Your Anger: How Transforming Your Anger Style Can Change Your Life*. Hoboken, NJ: John Wiley & Sons, 2003.

Golden, Bernard. *Healthy Anger: How to Help Children and Teens Manage Their Anger.* New York: Oxford University Press, 2002.

Goleman, Daniel. *Destructive Emotions: A Scientific Dialogue with the Dalai Lama.* New York: Bantam, 2003.

LeDoux, Joseph. *The Emotional Brain: The Mysterious Underpinnings of Emotional Life, Reprint Edition.* New York: Simon & Schuster, 1998.

Lerner, Harriet. *The Dance of Anger: A Woman's Guide to Changing the Patterns of Intimate Relationships, Reissue Edition.* New York: Quill, 1997.

McKay, Matthew, Peter D. Rogers, and Judith McKay. *When Anger Hurts: Quieting the Storm Within, Second Edition.* Oakland, CA: New Harbinger Publications, Inc., 2003.

Medea, Andra. *Conflict Unraveled: Fixing Problems at Work and in Families.* Chicago: PivotPoint Press, 2005.

Murphy, Tim, and Loriann Hoff Oberlin. *The Angry Child: Regaining Control When Your Child Is Out of Control.* New York: Three Rivers Press, 2002.

Novaco, Raymond. *Anger Control: The Development and Evaluation of an Experimental Treatment.* Lexington, MA: Lexington Books, 1975.

Petracek, Laura J. *The Anger Workbook for Women.* Oakland, CA: New Harbinger Publications, Inc., 2004.

Potter-Efron, Ron, and Pat Potter-Efron. *Letting Go of Anger.* Oakland, CA: New Harbinger Publications, Inc., 1995.

Reeve, Susyn. *Choose Peace and Happiness: A 52-Week Guide.* Red Wheel, 2003.

Rifkin, John R. *The Healing Power of Anger: The Unexpected Path to Love and Fulfillment.* Paraview, 2004.

Rosenwein, Barbara H. *Anger's Past: The Social Uses of an Emotion in the Middle Ages.* Ithaca, NY: Cornell University Press, 1998.

Spielberger, Charles D., ed. *Stress and Emotion: Anxiety, Anger, and Curiosity (Stress and Emotion).* Washington, DC: Taylor & Francis, 1996.

Tavris, Carol. *Anger: The Misunderstood Emotion.* New York: Simon & Schuster, 1989.

Whitehouse, Eliane, and Warwick Pudney. *A Volcano in My Tummy: Helping Children to Handle Anger.* Gabriola Island, British Columbia, New Society Publishers, 1996.

Wilde, Jerry. *Hot Stuff to Help Kids Chill Out: The Anger Management Book.* Richmond, IN: Lgr Publishing, 1997.

Resources

There is a lot more information out there about anger, its causes, effect, and what to do about it. To help you find what you need, I've compiled this list of websites, organizations, and other resources. It is by no means inclusive, but hopefully you can find it useful.

The entries in this appendix are divided into four sections, one for each part of the book.

Part 1: Understanding Anger

The Anger Project
www.angerproject.com

Angries Out
www.angriesout.com

The Brain Science Foundation
www.brainsciencefoundation.org
508-242-9830

Bully OnLine
www.bullyonline.org

Center for Safe Schools and Communities
groups.msn.com/CenterforSafeSchoolsandCommunities
1-800-221-4125

National Alliance for the Mentally Ill
www.nami.org
1-800-NAMI (6264)

National Brain Tumor Foundation
www.braintumor.org
510-839-9777

National Institute of Mental Health
www.nimh.nih.gov
1-866-615-NIMH (6464)

National Institute of Neurological Disorders and Stroke
www.ninds.nih.gov
1-800-352-9424

National Mental Health Association
www.nmha.org
1-800-969-6642

Students Against Violence Everywhere
www.nationalsave.org
1-866-343-SAVE (7233)

Part 2: When Anger Hurts

Dr.Driving.org
www.drdriving.org

Institute for International Sport Center for Sport Parenting
www.internationalsport.com/csp
401-874-2375

The National Center for Children Exposed to Violence
(NCCEV)
www.nccev.org/
1-877-49-NCCEV (62238)

National Clearinghouse on Child Abuse and Neglect Information
nccanch.acf.hhs.gov
1-800-394-3366

National Domestic Violence Hotline
www.ndvh.org
1-800-799-SAFE (7233)

National Institute for Occupational Safety and Health
www.cdc.gov/niosh
Job stress Internet site:
www.cdc.gov/niosh/jobstress.html
1-800-35-NIOSH (64674)

National Institute for the Prevention of Workplace Violence
www.workplaceviolence911.com
949-770-5264

Nicole Brown Charitable Foundation
www.nbcf.org/lobby.htm
1-800-799-SAFE (7233)

The Substance Abuse and Mental Health Services Administration (SAMHSA)
sims.health.org/Admins/

United States Department of Labor, Occupational Safety and Health Adminstration—Workplace Violence
www.osha-slc.gov/SLTC/workplaceviolence/index.html

Workplace Violence Research Institute
www.workviolence.com
1-800-230-7302

Part 3: Taking Charge

Albert Ellis Institute (Rational Emotive Therapy)
www.albertellis.org
1-800-323-4738

American Association of Anger Management Providers
angermanagementproviders.com
310-207-3591

American Psychiatric Association
www.psych.org
1-703-907-7300

American Psychological Association
www.apa.org
1-800-964-2000

American Psychotherapy Association
www.americanpsychotherapy.com/index.php

Anderson & Anderson Anger Management
www.andersonservices.com
310-207-3591

Center for Social and Emotional Education
www.csee.net

Cognitive Behavior Therapy
www.cognitivetherapy.org
718-636-5071

Emotion Focused Therapy
www.emotionfocusedtherapy.org

International Center for Aggression Replacement Training
www.aggressionreplacementtraining.org
011 46 380 472 00

International Society for Complementary Medicine Research
www.iscmr.org/

Mind/Body Medical Institute (in affiliation with Harvard Medical School)
www.mbmi.org
617-991-0102

National Center for Complementary and Alternative Medicine
nccam.nih.gov/
1-888-644-6226

New York Online Access to Health: Complementary and Alternative Medicine
www.noah-health.org/en/alternative/

Psychology Today Online Therapist Directory
therapists.psychologytoday.com/rms/prof_search.php

United Way of America
www.unitedway.org
1-703-836-7112

Part 4: Managing Anger in Your Life

American Association for Marriage and Family Therapy
www.aamft.org/index_nm.asp
703-838-9808

American Family Therapy Academy, Inc.
www.afta.org/
202-483-8001

BeyondIntractability.org
www.beyondintractability.org/iweb/

Campaign for Forgiveness Research
www.forgiving.org/

Communication Psychology
www.worldpsychology.net/World%20Psychology/
OriginalCorePages/virtuaps.htm

Conflict Resolution Consortium
conflict.colorado.edu/
303-492-1635

Conflict Resolution Information Source
v4.crinfo.org/

The Forgiveness Web
www.forgivenessweb.com

International Online Training Program on Intractable Conflict
www.colorado.edu/conflict/peace/index.html

North American Institute for Conflict Resolution
www.crtraining.org
780-465-1721

Index

Q–R